Praise for 31 Days to Purchasing and Renting Your First Investment Real Estate Property

"I was fortunate to read a copy of Rick Harris's book in advance, and I think it's a thorough and helpful quick-start guide to investing in real estate. Rick is a credible and knowledgeable investor and author, and he shares his wisdom from years of experience. He urges the reader to take action (something I also emphasize), and his thirty-one-day guide makes that very simple! Rick does not attempt to make real estate investing out to be a get-rich scheme . . . because it's not. He is very clear with setting expectations and laying out a realistic strategy. And he references dozens of helpful resources along the way. Highly recommended!"

Rachel Richards

Bestselling author of *Money Honey* and *Passive Income, Aggressive Retirement*

"If you are seriously entertaining buying your first investment real estate property, I would strongly recommend you read this book. I was amazed at the incredible detail the author has provided the reader, with an in-depth review of the many steps to buying your first investment property. In addition, the author provides many experiences he had in buying his first property and how his mistakes can make your experience a lot less stressful. By reading his book, you can feel the author's passion for investment real estate."

Robert Jeffery, AACI

Residential appraiser, retired

"I am an investor. I like to invest and have invested in many things, including real estate. I know that investment real estate requires planning and discipline. Rick's book is a no-nonsense, practical, and very informative step-by-step outline of the process required to make your investments count. If being in the top 2 percent of the real estate investing game interests you, then you have a practical reference that can guide you to this or any investment real estate goal. Rick's passion for what he and his family have achieved financially through investment real estate rings loud and true in this firsthand account. Rick is willing, able, and qualified to share this information with you so that you too can benefit from smart financial planning and investing. *31 Days to Purchasing and Renting Your First Investment Real Estate Property* is a detailed, resource-rich, step-by-step approach to achieving success with your very first foray into the world of investment real estate."

Leigh Matheson

Co-owner, Full City & Supply

"I have been a real estate investor for over twelve years. I started with one property and have since expanded my portfolio to three. In that time, I have met with Rick often and he has provided me with a wealth of coaching and knowledge. What I didn't have when I began as an investor that this book offers, beyond the worksheets and formulas for investment, is the mindset for success! Having the right mindset along with the right numbers will help a person go a long way in building their portfolio. This book is a gem that comes from someone with a lifetime of experience, knowledge, and a goal-directed attitude that is second to none! An easy-to-follow guide with many of the author's personal experiences woven into the fabric of the information, making it easy to read and follow."

Michelle Heyden Macdonald

Co-owner, Full City & Supply

"I've always had an interest in real estate and have watched the various markets as an observer with the idea of the possibility of owning an investment property. In reading various books and articles about owning investment property, I generally found them lacking in specific details regarding the necessary steps and more about personal experiences. When I read *31 Days to Purchasing and Renting Your First Investment Real Estate Property* by W. Rick Harris, I found a true guide for getting into investment property ownership. The book has some personal experiences listed by the author as an acknowledgement of experience to illustrate the main theme, and gives a very detailed walk-through of the steps and knowledge required to make ownership a reality. The bonus for me was learning about 'goal-directed thinking' and the steps that are required to move from a wish to a reality. The author continues to impress the importance of checking in and evaluating the process, which I found to be a great coaching model. I will continue to refer to this book as a guide for my journey as a new landlord and owner of an investment property. A great read and a great resource for anyone considering or planning on entering ownership of investment real estate."

Jim Mansell

Western regional sales manager, retired

"I am really enjoying this book. I can feel the author's enthusiasm as I read the book, and he is very thorough and detailed. Great job!"

Ted Hodgson

Lawyer and partner, retired

"I have just finished reading *31 Days to Purchasing and Renting Your First Investment Real Estate Property* and I have to tell you how wonderful I think it is. You know your stuff, Rick, and your knowledge comes through in the detail and straightforward narrative. It is a joy to read. CONGRATULATIONS!"

Gary MacLeod

Senior vice president, international and food service, retired

"When I started working with W. Rick Harris as his editor on *31 Days to Purchasing and Renting Your First Investment Real Estate Property*, I never expected that the book would lead me on my own investment real estate journey. But with the rich knowledge and expert guidance Rick provides, I realized homeownership was within my reach. The goal-oriented incremental approach makes diving into investment real estate less daunting, and knowing what to expect at each stage of the process gave me the confidence to move forward. Now, I'm the proud owner of a beautiful home on one of B.C.'s Gulf Islands, building my equity for the future while providing my aging parents with housing security at the same time. Thanks, Rick!"

Robin Schroffel

Editor

31 DAYS TO PURCHASING

and renting your first investment
REAL ESTATE PROPERTY©
by W. Rick Harris

The material in this publication is provided for information purposes only. Laws, regulations, and procedures are constantly changing, and the examples given are intended to be general guidelines only. This book is sold with the understanding that neither the author nor the publisher is engaged in rendering professional advice. It is strongly recommended that legacy, accounting, tax, financial, insurance, and other advice or assistance be obtained before acting on any information contained in this book. If such advice or other assistance is required, the personal services of a competent professional should be sought.

© 2021 W. Rick Harris

All rights reserved. No portion of this book may be reproduced or used in any manner without the prior written permission of the copyright owner, except for the use of brief quotations in a book review.

For permissions, contact: wrickh@vaulttoinvestmentrealestatesuccess.com

Edited by Robin Schroffel

Cover and layout by Konn Lavery, Reveal Design

eBook ISBN: 978-1-7774765-1-9

Print ISBN: 978-1-7774765-0-2

Published by Vault to Real Estate Success Corporation, St. Albert, Alberta, Canada

www.vaulttoinvestmentrealestatesuccess.com

To my wife, Brendalee; you are the most treasured person in my own Vault to Success.

TABLE OF CONTENTS

QUICK-START GUIDE	1
PREFACE	3
ACKNOWLEDGEMENTS	10
WELCOME!	13
VALUE	16
INTRODUCTION	24
How Investment Real Estate Touches Our Lives	24
Day 1 — What Is Investment Real Estate, and Is It Right for You?	55
Day 2 — "Ready, Set, Goal" for Your Investment Real Estate and Rental Property	65
STAGE I: READY	80
Call Out Your Investment Real Estate Purchasing Power and Mindset	80
Day 3 — Defining Your Financial Base and Purchasing Power	83
Day 4 — Entrepreneurial and Small Business Mindset	102
Day 5 — Don't Give Up Your Day Job, and Other Income Advice	124
Day 6 — All in the Family	136

Day 7	The Types of Investment Real Estate Property and Tenants That Match	146
Day 8	Home May Not Be Where the Investment Heart Is	159
Day 9	Going Further: Gross Domestic Product, Job Growth, and Population Growth	166
Day 10	Trends and Timing	172
Day 11	Decreased Vacancies and Increased Rental Demand	180
Day 12	FOCUS (Follow One Commitment Until Success)	190
Day 13	Financing: What Is Best for You?	205
Day 14	Financing: What Can You Afford?	217
Day 15	Financing: Tying the Elements Together to Meet Down Payment and Revenue Requirements	236
Day 16	The Costs to Purchase	251
Day 17	Funding: Your Source of Funds Determines Your Financing Needs, and How to Present Your Case	260
Day 18	SMART (Specific, Measurable, Acceptable, Realistic, Time-Bound)	274

STAGE II: SET — 284

Search for Your Investment Real Estate Team		284
Day 19	Identifying, Assembling, and Meeting Your Team REAL	286
Day 20	Entry Stages of Team REAL: Before Purchase, At Purchase, and After Purchase	305
Day 21	Which Lender Is Right for You?	312

Day 22	The Offer: Definition, Structure, and Process	330
Day 23	The Offer: Adding Conditions, Including Property Inspection	338
Day 24	The Purchase: Property Inspection Done and Conditions Removed	344

STAGE III: GOAL — 354

Crossing the Finish Line, Arms in the Air — 354

Day 25	Marketing Your Property to Renters	356
Day 26	Screening, Acquiring, and Retaining Quality Renters	379
Day 27	The Move-In/Move-Out Inspection Checklist	390
Day 28	Breaking Down the Rent Check and the Monthly and Year-to-Date Income Statement (Micro View)	399
Day 29	Rate of Return on Investment: Monitoring Revenue Success Elements (Macro View)	412
Day 30	Adding More Doors: Concerns and Possibilities	436
Day 31	The Exit Strategy	444

CONCLUSION — 457

The End, and Warmest Appreciation — 457

APPENDIX — 459

REFERENCES — 460

QUICK-START GUIDE

We live in a busy world. Often, we are so busy that we let others manage the money we are earning and investing into our financial future. We don't make the time to take control of our investments. Is it any wonder that our financial returns are often not as good as we had hoped?

In this book, I help you turn things around and take control over your financial portfolio through investment real estate.

When I wrote *31 Days to Purchasing and Renting Your First Investment Real Estate Property*, the plan was to get to the nitty-gritty and jump right into the action without giving you the *why* or sharing my personal journey and philosophy of investment real estate. But with the COVID-19 pandemic, there has been a strong movement toward online learning. People are taking the time to read more, slowing their lives down, and adding more personal development to their life's equation. I realized that real life is too important to gloss over, and that sharing my *why* with you will add invaluable depth to your understanding of real estate investment.

Part of this entails inviting you into my life and sharing just how real life can get in the way of many of our life decisions. Real life changes the trajectory of our finances, our health, our mental well-being, and our legacy.

I hope you will see the value in taking the time to read the first part of the book before you jump into the deep end and start on the thirty-one days and sixty-one coaching challenges. By skipping ahead, you'll miss out on lessons from real life experiences that will get you ready and set to bring investment real estate into your financial portfolio and reach your financial goals.

Real life can be fraught with challenges. My wife, Brendalee, and I have weathered both of our children starting families and then having those relationships fall apart, and joint venture partners getting into financial trouble and having to buy them out. We have overcome losing my job after almost thirty years in my career, aging parents with declining health, getting notice from joint venture partners that they would like to sell down the road, being chased by the taxman, riding the good times and the bad times of the economy, and experiencing other difficult situations.

I've been honored to speak about these experiences, investment real estate life lessons, stories, insights, and more as a guest on several podcast shows. Listen to my guest appearance on The Everyday Millionaire podcast, hosted by Patrick Francey, to get a real sense of who I am and what I bring to the party.

For those of you who want to skip this valuable information and jump right to the first day, I have created a quick-start method: a digital workbook and planning guide to support the content in this book.

Click on this link to purchase your copy of the *31 Days to Purchasing and Renting Your First Time Real Estate Property Workbook and Planning Guide.*

> *"Let your journey to investment real estate success begin."*

PREFACE

Throughout history, great leaders and academics such as Aristotle, Einstein, and many others have discussed achieving success through setting goals.

In his book *The Richest Man in Babylon*, George Samuel Clason talks about how each of us can achieve success through our own efforts and abilities. Clason says the key to success is the proper preparation. One way you can prepare to succeed in investment real estate is to invest your time in reading this book and faithfully follow the process it outlines. The goal at the finish line is simple: to purchase and rent your first investment real estate property successfully.

When I first started to think about achieving investment real estate success, the words of Henry Ford came to mind: "Whether you think you can, or you think you can't—you're right."

Why I Wrote This Book

Over the last several years, I noticed that most of my coaching clients and joint venture partners were reaching out to me for one reason: they were interested in adding investment real estate into their financial portfolio but did not have a clue how the process worked or how much time it might take to complete. Being contacted by these folks was one of the catalysts to writing this book.

The first question they'd usually ask was, "I heard you own investment real estate. Is this true?"

My answer, of course, was yes.

The next two questions were, "How did you buy investment real estate?" and "How long did it take to make the purchase?" followed by, "How did you find tenants for your property?" and "Can you coach me on this entire process?"

My first couple of investment properties were purchased within thirty-one days, so I had a good idea of the timeframe, and I had learned from one of my investment real estate mentors that it would be possible to rent out our first property before we even took possession.

Seeing a need for this type of information and wishing to inspire people on their own investment real estate journey, I decided to write this book. My experiences led me to title the book *31 Days to Purchasing and Renting Your First Investment Real Estate Property*.

Who This Book Is For

Although anyone can benefit from this book, I have tailored the content toward those who are investing in investment real estate for the first time.

Many people, especially boomers, purchased their first home when they were in their twenties for less money than it takes to buy a set of stainless-steel top-end appliances or a Harley-Davidson motorcycle today. If that's you, you may have lived through times when interest rates skyrocketed just as you bought your first home or had your first mortgage renewal come up, and the thought of a return to high interest rates might scare you silly. It's no wonder—many boomers saw mortgage rates as high as 21 percent, and it was painful for those of us who experienced it.

Thankfully, it seems that, in a few years, high interest rates may become the stuff of urban legend. Recently, I renewed a mortgage on an investment income property. The bank honored a .75 percent discount off their prime rate of 2.60 for an annual rate of 1.85 percent. A low-interest-rate environment has great appeal. Although this low-interest environment may be all that younger readers have ever known, I don't take these low-cost rates for granted—the mortgage rate on our first home was 10.75 percent!

Low interest rates are significant because it means the cost of borrowing is not a major barrier to purchasing property like it was in the past. And today, you have an excellent chance to enjoy low interest rates for the foreseeable future.

With the coronavirus pandemic creating global economic uncertainty, low interest rates will be a mainstay of our world for some time to come. Simply listen to the direction of the American Federal Reserve, which conducts monetary policy in the United States, directly affecting short-term interest rates and indirectly impacting long-term rates; most countries are following its lead.

Perhaps your experience with real estate is through a friend of a friend who owned investment real estate that was trashed by tenants, causing the investor to lose their shirt. Rest assured, there are practices in this book that will keep you from experiencing this.

For boomers who have only owned a principal residence, the thought of investing in real estate may be relegated to the dustbin because of your age. Well, I believe that investment real estate is a worthwhile endeavor no matter how old you are. Medical science and technology are making advances in longevity, and there are many recent success stories about the positive side impacts of the search for the coronavirus vaccines. The intensive research is uncovering new methods for treating other diseases such as cancer. You never know how long you'll have.

In addition, many people are being inundated with the story that investment real estate is overpriced and that a cooling-down period is about to happen. (Boomers have heard this story before.) I will talk more about this later in the book, but for now, know that there are many investment markets in every part of North America and worldwide. Hot, cold, just right—you can find a market that works for you.

Investment Real Estate vs. Real Estate Investment

You might be wondering why I'm talking about investment real estate versus real estate investment. It's because there is a big difference. I want you to think of investment first, and real estate—as the vehicle—second.

Investment real estate is a way of saving, sharing, securing, investing, and getting a return on capital. All these words represent stable concepts, unlike the terms typically used to talk about most other kinds of investments. Speculation, outlay, deal, and venture capital . . . these are all words that carry a connotation of risk. Investment real estate shouldn't be overly risky; rather, it should be boring, so you have no problem sleeping at night, and you make money while you get a good night's rest. It should help you capitalize, participate in, and advance your investment funds forever.

Play out your own thirty-one-day journey to purchasing and renting your first investment real estate property in your mind, and then ask yourself some questions. Why investment real estate now? What factors, personal and financial, might be driving your curiosity?

This book will help you purchase quality investment real estate, giving your tenants a great place to live and you, your family, and your joint venture partners an excellent return on your investment.

My Approach

I am a big fan of the idea of "learners who lead leading learners," as Natalie Sisson talks about in her book *The Suitcase Entrepreneur*. During the recent coronavirus pandemic, many people had to rely heavily on the government for help, causing worry and stress. Although my wife and I were able to avoid this, thanks in part to our investment real estate's health, we also had some challenges. We learned from these experiences through doing and growing with our tenants, lenders, service providers, and property management team. It worked out better than we expected, and I am pleased to pass these learnings on to you.

Ready, Set, Goal

*If you want to live a happy life, **tie it to a goal**, not people or things.* — Albert Einstein

This book will introduce you to a process I call Ready, Set, Goal. If you follow the Ready, Set, Goal process, I know you'll be successful in purchasing your first investment real estate property.

Ready, Set, Goal is the baseline achievement, direction, and action that you'll be asked to examine on your way to purchasing investment real estate. Even though you might think of real estate as a thing, it is much more than that and can lead you on a path to a happy life. In a moment, I will introduce you to Happy Place. She is part of my inspiration and brings a smile to my face.

Having a clear goal is essential in investment real estate investing. The book's title, *31 Days to Purchasing and Renting Your First Investment Real Estate Property*, clarifies your goal, and joining our community will help you watch your progress. You'll have the opportunity to set the foundation for your economic health and learn how investment real estate can be the key to growing your skill set and earning power.

The first eighteen days of this book are all about knowledge acquisition and laying a foundation—what I call the Ready phase. If you are expecting to purchase your first investment property on the first day, in the first week, or even in the second week, then I'm sorry to disappoint you.

Don't worry—we do get to the purchase somewhere around the third week. There's no question that following the method and process outlined in the book will lead you to this goal.

Patience is needed in the big picture, too. The long-term buy-and-hold strategy I advocate means you will likely be involved in investment real estate for years or decades. Day 31 is about having an exit strategy. Stay the course and you will see how this all ties together, day by day, week by week, until Day 31.

The Ready, Set, Goal process will also help you if you have already purchased your first investment real estate property and are looking to add some life and energy into your current investment real estate portfolio.

You can set many commodities and possessions as goals to acquire in your everyday life if you have the wealth or credit. Time is your most important commodity, but you can't buy more time. Meeting your goal of having more financial freedom allows you to decide what to do with your time.

Why This Process Works

When it comes to investing, most traditional methods have you making contributions over time. You will probably hear the phrase *dollar-cost averaging*, which means how much money you will contribute to your investment each month, each quarter, or each year.

If you follow the Ready, Set, Goal process, you will eliminate this part of investing because, through your rental income, your tenants will be the ones contributing monthly to your goal and your success.

And because you have a mortgage tied to a term and amortization length, you can easily determine your expected growth on your investment. Later, on Day 15, we'll talk more about how aggressively or conservatively you want to invest. On Days 3 and 5, I also talk to you about what I call "Uberizing" your investment, a simple method to accelerate your investment growth.

Will there be bumps along the way? Yes! How do you recover from an economic downturn and catch the next wave up? We will discuss some little tricks, including how you set up your financing; if you simply ask, many lenders have ways to help you not only through the good times but the bad times, too. Lenders don't want to be landlords; this is a job and an investment role you have chosen. On Day 15, we will discuss financing, protecting your investment real estate, and compounding your growth through different financing techniques.

You may have heard of the power of compounding. This refers to investing your money in an investment that creates interest, and the interest is then reinvested into the original investment to earn more interest. It is like planting a tomato plant; the tomatoes grow, you harvest the first crop, more tomatoes grow on the same plant, and you get to harvest again.

The magic of compounding in investment real estate is that your investment real estate portfolio flourishes as the mortgage principal is reduced through tenants' rent.

On top of investing your own efforts and funds to grow your investment real estate value, you'll benefit from the time and revenue contributed by your tenants. I call this value growth your Happy Place. Compounding is just one of the value growth techniques to get you to your Happy Place that you will uncover in the book.

 SAY HI TO HAPPY PLACE ICON!

She will guide you on your investment real estate journey. Look for Happy Place bullet points throughout this book.

ACKNOWLEDGEMENTS

Spirit, Growth, Success —school motto, Sir George Simpson Junior High School

First, I would like to thank you, thank you, thank you and acknowledge you, the reader—whether you are a boomer, a Generation Xer, a millennial, or a member of Gen Z. (This includes my daughter, who is an Xer, and my son, who is a millennial.)

If you purchased this book as an Xer, millennial, or Gen Zer, a special thank-you to you. It is my wish that this book will motivate you beyond your years of investment and help you encourage your mom and dad or grandparents that it is never too late to begin using investment real estate to create a strong financial foundation that unlocks sustainable wealth and a living legacy. I love my children and their children, and through investment real estate, I have a bigger purpose in life than just creating my own wealth.

I would also like to thank my mom and dad for the greatest gift they ever gave me: them. My parents have passed away, and I hope they knew how much I appreciated them and how much of an influence they had on my life. My mother was very much a modern woman; she was a working administrative professional for most of her life. My dad gave a big part of his life to the Armed Forces and was proud of his contributions until the day he passed away. We celebrated my dad's life at the legion he belonged to, and he received an honor guard for his service to his country. His military career had a big influence on how I live my life and view the world.

That my brother and I grew up in the sixties and seventies as part of a dual-income family is proof my parents were ahead of their time, and this ensured we never had to go without. We were latchkey kids who were very much loved, and I think we turned out great.

Being a strong working woman, my mother also served as a good role model for her granddaughters, proving we are all people, and anything is possible.

I was fortunate that my dad's military life allowed me to see most of Europe and Canada by the time I was eighteen. These travels helped shape who I am today. I experienced living in Europe when the Beatles and the Rolling Stones were just starting their careers, and the Cold War was still real. Back then, the Berlin Wall was dividing Germany, and politics was just a twinkle in Ronald Reagan's eye—he was not yet tearing anything down. Living in Europe opened my eyes to different cultures and languages, giving me an appreciation of how different nationalities can live together in harmony.

Our years in Europe exposed me to investment real estate for the first time. There, my family was renting and we relied on good investment real estate owners to provide us with a safe and secure place to live. Moreover, seeing the armed guards and high walls that kept Eastern Europeans from living a more open life gave me a greater appreciation of our freedom as North Americans.

My parents loved to travel. We spent our family vacations visiting different countries and embracing the food, the art, the architecture, the festivals, and the daily lives of other cultures. Our school trips were to incredible European cities like Vienna, Berlin, London, and Paris; it gave me a spirit of adventure that has stayed with me throughout my life. I played hockey all over Europe and, as a Scouts member, attended a World Jamboree; these experiences taught me that we as people, no matter where we live in the world, have more similarities than differences. There is no question that I am more outgoing, more tolerant, and more appreciative of art and history because of my four years living and traveling in Europe.

This background impacted how my wife and I raised our family. Our two children have allowed me to live out many of the ideas in this book and have humored me as a father. They have both built strong families of their own, but not without some challenges. These challenges have brought more members into our extended family, and by embracing all members, we all benefit.

To my grandchildren, your influence on our lives is beyond words and our time together allows me to be a kid again; it's pure fun. You help me to push my physical, mental, and spiritual health to new levels.

To Don R. Campbell, who has written many informative books on real estate investing, and REINCanada.com, the Real Estate Investment Network. I had purchased investment real estate before ever hearing of Don R. Campbell or REIN; however, Don and REIN inspired me to know when to hold 'em, avoid cashing out too soon, and expand my purchasing beyond just lifestyle. His work has given me many of the foundational tools in my investment real estate toolbox.

Last, it is my real pleasure to acknowledge my wife, Brendalee, who has been the most encouraging person in my life, cheering me on in this writing journey.

P.S. Over the last twenty years, I have learned much from my joint venture partners, friends, colleagues, and fellow members of REIN; the publisher of my investment real estate magazine articles, Don Loney; and many of my podcast guests. I have always said I have a great memory — it's just short. It is never easy to remember exactly who said what and who provided me with what information. Should I have failed to give someone credit for a piece of information I have included in this book, please make me aware of this so I can update the credit. And to all my investment real estate friends, I owe you a great thanks for sharing your investment real estate knowledge.

P.P.S. Location, location, location was important to writing much of my book. I have never met a venti low-fat no-foam latte I could resist. I wish to thank all of the Starbucks locations in my hometown of St. Albert for allowing me to write away in an atmosphere I found conducive to churning out the words to my book.

WELCOME!

Thank you for taking the time to share your investment real estate journey with me. If you aspire to live a happy life with more financial freedom, and your goal is to purchase and rent your first investment real estate property in thirty-one days, my process will take you to your Happy Place.

You already have the ability to purchase and rent your first investment real estate property inside you. I'm just the person who will help you take the first step and unlock your potential.

My goal is to guide you every inch of the way, giving you as many tools as I possibly can to ensure your success. At the end of the day, I will challenge you to keep everything you do as simple as possible—don't complicate or let others complicate a simple system.

I will support you on your journey through detailed information in this book's chapters, separated into thirty-one days; coaching challenges to get you to take action; worksheets to get you clear on your financial position; social media platforms; a shared community; videos; podcasts; and more.

You might notice some familiar references throughout the book. I have always felt that authors of fairy tales based their work on real situations and disguised timeless life lessons in a fun and entertaining way. I hope that using fairy-tale analogies and real stories from my ten-thousand-plus hours of real estate investment education, knowledge-gathering, and action-taking will help you create memory triggers to store valuable principles, lessons, and methods.

Before we get into the thirty-one-day plan, there are a few things I want to cover that will help you get the most out of this book and your investment real estate journey at large. In the following section, we will discuss vision, mission, and values, and you'll learn about my company, Vault to Real Estate Success Corporation. I'll talk about my purpose; introduce you to investment real estate; tell you how this book will work for you, give you instructions for using it, and teach you how to navigate it;

show you how to write your own investment real estate mission statement; and offer you access to our free Facebook community. Finally, I'll introduce you to some supporting materials I've created to help you on your journey to success, like the *31 Days to Purchasing and Renting Your First Investment Real Estate Property Workbook and Planning Guide* and the supporting online course, "31 Days to Purchasing and Renting Your First Investment Real Estate Property." All of these different learning tools will teach you the principles of investment real estate in whatever way you love to learn.

My Approach

There's a lot involved in the investment real estate purchasing and renting process. That's why I'm committed to leading by example: **doers do, doubters don't**.

As you read this book, you will discover more about me and how my half-marathon training, running, and competing background has influenced how I share training and coaching methods and processes with you.

For example, you will learn I have had several half-marathon running coaches, and recently, I decided to switch my sport of choice to sprint triathlons. I am using two online coaches for my training: one is in New Orleans, Louisiana, and the other is in Victoria, British Columbia. We live in a global world, and to be able to access support and resources from people all over the world is a pretty cool thing.

I'm telling you this because, like my training coaches, I work with people throughout Canada, the United States, and further afield via the power of online connection. Connect with me through YouTube and Facebook, or you can visit my website to explore my course offerings and coaching services at vaulttoinvestmentrealestatesuccess.com.

One of my coaches, Melanie McQuaid, wrote an article entitled "Staying Motivated, Commitment" for *Triathlon Canada*'s July/August 2020 edition. The article listed six ways to build commitment that also apply to your investment real estate journey. They've been adapted, with permission, below:

- ⇧ **Be accountable to someone.** Finding an accountability partner, joining our Facebook community, or working with a coach are all great ways to keep you on track.
- ⇧ **Create process goals.** This book has a thirty-one-day goals process and sixty-one coaching challenges to complete
- ⇧ **Have a routine.** Each of the thirty-one days has approximately two coaching challenges so that you can get into a daily routine and habit.
- ⇧ **Find inspiration.** Having a group like our Facebook group helps you find inspiration with like-minded people; remember, there are countless books, articles, and podcasts about successful investment real estate investors. Do your own research to find inspiration.
- ⇧ **Take breaks.** Even though the book has a thirty-one-day plan, it doesn't mean you have to complete the steps consecutively. You may need to take a break. When taking on a big task, it is easy to suffer burnout and then never return to the goal at hand.
- ⇧ **Be confident.** There is much to learn, but the knowledge, skills, and methods you gain from this book will build your confidence.

Many of the supporting resources mentioned in the book and on the website are free. Your success is my motivation; that's why I encourage you to not only choose me as your investment real estate coach or consultant, but I will recommend other people and resources that have helped me on my journey.

VALUE

As I'll frequently discuss throughout this book, investment real estate is a business, and you should begin to think of yourself as a businessperson from the very beginning. Before we launch into our journey, I'd like to talk a bit about the importance of mission, vision, and values.

Your Mission and Vision

Many times, when entrepreneurs start a small business, they don't have a clear mission or a vision.

According to author Susan Ward, a vision statement "is sometimes called a picture of your company in the future but it's so much more than that. Your vision statement is your inspiration, the framework for all your strategic planning." She goes on to say, "What you are doing when creating a vision statement is articulating your dreams and hopes for your business. It describes what you are trying to build and serves as a touchstone for your future actions."

I hope to help you articulate your dream of owning and renting your first investment real estate property. The book can take you from hope to reality by clarifying what you are trying to build and helping you with your future actions to reach your vision.

Creating Your Personal Vision and Mission Statement

An example of a **vision statement** for you might be as simple as this book's title: "To purchase and rent my first investment real estate property in thirty-one days." Or, it could be a little more detailed: "To create a financial portfolio that owns and rents investment real estate, building a stable economic base, and creating income for myself and my family."

An example of a **mission statement** might be: "To purchase and rent investment real estate as a means to gain more financial freedom and create income and wealth that my family and I can enjoy for years to come."

My Company's Vision and Mission Statements

To give you some inspiration, here are the vision and mission statements for my company, Vault to Investment Real Estate Success Corporation.

Vision: A world in which investment real estate builds a strong financial foundation, unlocking sustainable wealth for you and generations to come.

Mission: To provide investment real estate guidance so that you may successfully build a strong financial foundation and unlock sustainable wealth and a living legacy for you and generations to come.

Your Value Statement

In addition to vision and mission statements, companies also frequently have a value statement that informs the way they do business.

Creating your own value statement helps you to develop personal responsibility. Teachers, coaches, mentors, and consultants can lead you to a wealth of teaching, knowledge, processes, methods, and tools, but unless you take personal action, nothing will happen for you.

My Company's Value Statement

You guessed it—Vault to Investment Real Estate Success Corporation also has a value statement. This statement helps me ensure I am living up to my values with every business decision I make.

How will I know if I have succeeded with the value statement I show you below? The answer is easy. You will have purchased and rented your first investment real estate property through my ability and methods to get you to act.

Value Statement: Give someone your words, your money, and your knowledge, and they will totally rely on you. Give someone guidance through training, encourage them to develop their own investment real estate goals, and be a catalyst for them to act, and they can build a strong financial foundation that unlocks sustainable wealth and a living legacy for themselves and many generations to come.

Value: Volume, Action, Learning, Understanding, Expectation

The word *value* is thrown around a lot and is one of the most overused and abused words in the English language.

How do you recognize value?

First, you must understand what makes up value: worth, importance, quantity, appeal, appreciation, and assessment.

The one word left out of understanding value is the word *you*. If you don't see value in the offer, then it has no value.

I am reminded every day that people only recognize value if they are prepared to part with their hard-earned cash to pay for your service or product. In the same breath, we are reminded that money tends to be the easy part of your commitment. There is a saying: "A fool and his money are soon parted."

Many studies have proven that people frequently recognize value in books and courses and make the investment, then fail to implement any of the principles they learned.

Once again, it all comes down to time. The element of time is the true investment. Time is what you need to invest first, and time is much more valuable than money. There will always be more money; what we will run out of and can't earn more of is time. Time is the world's most precious commodity. At the end of the day, the value of investment real estate is not a monetary result; instead, it is what it affords you to do with your time. Whatever you want to do with your time should be your choice, and my goal is to show you the value of investment real estate—it's time well invested.

Building Value Throughout the Book – Value Bricks

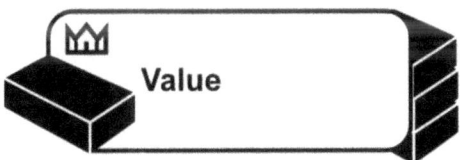

Wouldn't you like to be the landlord over your own money?

Investing money is serious business, and many of us shy away from taking daily responsibility for managing our money. We are happy to let our employer or the government just deduct it off our paycheck and invest it as they see fit. Then, we wake up surprised to see little, if any, return on our investment. As I mentioned earlier, some of us have read about and practice dollar-cost averaging. Dollar-cost averaging is how our investment advisors and planners deduct money each month from our bank account and invest these funds into many different vehicles like ETFs, mutual funds, stocks, bonds, etc. Again, we're leaving our returns up to someone else! I am not saying you shouldn't use any of these financial vehicles; rather, I am asking you to take control over some of your own money and manage it monthly.

My purpose? Prosperity for all aspects of your life forever.

Tell me and I forget, teach me and I may remember, involve me and I learn. — attributed to Benjamin Franklin

The 31 Days to Purchasing and Renting Your First Investment Real Estate Property book

This thirty-one-day journey to purchasing and renting your first investment real estate property is based on sixty-one coaching challenges. These challenges are for you to complete and take action.

The book is supported by free and paid resources, including our website, vaulttoinvestmentrealestatesuccess.com, to help you in each step of the thirty-one-day process.

The Vault to Real Estate Success website contains many resources to support your investment real estate journey, including financial calculators, worksheets, podcast episodes, and guest episodes with investment real estate experts, small business leaders, and entrepreneurial professionals.

Gut Feel

If you feel you have not been going down the right path when it comes to your financial foundation, this book will get you grounded and focused. It will show you how to purchase and rent your first investment real estate property in just thirty-one days.

What does it take to purchase and rent an investment real estate property in thirty-one days?

It takes an entrepreneurial mindset.

On Day 4, we go into depth about how to think like an entrepreneur and adopt the right mindset that will lead you to investment real estate success.

It takes patience.

As I've already mentioned, the first twenty-one days of your journey are critical. Throughout the book, we discuss the need for a strong financial foundation, but it is more than your finances that build your foundation.

Have you ever noticed that, when they are building new construction, the majority of the time spent in assembling the building takes place before the construction equipment is brought to the worksite? The majority of the time goes toward ensuring the building is zoned properly, completing the legal work to make the purchase, designing the blueprints, buying the materials and lining up the trades. The actual time on-site to build the new construction is only a small fraction of the time it takes to complete the work.

All this time spent before you actually see the construction is what I call the Ready phase, and you'll need patience to get through the thirty-one-day journey to purchasing and renting your first investment real estate property. No Ready detail can be missed. The first twenty-one days of this book are all about knowledge acquisition and laying a foundation.

Patience is needed in the big picture, too. The long-term buy-and-hold strategy I advocate means you will likely be involved in investment real estate for years or decades.

It takes action.

I'll show you in detail the process required to act on, purchase, and rent an investment property in thirty-one days. The daily coaching challenges will be a chance for you to put your learnings into action and take real steps toward your dream.

It takes a financial purpose.

The book will help you clearly define your financial purpose so you can focus on achieving the purchase and rental of your first investment property.

It takes preparation.

You'll learn everything you need to know so you can prepare and present the information required to purchase and rent your first investment real estate property.

It takes time.

Time, as we've discussed, is our most important asset. I'll show you how to use your time productively to learn all you need to know about investment real estate. We'll talk about how to organize your thoughts and how to outline your investment real estate goal before you make a purchase or rent the property. You'll learn, step by step, how to purchase your first investment property and rent it out in just thirty-one days through the coaching challenges each day.

So Where Do We Start?

You can either review the entire book from cover to cover first and then go back to each day's exercises and coaching challenges, or just jump right into the days and coaching challenges as you come to them.

I challenge you to do each day in order and not to move ahead until you have completed all the exercises and coaching challenges for that day. Make sure you have a notebook and pen handy, and there's also the option to purchase the accompanying workbook and planning guide created especially for this course. Keeping these resources close at hand as you go through the investment real estate purchase process will be an invaluable resource. What's more, the workbook and planning guide contains additional bonus questions and quizzes to help unlock your investment real estate learning. (Download the workbook and planning guide from our website or Amazon.)

Once you have made your first investment real estate purchase and rental, I invite you to contact me. I would love to hear about your success, learn whether I can help you in any way, and see if you need more coaching help. I will be waiting on the porch.

With warmest appreciation,

W. Rick Harris

Author, 31 Days to Purchasing and Renting Your First Investment Real Estate Property

INTRODUCTION

Every stage of life provides us with different opportunities. My current stage of life got me thinking about the opportunity I now have to share my investment real estate knowledge and expertise to benefit others. I believe strongly that including investment real estate in your portfolio can be a significant contributor to your overall financial success, and the level of that success has a lot to do with the stage in life when you start purchasing investment real estate.

My goal with this book is to lay out advice tailored to help Generation Z (born 1995–2009) millennials (born from 1979–1993), Generation Xers (1965–1978), and baby boomers (1946–1964). When general advice won't apply across the board, I offer specific strategies that suit each group. This is because I believe that each age stage involves some personal growth: Gen Zers and millennials entering adulthood, Gen Xers entering parenthood, and baby boomers entering a time that's focused more on living than on accumulating more wealth.

Adding financial investment pressure is not always prudent, and in this book, I will help you recognize when you, as an individual or as a couple, are ready. Your family and community circumstances will have an impact on when you purchase investment real estate, the type of investment real estate you purchase, why you might purchase investment real estate, and how you go about purchasing investment real estate.

HOW INVESTMENT REAL ESTATE TOUCHES OUR LIVES

The path to investment real estate success is different for everyone. This book is intended to help you explore and make the most of whatever stage of investment real estate you are in. The stage you're in is determined by more than just your age. Your age can indeed be a major determining factor, although there are many others, including how you invest.

As I discussed in the "Welcome" section, the majority of your financial investments are likely controlled by second- or third-party folks, most of whom you have never met and perhaps never will meet. Investment real estate, however, is not a passive endeavor, and so when you start down that path, you may be taking firsthand control of how you invest your money for the first time in your life. You will need to be hands-on and consider many factors, including the type of real estate you consider, the length of time of your mortgages, your financing options, where you invest, where you source funds to invest, whether you take on partners, how your investment decisions affect your family, and how much risk you're willing to take on.

In this section, I will review, by stage of life and generation, how investment real estate decisions will impact your accumulation of wealth for future prosperity. I hope you'll return to this chapter more than once, and that each time you read it, you'll turn another thought into action.

As infants, we rely on someone to feed us, clothe us, protect us, love us, educate us, shelter us, and meet our financial needs. Our parents usually fill this role, and in many cases, the whole thing is new to them as they are just starting their adult lives when we arrive in this world. Most of our parents relied on rental property to shelter their families in the early stages of parenthood until they could build a nest egg to purchase a family home. Having children is one of the main reasons people purchase a home, so that they can start assembling a form of family wealth.

It is interesting how, as young adults, many of us move out of our parents' home to start our lives and we become tenants in someone else's investment real estate, only to return to our parents' home shortly thereafter. This happened to me, and it happened with my children. Many of us have returned to the family home at different phases of our lives. The *why* is generally economic in nature: we no longer have enough cash or cash flow to pay our rent, or we move back home to save enough money to purchase our own home. Generally speaking, today's young adults aren't rushing into getting married or starting a family of their own, and they are not giving investment real estate much thought.

My hope is that, regardless of your age or generation, *31 Days to Purchasing and Renting Your First Investment Real Estate Property* helps you build your financial foundation, unlock your sustainable wealth, and create your living legacy. The keys to your vault are a combination of goal-setting, motivation, embracing failure, discipline, education, and planning. Let's explore each of these keys to your vault.

Goal-Setting

Throughout the book, I talk about the importance of goal-setting.

"Done is better than perfect" is a philosophy I try to use as a guiding light, and I encourage you to do the same. By getting started with purchasing and renting your first investment real estate property and following the book's suggestions, you will learn by doing along the way. Soon, you'll be confident you are ready and set to go after your goal to purchase and rent your first investment real estate property.

Right from the start of the book, I introduce you to the optional workbook and planning guide. Why? The biggest reason is goal-setting. Some of the information I use regarding goal-setting was developed by USA Today. According to research from USA Today, folks who made New Year's resolutions were divided into two groups: people who not only made resolutions but wrote them down, and people who made resolutions but never wrote them down.

The researchers followed up with both groups a year later and, surprise, surprise, 44 percent of the folks who wrote down their goals acted on them, while just 4 percent of the people who never wrote their goals down acted on them. This meant those who wrote their goals down increased their chances of success by 1,100 percent.

In the book, you'll discover several effective goal-setting methods that will help you purchase and rent your first investment property in thirty-one days.

You don't have to spend a crazy amount of time searching for an investment goal; the framework is provided in the workbook and planning guide, making it easy to write down your goal. Best of all, you don't have to wait a year like in the research on goal-setting discussed by USA Today—you will know within thirty-one days if your goal has been achieved.

We discuss several goal-setting methods in the book. They include: Ready, Set, Goal; Base, Better, Best; and SMART. These are the methods you'll use to achieve the goal of purchasing and renting your first investment real estate property.

The Base, Better, Best System

Goal-setting has played an important role in my athletic life. Using the Base, Better, Best system of goal-setting not only helped me as an athlete but has been indispensable in our investment real estate business.

To help you understand what the Base, Better, Best system is, I will give you an example below and explain how I used the system in my half-marathon training regimen.

Think of anything you might do in life. It can be as basic as being a baby learning how to walk. First, a baby learns to crawl; this is the mobility base, getting from one place to another. Within several months, the baby learns to walk; their original baby movement base was crawling, and now that they've learned to walk, walking is now their better. For a couple of months, they crawl more than they walk, so crawling remains their base. Eventually, the baby stops crawling and walks most of the time. Now, walking becomes their new base of movement.

With anything you learn in life, your base is always your original method to the skill, and then, as you progress in the skill, your base of the skill changes.

I look back on my original base to run: the farthest distance I had ever run was five kilometers. Over an eighteen-week half-marathon training program, I gradually moved from a base of five kilometers to a new base of 21.1 kilometers.

Each stage of life and generation sees our plans evolve.

My original running goal was 5K. After I achieved my goal of 5K, it was easy to start evolving as an athlete and build my 5K base into a larger running base of 21.1K.

In each of the running clinics I have taken, the first thing they ask you is, how do you run your first kilometer? The answer is one step or stride at a time.

Think of your financial base like an athlete starting to train. Start by saving one dollar at a time. Your financial training might be first developing a system of savings. Do you have any money left over at the end of each month after meeting all your financial obligations?

On Day 3, we will spend time reviewing your funds available at the end of each month to help you acquire your down payment amount; if no funds are available at the end of each month, we will create a base of positive cash flow. Developing a positive cash-flow mentality—a mentality in which you always bank a portion of your income after all expenses—is the foundation of owning investment real estate. Even though you will get financial advice about what constitutes positive cash flow, for the purpose of this book, only purchase properties where the rental income covers all expenses, including principal paydown.

We will also discuss on Day 15 how to create different sources of down payment funds.

Your financial base might start with your down payment amount in mind. In calculating the amount you require for your down payment, your base amount could be 5 percent, better could be 10 percent, and best could be 20 percent of the investment real estate property's total price.

Setting SMART Goals

On Day 18, we introduce you to the SMART goal-setting technique. SMART goals are specific, measurable, acceptable, realistic, and time-bound.

Folks, I believe in goal-setting so much that I ensured this book's title passed the SMART goal-setting test. The title is **specific**: purchase and rent your first investment real estate property. It's **measurable**, against a method outlined of thirty-one days, with day-by-day challenges. It's **achievable**, because I have personally done this several times, and **realistic**, because it is not only myself but others before and after me in the investment real estate field who have done this. Finally, it is **time-bound**: you'll achieve your goal in thirty-one days.

I also mentioned the importance of goal-setting and how Albert Einstein recognized this during his incredible life. Thanks in part to Einstein's practice of writing down his goals, the world gained some of its most important scientific formulas.

Motivation

In his book *Before Happiness*, Shawn Achor talks about the hidden keys to achieving success, spreading happiness, and sustaining positive change. Notice that Achor ties spreading happiness and sustaining positive change together with achieving success. The book you are reading now contains facts, events, and actions related to investment real estate that will help you build a successful foundation, sustain positive change with those you encounter as a result of your investment real estate journey, and spread happiness for years, decades, and generations to come. In short, you'll create your living legacy.

Many authors use parables, personal stories, or sports illustrations to guide readers and help them understand that our efforts, abilities, and actions lead directly to our success. Achor is one of those authors, and I really enjoy his work.

In *Before Happiness*, Achor speaks about what he calls X-spots. As he explains, the X-spot for a marathon runner occurs near the end of a race, when you would think the runner would be almost out of gas and ready to call it quits. But instead, with the finish line in sight, the runner reaches down deep and musters the energy and will to sprint to the finish line. Achor suggests that there are many X-spots in all facets of life and that they help your brain believe that success is close, possible, and worthwhile. He goes on to say that X-spots need not be near the end of completing a project; they can be found all along the way. As a half-marathon athlete, I could not agree with this more. I have realized, even in training, that X-spots are just around every corner. Recently, I was doing hill training on eight hills, and when I reached the eighth hill, I noticed that my pace picked up while running up the incline; I was almost in sprint mode.

Achor suggests that people design mini-goals they can achieve daily and focus on progress to date rather than what's left to do, especially for challenging or mundane tasks. He also talks about how this will cue your brain to release productivity-enhancing chemicals to speed up your progress. You should also create a to-do list and check things off as you go through your day. These actions will increase the likelihood of an X-spot experience. I will add that you can also develop a mental checklist and check off your progress mentally if you are working on a long-term project, like training for or running a marathon. I have run more than fifty half-marathons, and the training regimen is etched in my mind. However, I do make changes to my training from time to time to work on getting a better result. It took me several races to break a time threshold I had desired, and part of my training involved building a strong physical foundation while recognizing when I needed to change things up.

Don't be afraid to modify the processes I outline in this book; there is lots of time to peak. And in the meantime, there's nothing like the feeling of mentally checking off your progress—you get an instant rush without having to look for paper or a pen (try running eight hill repeats and you will know exactly what I'm talking about). By using the consistent processes that I outline in each day and each coaching challenge, following investment real estate best practices will become more natural to you. You'll start noticing X-spots and having success rushes.

In addition to helping you monitor your progress, I've included illustrations of what I call Value Bricks throughout the book. Value Bricks are action triggers. Why bricks? Bricks are laid in courses and patterns known as bonds, collectively known as brickwork, and they may be laid in various kinds of mortar, which holds the bricks together to make a durable structure. Humankind has been making and using bricks for over five thousand years. Keep an eye out for Value Bricks as you read and use the information to help you build a strong financial foundation. You already saw an illustration of a Value Brick in the Value chapter.

Embracing Failure

Most of us have seen at least two major upturns and downturns in financial market conditions during our lives, whether it be in our own city, state/province, or country, or elsewhere in the world. Currently, we are in a global downturn that is more persistent than we've seen in the past. However, like everything else in life, this too shall pass. It's what you do in tougher times that defines your character and creates success. Have you ever noticed we all love to hear stories about people who have failed and bounced back to build an admirable life?

In my own life, I've had to learn from my failures in order to succeed. I will cite examples of this throughout the book; for now, I'll share a lesson that I learned early on, when my wife and I purchased our first investment property and sold it within a couple of years. Instead of reinvesting the gained equity and mortgage paydown on more investment property, we spent the money on diminishing-value toys and other "stuff," meaning that, in the end, we had very little return to show.

At the end of the day, the guidance I offer you is tried and true, but at times, you will want to explore the truth on your own. My parents gave me great advice growing up, and yet, nine times out of ten, guess what—I didn't take it. I had to learn the hard way and let the history of failures repeat itself. Many of us feel that failure is a rite of passage and that when life throws a new adventure at us, we must sometimes take the journey on our own. I hope to at least give you some caution signals to learn from; it is up to you to yield.

Remember, my goal is to get you to take that first step into investment real estate, and I'll always be available to help you through my website, vaulttoinvestmentrealestatesuccess.com. Your continued path forward will come from your ability to take continuous action; failure is part of your path.

"Failure is success in progress."

Albert Einstein was one of the greatest minds of our time, and in this quote, he summarizes the value of failure to our future success.

The biggest investment real estate failure my wife and I experienced was a false start that took us over a decade to recover from. We had the resolve to overcome the challenge. It wasn't easy, but in retrospect, that failure had a silver lining: it was a critical learning experience that made it possible for me to effectively coach, guide, and support you on your journey. In many ways, that experience directly led me to create this book as a guide so you can invest in real estate for yourself while avoiding some of the pitfalls we encountered.

Through our story and the stories of others, you will receive guidance that enables you to build a strong financial foundation, unlock sustainable wealth, and create a living legacy that follows your heart.

Discipline

In his book *No Excuses!: The Power of Self-Discipline*, Brian Tracy discusses how discipline can be the difference between winning and losing, between greatness and mediocrity.

Through discipline and following our thirty-one-day system, you can take yourself from failure to accomplish your financial goals to a strong start on building sustainable wealth. By working through the thirty-one days, you can go from being a possible victim of the long-term care system, a situation many of our seniors have found themselves in during the COVID-19 pandemic, to living independently on your own for your entire life.

Tracy also discusses the power of discipline in seven critical areas of your life. These areas are goals, time management, finances, responsibility, character, personal health, and courage.

Even though our thirty-one-day system is not focused on every discipline outlined in Tracy's book, by following the system and taking action through the sixty-one coaching challenges, you can get in the habit of treating investment real estate as part of your foundational financial journey.

You will develop the habits behind goals (purchasing and renting your first investment real estate property), time management (thirty-one days, sixty-one coaching challenges), finances (building your financial foundation), character (your legacy), personal health (I used some of the methods in the book to train for half-marathons), and finally, as Tracy outlines, courage (do you have the courage to purchase and rent your first investment real estate property?).

Part of my goal is for you to have prosperity for all aspects of your life forever. The guidance I offer through the thirty-one-day system can help you create a disciplined path.

The pathway to purchasing and renting your first investment real estate property may not be paved with gold, but following the thirty-one-day system, including taking action on the sixty-one coaching challenges, can lead you to sustainable wealth and help you build habits to take action.

My website holds a wealth of sustainable investment real estate knowledge, resources, execution strategies, ideas, principles, and processes to help you in your investment real estate journey. The website is part of this book's strong foundation, sustainability, and living legacy. The saying "actions speak louder than words" has been a catalyst motivating my wife and me to move from analysis paralysis to the purchase of investment real estate. With the worksheets and templates available through my website, you can create your vision and follow through to success, just like we have. Visit vaulttoinvestmentrealestatesuccess.com to learn more.

Education

We are composed of the conscious and unconscious influences of the many points of contact in our lives. It starts with our mother, father, and family; then our friends and social and educational contacts; then traditional media, such as TV, print books, and magazines; and now an explosion of social media, such as Facebook, Twitter, LinkedIn, Instagram, Snapchat, Periscope, and TikTok, with many more social media platforms on the horizon. We are inundated with so much information that it's hard to know if we are having an original thought.

I don't profess to be the only one who has expertise in investment real estate, and I will introduce you to others who are researching how to succeed in this area. I have read hundreds of books and thousands of articles and listened to thousands of hours of recordings, podcasts, and live seminars in my effort to continue my personal growth and investment real estate education. I am happy to share those references and links to ideas and thoughts that influenced my beliefs, with thanks to all my peers who have helped me transform my thoughts and ideas into actions and outcomes. They have been of great value to me, and I believe they will be of great value to you, too.

My sincere wish is to add to this wealth of educational materials by creating new ideas and processes to help you develop your strong financial foundation, unlock sustainable wealth, and create a living legacy that is uniquely yours.

Planning

My journey to becoming a half-marathon athlete was instrumental in my ability to plan successfully, and I'll reference this story throughout the book.

As you read this chapter, I hope you are starting to think about the stage and phase of life you are currently in and how it will affect your investment real estate strategies. What will your investment blueprint look like? How will you use it to build your investment real estate portfolio? How do you utilize your current financial portfolio to preserve its value and encourage it to grow, providing you with additional revenue now or in the future?

Generational Reasons to Succeed

Whether you are a member of Gen Z, a millennial, a Generation Xer, or a baby boomer, sometimes certain investment real estate purchasing strategies or processes might be more meaningful to one generation than another. In this book, I offer specific strategies tailored by generation; however, please note that I don't mean to pigeonhole all people according to their age. It's just that identifying the common characteristics of the different generations allows me to help those in different stages of life to build a strong financial foundation that's right for them.

Members of Gen Z are often labeled "digital natives," and, like the millennial generation, they get painted negatively because of their screen time. Again, I am not a big fan of labels and trying to fit a whole generation into a tidy box. Gen Z will bring leadership to the world coming out of the pandemic. Investment real estate will see transformations in how it is used because of Gen Z. I see opportunities for what I call the "Gen Z Suite," a strategy built on income suites with their grandparents.

If you are aged twenty-seven to thirty-seven (a millennial), you might be considering starting your first career, getting married, or starting a family. Your focus should be to accumulate wealth for your future prosperity. There are many options available to you, and I recommend you give up certain lifestyle niceties. You should sacrifice some of your privacy for short-term gain and start to realize that, for most of you, time is your champion if you use it properly. You need to develop financial discipline and understand the good, the bad, and the ugly of debt.

Toward the end of the book, on Day 30, we will discuss the "Buy, Invest, Remortgage, Buy, Invest, Re-mortgage" strategy. This strategy helped my wife and I build our investment real estate portfolio.

Those of you aged thirty-eight to fifty-five (the Gen Xers) are entering the earning power stage of your lives. It is a time when many families and children are maturing. You are at the point in your life when you should be seeking wealth maximization and planning further for retirement. You are realizing that a significant reduction in annual income is likely unless you develop a strategy that offsets your income source from your employer, and that investment real estate could be a key part of this strategy. You have other investment vehicles, but realize you don't have much control over the returns they deliver. You are looking for greater control.

Those of you aged fifty-six to seventy-four (the boomers) are in an interesting position. If you're still working, you might have spent decades saving and watching and hoping your hard-earned money was growing. Now you might be staring in the mirror and realizing you have not paid enough attention to the returns and income you will have at retirement. You know you are coming up short, and so you're looking to find an investment vehicle that can mature in the next ten years.

Some boomers will have already retired and left the workforce, and you may be finding that the golden years don't provide the level of golden returns you had expected. The financial future you had envisioned in retirement is not reality, and there is a growing need to supplement the retirement life you desire. This desire to live a more prosperous life has you driving the fastest-growing segment of the workforce and returning to work to supplement the shortfall between what you thought you could live on and what you actually can live on. You don't want a meek retirement existence; you want to have a lifestyle similar to the one you had before retirement. You are also beginning to realize your health-care costs, travel, and other recreational expenses are higher than you had calculated.

Many boomers are at a point where we have a lot more life to live and are looking for ideas or to get out of our comfort zone, perhaps a little or perhaps a lot. We are also the parents of Generation Xers and millennials, and grandparents to Gen Zers, who are changing the investment real estate landscape. Gen Xers are the "family action" generation; unlike their parents, especially their fathers, Xers walk their talk and invest time in their families. The "living legacy" part of this book might be an area where you, as a boomer, may do a little more reflection and learn from the younger generations.

Millennials are often called the Boomerang Generation because they return home after leaving the nest. As boomerangers, they tend to communicate with their parents more than previous generations, but they do so through technology; in fact, they are using technology more than any other generation. I know this because texting is by far the easiest way for my wife and me to reach our millennial son and daughter-in-law; for them, the cell phone is only a text communication device and a way to use the Internet. Gen Zers and millennials are helping the world embrace technology, and I say, as boomers, let's jump on board and enjoy the ride.

Boomers: The Impact of Longer Lives

In North America, over eleven thousand boomers turn sixty-five every day, and a person turns fifty-five every seven seconds. Many recent employment numbers show that the fastest-growing age group entering the workforce is fifty-five to fifty-nine. I will talk about the additional resources boomers can generate with investment real estate and how to build on these revenue streams.

Boomers have parents who have lived with or are living with health issues into their late seventies to mid-nineties. Currently, in North America, there are just over 100,000 people over one hundred years of age, and this number is projected to increase more than tenfold to more than a million people between 2040 and 2050. Many boomers, including myself, are healthier than our parents and are living proof we will live longer; living to and past one hundred and staying healthy will not be unusual for many of us.

You'll find many references to boomer health in this book; we are on the verge of what I call "leapfrog health care" and medical advances that will extend your lifespan. Study and practice the techniques and references mentioned in this book, and you will see why you need a strong financial foundation, sustainable wealth, and a living legacy. The financial consequences of this longevity to boomers personally and to our country's economic infrastructure are going to be major. Deficit spending is the norm for most countries, and this meal ticket will be a Greek salad for many other countries in the future. The United States and Canada are not immune to continued deficit spending, and with the severe financial pressure put on all nations because of COVID-19, deficits are going to be a mainstay for a very long time.

Boomers will be around to see the consequences of our government's spending actions. We need to protect ourselves more than ever.

Many boomers have taken a beating with their financial investments and are seeing poor, if any, returns on our investments. We have seen two economic downturns in the last ten years, just as we are getting ready to enter our golden years. We need to find a more reliable investment vault. This vault must increase our cash flow and the return on our investments. My book will open the vault that is right under our feet.

In an article for the community newspaper *Metro* entitled "The future will be the good old days," author Mike Goetz talks about how car manufacturers are already discussing longer life expectancy. He gives much credit to Sheryl Connelly, who serves as the resident "futurist" at Ford Motor Company in Dearborn, Michigan. She talks about having to relinquish your driver's license at age 80. This is one thing when your life expectancy is 85, she notes, but it is entirely another thing if your life expectancy is 105. What does this mean? Car manufacturers are paying attention to life expectancy rates. Connelly says nobody wants to drive a vehicle designed for old folks, but this is where technology steps in and serves everyone. Technology is making driving safer for the elderly, but we all get to enjoy the benefits of blind-spot warnings, cruise control with automatic gap control and braking, and around-the-car camera monitors.

You may be wondering what driving a vehicle well into your nineties or hundreds has to do with investing in real estate. For many of us, our vehicle is our second-largest monetary investment. Vehicles are getting better shelf life, but if we all live and drive well into our hundreds, how many vehicles will we need to maintain and/or purchase over that time? If you retire at sixty-five, it will take a strong financial foundation with sustainable wealth to keep you in the driver's seat in the future.

The Health–Wealth Connection and the Coronavirus Pandemic

When I started to write this book, I never for one moment envisioned that a worldwide pandemic would bring not only the health of the globe to its knees but take the world's economy down with it.

My hope is that by the time I have this book to market, the pandemic will be in the late stages of winding down and we will have a vaccine. I have a ton of confidence in the scientific, medical, and technological communities that a cure will be found.

I know the lessons learned from this pandemic will mean the chances of another one crippling the world's health and the economy will be much lower in the future.

In their book *Transcend: Nine Steps to Living Well Forever*, authors Ray Kurzweil and Terry Grossman, MD, talk about how health and medicine are moving into the new information technology era. Kurzweil, who has written extensively about a key characteristic of information technology called "very rapid exponential growth," talks in the book about how we now can dramatically reduce the risks of our biggest killers—heart disease and cancer—and dramatically slow down the aging process. The purpose of *Transcend* is to explain how you can take full advantage of the available information to help you eliminate your chance of disease and dramatically slow the aging process, starting right now.

Kurzweil and Grossman's biggest fear is that most conventional health-care practitioners are caught up in the old health-care paradigm. Many national governments are stuck in a similar paradigm regarding aging, retirement, and funding the medical and retirement systems.

The Canadian government recently repealed the eligibility age for Old Age Security (OAS) from sixty-seven to sixty-five—short-term political gain for long-term pain of more overspending by the government and more Greek on the financial government-spending menu.

All of these factors are compelling reasons for us to take control of our retirement income into our own hands, rather than relying on the government or other institutions to provide us with the quality of life we want in our old age.

Medical Technology's Impact

We are seeing pharmaceutical companies, medical research labs, and medical universities stepping up to work on COVID-19 like they've never stepped up before. There is going to be much good news as the pressure mounts to find a cure for COVID-19.

I call the many advances in medicine and health-care technology "leapfrog healthcare." The medical advances are coming at an exponential rate, and things that took years in the past will take a matter of months going forward. As a society, we can't live in the past. We are living in the past regarding aging, and we are still living in the past when it comes to our estimates of how long it will take to bring medical advances to market.

I believe the global population is going to reach well beyond ten billion, pandemic or no pandemic. Think of the pressure on the planet's resources. Are we ready for this additional pressure, and will you as an individual be in a position to survive financially? We know that governments are too slow to react and that too many decisions are made for political ambition, not for practical reasons.

Recently I read a blog by Preston Ely titled "How to Make Money by Staring at the Ocean." (Later, I'll show you how my wife and I made money staring at the Rocky Mountains.) Ely writes for *Success Magazine* and has access to a list of over 250,000 e-mail subscribers. He asked them what they were most concerned about in life right now. The options he gave were a) physical health, b) money, c) spirituality, d) mental/emotional health, and e) all of the above equally. Ely was amazed to discover that 93 percent of responders were most concerned about money. Even more interesting, those who answered "all of the above equally" had a 75 percent higher chance of becoming wealthy! The blog goes on to say that wealth is naturally attracted to people who are physically, spiritually, and mentally healthy—in other words, whole.

Studies have shown that physical health and mental health go together. Throw in a little spirituality and a little money, and you have the magic elixir for success. It is not a tough pill to swallow should you prescribe your own preventative medicine.

Have you noticed that we as consumers are getting ahead of the game when it comes to our health? Many of us are wearing technology, such as the Apple Watch, Fitbit, Polar, Garmin, and many other devices, to monitor our health and out-doctor the doctors. This wearable technology is just the beginning. We all know that no one will take better care of us than we will. With all the Wi-Fi-enabled devices and the Internet, don't you think our doctors should be doing a much better job of using the information from our devices and working in partnership with us regarding our daily health?

Even though my doctor has embraced technology in his office, he has shown no desire to use technology that would allow him to share information with his patients. All my personal health information stays within the four walls of his office—I don't have access to it. With the technology I own, I can measure my health by collecting data multiple times a day; unfortunately, though, what I collect daily does not connect with my doctor's technology. I end up being my own medical practitioner with health data I collect on myself.

I have read that, soon, many of us will be able to do our own bloodwork at home and immediately access our results. I believe these advances in personal health care will come with recommendations that will be more reliable than those given by our physicians, and timelier. Our personal use of technology will keep many of us ahead of the grim reaper. The health-care systems and the government will not be paying enough attention to people using technology to maintain better personal health and longevity. This groundswell of people living much longer than expected will, again, put much pressure on society.

You might be wondering what all this has to do with investment real estate. It's simple: I believe that if you are taking care of your health on a daily basis, you need to become more engaged in your financial well-being and use investment real estate to protect your daily wealth.

The Truth About Pensions

If we are making strides toward living longer, healthier lives, we will soon realize the lucky ones are those with a defined-benefit pension they can draw on for many more years than the years they worked with their employer. In the United States and Canada, defined-benefit pensions are going the way of the dodo bird and being replaced with defined contribution pensions. I personally saw the company I worked for implement this strategy. Luckily, most of the company's boomers escaped the program, but those coming after us are being forced to accept a defined-contribution program.

The Problem with Pensions

In the simplest terms, a defined-benefit pension is a pension that keeps paying you money until your death. You can't outlive this pension. If you have this type of pension, count yourself lucky.

If you have a defined-contribution pension, you have a good chance of outliving it, mostly because of the poor returns on your investments in the pension. In addition, many companies have employees self-direct their pension, in which case, unless they are watching the stock market all the time, they end up with low returns.

What if you have no pension except for your government pension? There is lots of advice out there on how to build a complete financial portfolio, but there is almost always a catch to this advice because those who give it tend to have a financial incentive to get you to purchase specific products for your portfolio.

I think you have figured out by now that I am passionate about investment real estate. Please remember, though, that I don't sell investment real estate. I am one of the lucky ones who have a balanced financial investment portfolio, but I also experienced the two most recent economic downturns. I watched our RRSP contributions take a licking, and my company pension has been under siege, as the company I worked for tried to catch up on underfunding. What I know is that there is a strategy you can follow to ensure your money will outlive you. My wife and I are currently using this as part of our investment strategy, and it is working for us.

I jump between "I" and "us" because, as those in a relationship know, both people need to be on board with any financial decisions. If you are married or have a significant other, don't take this investment real estate journey unless there is a shared feeling of "us." My wife and I have seen and continue to see greater returns through our investment real estate than are realized from my company pension or my wife's RRSP contribution program.

If you have no pension, then you need this investment strategy more than ever. For Gen Xers and millennials, defined-benefit pensions will be a rarity. Any type of pension will become harder to earn as part of your compensation, so self-responsibility becomes a big part of your vault to any type of wealth creation. Whether you are Canadian or American, these pension issues affect you the same way. I am not worried about Xers' and millennials' current lifestyle and their ability to enjoy life to the fullest; rather, I'm concerned about their future. Many studies indicate that the children of boomers may not have the same level of financial security in their retirement as their parents. But children and grandchildren shouldn't have to have a retirement life that is less enjoyable than that their parents or grandparents enjoyed.

Recently in Canada, the federal government and most of the provinces agreed to make changes to the Canada Pension Plan (CPP) that will have very little impact on boomers because the changes were phased in starting in 2019. As of 2019, there were more boomers drawing CPP than contributing to it. It amazes me that we try and protect the lower-income earners but they continue to get sideswiped; for those earning below the income cap, these increased contribution rates will result in higher deductions and lower take-home pay.

There is a little glimmer of hope when it comes to wealth creation. According to a CBC News article by Dean Beeby posted on February 24, 2016, a new analysis from the federal finance department determined that Canadians aged twenty-eight to thirty-four are the wealthiest such generation in the country's history. This is great for Canadians, but it's not a trend worldwide. Youthful Canadians are prospering far more than their counterparts in the United States, Australia, and Britain, where, according to Beeby, the younger generations are no longer successively wealthier. And in the United States and Australia, the rate of investment real estate ownership is double that of Canadians. Americans and Aussies, though, tend to have more difficulty keeping their investment real estate in a positive cash-flow situation. If you are not seeing positive cash flow, then all is for naught. We will talk about positive cash flow more as we get further into the book. As I mentioned earlier, the lower-income folks seem to take any changes to government-driven savings programs on the chin, and this new analysis referred to by Beeby confirms the growing inequality of wealth between the rich and everyone else. Through investment real estate, we can work to close that gap.

We are starting to see a few trends wherein the boomers are stepping up to help replace the lack of government help in housing; I will talk more about this later in the book. Not every boomer is out to bankrupt the system for their children and grandchildren.

I have noticed that each time there is a financial downturn, we see retirement programs under siege. To protect your future, I will guide you to build a vault that will reduce your worry and help you sleep at night. In fact, one of my main objectives is to help you earn money while you are sleeping—passive income.

The Value of Legacy

I challenge you to honor those who are no longer with us and take stock of and enhance or create markers of the impact your loved ones left on your life. I am a firm believer that we cannot grow in the future if we don't appreciate the past. We must take some responsibility to remember the legacies of those who went before us.

For the boomers among you, I challenge you to open your personal Vault to Investment Real Estate Success and impact the lives of Xers, millennials, and Gen Zers by giving them a hand-up, not a handout. Use the ideas outlined in this book to build a strong financial foundation, unlock sustainable wealth, and create legacy roots while you are still living. A good friend of mine, Jim Mansell, a former sales manager for a large food manufacturer, would tell his salespeople they should see evidence that they had made a sales call when they left the call. His underlying message was to challenge his sales team to notice if they had left a positive impact on the customer and created a living sales legacy. The sales legacy Jim was referring to was one that helped the profitability of the store, attracted more consumers, added point-of-sale materials to displays to create impulse buying, left the store staff in a better frame of mind, added value to every point of contact, and saw the salespeople engaged in a friendly manner with the store's customers. Many of Jim's salespeople did have a lasting effect on their customers, and many of the stores truly enjoyed the sales calls; therefore, he had created a living sales legacy.

What will your legacy look like? Are you investing your time in staying in contact with your family and friends? Are you leaving evidence that you have had a positive impact on their lives? What are you remembered for in each visit? Do you even wonder what you'll be remembered for? Invest some time and think about the impact you have on others. Will there be positive markers that people will see and reflect on that will cause them to know you are and were a positive influence on them and this earth?

Lifelong Learning Can Start at Any Age

I achieved the designation of Real Estate Investment Advisor (REIA) through the Real Estate Investment Network. I continue to walk my talk, and I look to continuous improvement and learning to support myself and those interested in using investment real estate to build a strong financial foundation, unlock sustainable wealth, and create a living legacy.

If you're like me, you are also committed to learning and appreciate it when an author updates their work to reflect new knowledge. Personally, I don't mind making another financial investment to obtain this new knowledge, but I believe it should be an investment in only new material. I also believe that, in today's technologically advanced world, a book should be a living and breathing resource that grows and changes with the times and that readers should have instant access to these changes. Therefore, if you send your e-mail address along with the words "Living and Breathing" to me at wrickh@vaulttoinvestmentrealestatesuccess.com, when I make any changes to this book, I will send you the latest e-book of *31 Days to Purchasing and Renting Your First Investment Real Estate Property* at no cost.

The *New Webster's Dictionary* describes the noun *vault*, in part, as meaning a "storage room for valuables." It defines *success* as meaning a favorable termination; however, I prefer the word *outcome* as opposed to *termination* as, rightly or wrongly, *termination* carries a negative connotation. My goal is to show you how to use the strategies in your Vault to Success to create the outcomes of a strong financial foundation, sustainable wealth, and a living legacy.

When you first hear or see the word *vault*, some of you might think of it as a verb, and you, too, are correct. You can think of vaulting as the ability to jump, leap, spring, hurdle, or bound. With investment real estate, you can look to jump-start your financial foundation; you can see investment real estate as a leap of faith into an area of financial belief you have never before experienced. You also can spring into financial action you never envisioned, hurdle financial challenges, and bound like a superhero into an area of financial risk that has many rewards for you, your community, and generations to come.

Whether you think of success as a noun or a verb, the key to your financial foundation, sustainable wealth, and legacy is learning. It requires a continuous process of investment real estate education that starts whenever you're ready to begin the journey and transcends to the great beyond.

The purpose of this book is to help you achieve prosperity for all aspects of your life forever. On Day 3, I will give you tools to recognize your financial base through The Investment Real Estate Way. Using investment real estate as your financial base is the first step in vaulting your way to prosperity through portfolio success.

More on Why I Wrote This Book

Over a decade ago, my employer at the time was concerned that few employees were joining the company pension plan. It was a defined-benefit pension plan, and I was a member. I had joined it because I was a poor saver, and I saw the company pension as a forced savings plan. The money would come off my paycheck every two weeks, and I couldn't access these funds until I retired.

Our VP of human resources traveled across the country to explain to employees the importance of joining the plan. The company was going to give every employee who had chosen not to join the pension plan when they had the opportunity to do so one more chance to join. It was a limited-time offer.

The VP's story was compelling. He explained that even though there were government pension plans, those plans were only set up to provide the basics of life's needs when you retired. He described what he referred to as the "three-legged stool," which is composed of three parts: (1) government retirement funds (e.g., 401K, CPP, and OAS), (2) registered savings accounts or other types of non-registered investments (e.g., bonds, stocks, etc.), and (3) company pension plans.

Even though I had joined the company pension plan, had a registered savings plan account and a few other stock investments, and was contributing to the government retirement savings plan, I felt a void.

The company and government retirement savings vehicles were controlled by the folks who ran the funds, and the registered savings funds were administered by others, too. Each of these retirement vehicles was funded by me and, if I contributed, the accounts grew modestly. The void I felt came from the fact that I had no control over any of these savings vehicles.

Over the years, my wife and I changed our principal residence to suit our growing family's needs. Each time we changed residences, we gained financially, which contributed to our modest financial portfolio. The equity growth in our real estate over time was awesome, but we needed a place to live and raise our family. Our home was another forced savings account, as we could not access this equity unless we sold our home. (Sure, we could have borrowed against the home, but paying interest on these funds without a plan just made no sense to us.)

Around this time, I had a conversation with a friend who mentioned how nice it would be to have a rental property and have your renters pay into your forced savings account. At first, I wondered what the heck she was talking about. She explained that you get a mortgage and collect rent and use the rent to pay the mortgage on that property, meaning that someone else would be paying into a forced savings account for you. It almost sounded too easy, but my wife and I took our friend's suggestion and bought investment properties.

We now have tenants paying rent and we are paying down the mortgages with that rent, thus creating a forced savings account. Today, our monthly gross income from our investment real estate represents a large portion of our monthly revenue. Down the road, this revenue will be the most considerable portion of our retirement income, exceeding the four other sources (company pension, registered savings, stocks, and government retirement programs).

A casual conversation with a friend turned into an "aha" moment for my wife and I, and it has put us in the strong position we are in today. Now I want to share our secret and help you to unlock your own Vault to Investment Real Estate Success and purchase your first investment real estate property in thirty-one days.

Why You Should Read This Book

I'm guessing you picked up this book because you had a gut feeling. Perhaps investment real estate is an area you have thought about over the years. Many of us start out as renters; we may have even paid Mom and Dad some rent while we worked, trying to figure out what our future was going to look like. During your time as a renter, you may have shared accommodation with others and rented near the college or university you attended. Or perhaps you rented with a friend whose parents had bought a property near the college or university, and they rented to other students as a way of offsetting the investment to house their child who was attending that school. Once you finished college or university and got a job, you likely started renting a place again, dreaming of the day when you could own your own house. If you were one of the many whose first rental experience was renting a basement apartment or a side-by-side, there was a good chance you knew the owners of the rental property. I am sure that, from time to time, you thought, "These folks are getting rich off my rent." You may have also thought, "If only someday . . ."

The Secret Sauce

The further you get into the book, the greater the detail you'll find. In fact, you might even say to yourself, "Didn't I already read this information earlier in the book?" You'll be right. This is the secret sauce.

The inspiration for this technique comes from Toastmasters, a group dedicated to improving your communication skills. At Toastmasters, you learn to give a series of speeches or talks. The secret sauce as you formulate your speech is, "Tell them what you are going to tell them. Tell them, and then tell them again."

Part of my goal is to get the basics of investment real estate investing to stick. I want you to take action—and remember, much of the responsibility is on you.

And so, let me ask you now: Is today your someday? Are you ready to be the owner to whom others pay rent every month and aspire to one day be like? Do you like the thought of earning higher returns from your investment real estate than the low interest rates paid by your bank or other investment vehicles? Do you feel that the government retirement programs or company pensions will not give you the income you would like to have in your retirement? Do you want some control over at least one of your investment vehicles? Do you like the idea of someone else paying down one of your mortgages or providing some additional monthly positive cash flow or equity growth you can access in the future?

If so, then this book will be of tremendous value to you.

Can you purchase and rent an investment real estate property in thirty-one days? Yes—I am living proof of this. When we first started our journey in adding investment real estate to our financial portfolio, we purchased two properties in thirty-one days. Many other investment real estate investors have purchased an investment property in less than thirty-one days. It can be done. You can do it. This book will show you how.

How This Book Is Organized

I've organized this book into three stages containing a total of thirty-one chapters, each representing one day, with sixty-one coaching challenges spread between those days.

Each day focuses on a specific part of your investment real estate journey and is presented in a logical order that guides you through the necessary steps. You'll find supporting information, knowledge, research in the area of investment real estate, and practical coaching challenges at the end of each day. Each challenge will get you to take action, moving incrementally toward your goal.

By the end of the thirty-one days, you'll have purchased and rented your first investment real estate property!

Generally, each day comes with two coaching challenges. Many people will think of a day as a day of work; the normal workday is eight hours, with a morning break, lunch break, and afternoon break. The amount of time you spend on each day and each coaching challenge is up to you. There is no right or wrong length of time; this is your journey, and when it comes to how comfortable you feel with your learning and progress, everyone is different.

Each day, you will notice whether or not the coaching challenge is working. But how will you know if it's working or not?

Easy—you must ask yourself if you are **closer to or farther away** from purchasing your first investment property. If you feel farther away, don't hesitate to reach out to me at wrickh@vaulttoinvestmentrealestatesuccess.com, detailing which coaching challenge you are working on and why you think you are moving farther away from your goal of purchasing and renting your first investment real estate property in thirty-one days. We might have to **change your approach.**

Is Audio Your Learning Mode of Choice?

If audio is your thing, please send your e-mail address to my e-mail above, and once the audiobook is available, we will advise you.

The 31 Days to Purchasing and Renting Your First Investment Real Estate Property Timeline

This book will teach you all you need to know to purchase and rent your first investment real estate property in just thirty-one days, divided into three stages.

Days 1 and 2 will explain what investment real estate (IRE) is and why you should make it part of your life.

Then, we'll dive into the "Ready, Set, Goal" concept for your investment real estate and rental property.

We will also look at how your age or stage of life impacts purchasing investment real estate. There are specific strategies for millennials, Gen Zers, Gen Xers, and baby boomers to help you get the most out of investment real estate at any stage of life. I will challenge you to fully appreciate the role that investment real estate can play in your life, and I will introduce you to a complete investment real estate system composed of a disciplined path of strategies and processes that will lead you to success.

You will realize that it is never too late, no matter where you are in life, to unleash the power of investment real estate in order to build a strong financial foundation, unlock sustainable wealth, and create a living legacy.

We will also explore how to unlock the equity in your principal residence to build your investment real estate portfolio. I will discuss how to release capital to work harder for you and how you can utilize this capital to grow your financial foundation and provide you with tax advantages you may never have thought were possible.

Stage I: Ready calls out your investment real estate purchasing power and mindset. I teach you how to create an overview of your financial portfolio that will position you favorably in the eyes of financial lending institutions so they will be more likely to support you. I also examine how to purchase your first investment property from your current financial base while ensuring that base does not get in the way of purchasing your second investment property and beyond. Finally, I help you to understand the role that government programs can play in helping you with your investment real estate journey, and how you can use your investment real estate portfolio to supplement government retirement programs that only help you with a minimum financial base in your retirement.

The Ready stage is set over days 3 through 18, and comprises over 60 percent of the book. That's no accident. Many people miss this stage, yet it is the part of the process that demands your greatest efforts, as it is foundational to your success.

In this stage, you'll learn why you should keep your day job, recognize there will be setbacks and learn how to build on them, and discover that investment real estate can come into your life when you least expect it. You'll also gain strategies for doubling down to jump-start or build upon an investment real estate portfolio that came into your life a little late.

Stage II: Set talks about how it takes a village of people to help you build a successful investment real estate portfolio. You'll determine who the members of your team should be, what their roles are, where you might find them, at which stage you need them, why they all have a role, and how to assemble the best team for you.

Many folks try and go it alone. If you have ever belonged to a sport, academic, or activities team, you know there is no "I" in team.

There is a common misconception that assembling a team comes with huge costs. The reality is it's not as expensive as people think. Often, all you have to do is watch someone's YouTube channel to get coached for free.

We will go into depth on creating your own Team REAL (Real Estate Advisory League). In most cases, the cost of assembling a great team is only paid when you use their services.

At the end of Stage II, you will make your first investment real estate purchase and begin your journey as an entrepreneur and small business owner.

Stage III: Goal makes it clear that investment real estate is not a get-rich-quick scheme and that it takes time to realize the potential in investment real estate. This section is all about making the most of the purchase of your first investment real estate property and setting things up to reap the benefits for years to come.

We will also discuss your exit strategy. At some point, your investment real estate journey will end, and there will be many ways to view your exit.

You'll learn how to use the legacy of inheritance while you are alive and have a say in how your legacy can make a bigger difference for your family and/or your community. The neat thing is that you are involved in the decision-making and get to enjoy the satisfaction of improving people's lives now. Building a strong real estate foundation can positively affect generations of your family and community, causing effects that live on long past your time in this world. This stage will help you set in motion clear strategies to build your own brick investment real estate house that can't be blown down.

To get the most out of this book, you must be an active reader. Throughout the chapters, I will ask you to participate and interact. Whether you are new to investment real estate and looking for a system to take you from the sidelines and onto the playing field or have already done some investing but aren't happy with your progress, you will learn how to achieve great results.

By the time this book reaches your hands, you will find many supporting blogs, numerous podcasts and guest podcast episodes, and a resource-rich website that will supplement this book. The Vault to Investment Real Estate Success website will be regularly refreshed with helpful information you can rely on to support your investment real estate portfolio development.

In addition, the book will be supported by an online course and a workbook and planning guide.

As I say during many of my podcasts . . . Let's get on with the show!

DAY 1 WHAT IS INVESTMENT REAL ESTATE, AND IS IT RIGHT FOR YOU?

Use this day to learn about what investment real estate is and determine if it's right for your financial portfolio. At the end of the chapter, complete the coaching challenges to define what your investment real estate success will look like. You'll use this information to build your foundation for purchasing and renting your first investment real estate property.

How Dreams Are Made

Real estate can have an incredible impact on our lives. We all need a place to live and lay our head at night; in part, that's why real estate has been and continues to be what dreams of wealth are built upon. How often have you heard of folks becoming rich in one area of their life and the first thing they do is to secure real estate to protect and grow their personal wealth?

According to Ray Kroc, the genius behind the success of McDonald's, getting involved in real estate was the "beginning of real income" for the company.

But what exactly is investment real estate? Simple—it's a property that generates income or brings us a profit or material result.

Ray Kroc saw that McDonald's success went beyond the billions of hamburgers sold. Owning and controlling the real estate that each McDonald's restaurant stands upon is the core of the true value and prosperity of McDonald's.

Investment Real Estate Can Be Your Genius

The beauty of investment real estate is that it can help us to gain financial returns, build equity, and leave a legacy for our children and loved ones for generations to come. It can give us a new career, one in which we work for ourselves. And it can go even deeper than that: for many, investment real estate becomes a calling.

Investment Real Estate as a Calling

Many of us identify deeply with social causes. Going green is an easy one; many folks tie their beliefs to this cause, which is crucial for the planet. As I mentioned already, when I was growing up, my father's Armed Forces career meant we relied heavily on good landlords with investment real estate to rent.

Much later, while on a road trip to watch the Toronto Blue Jays, my dad and I discussed our frequent moves and tallied up how many rental homes we lived in during my first twenty-one years in this world. It turns out we lived in twenty-one different rental homes!

This reliance on investment real estate owned by others is a big part of why investment real estate has become a social calling for me. Living in twenty-one different rental homes from infancy to young adulthood had a remarkably positive impact on my life.

Having a safe and secure place to live should be a given for all of humankind. My early life was filled with many safe and secure places to live thanks to investment real estate investors. Because of this, I believe that providing a safe, secure, and happy place for people should be part of your definition of investment real estate.

When you expand your definition of investment real estate, you begin to understand its true significance beyond just a wealth generator and see the real value investment real estate brings to the world.

Investment Real Estate as a Business

That said, there is still a business side to investment real estate, and I don't want to minimize this aspect. After all, it is hard to answer your social calling and provide great rental homes if you can't run a successful business.

In his book *The Canadian Real Estate Action Plan*, Peter Kinch talks about how few Canadians buy real estate as an investment. Only about 4 percent of the population ever purchases investment real estate. In the United States and Australia, the number is closer to 8 percent—still not huge.

Kinch goes on to note that roughly half of the 4 percent in Canada only buy two or three properties as a way of supplementing their financial portfolio and investments. If you buy more than three properties, you move into the top 2 percent of real estate investors in Canada—a very elite category.

How many times have you heard about such a small percentage of people taking action in any field and standing out from the crowd?

How to Determine if Investment Real Estate Is Right for You

Life is like a combination lock: your job is to find the right numbers, in the right order, so you can have anything you want. — Brian Tracy

When author and motivational speaker Brian Tracy compares life to a combination lock, he's on to something. Finding the right numbers means figuring out the right strategies and processes that will lead to success, and using them in the right order. Finding the right combination to your successful investment real estate vault is no different. Figure out the right strategies and processes and use them in the right order, and you'll be well on your way to achieving financial independence through investment real estate.

But first, you need to figure out if investment real estate is right for you. Determining that means asking yourself some hard questions. How would you assess your current financial situation? Are you building a strong financial foundation? Are you unlocking your sustainable wealth and a living legacy?

Earlier, I talked to you about my biggest why: my wife and I wanted an investment we had control over, and that captured our entrepreneurial spirit. What about you? Why do you want to go on this journey?

The answers to these questions will become clearer as you work your way through The Investment Real Estate Way.

The Investment Real Estate Way

The Investment Real Estate Way is a complete system tied to a disciplined use of strategies and processes. Purchasing your first investment real estate property requires you to find your way, and one of my goals is to guide you through this unique methodology.

The Investment Real Estate Way
- creates the conditions that will allow you to build your financial foundation;
- shows you revenue methods to sustain your wealth; and
- enables you to build a living legacy through investment real estate processes and principles that protect and preserve revenue and wealth for generations to come.

By now, you know that investment real estate is a way of life for myself and my family. It enables me to be socially responsible to others by providing a safe, secure, and happy place to live, and it helps me be a good steward of my own financial life. The Investment Real Estate Way takes things one step further. It allows me to share with you, my readers, how you, too, can create sustainable wealth and look after future generations of your own family.

The Investment Real Estate Way is a constant theme in this book. More than that, it is a way of life that can lead to a strong financial foundation, unlock sustainable wealth, and create a living legacy.

Residential Property: A House or a Home?

Most folks identify residential property as their home, a place where they live permanently as a member of a family or household. Many people have an emotional attachment to their home and refuse to call it a house. The word *home* has a more personal feel to it than the word *house*. The home is their private residence, and they are very protective of it.

Recently, I read a book by Alexis LeClair called *Retirement Groove: Finding Yours!* LeClair talks about your home being either your sanctuary or a place to hang your hat. Whatever your definition, your home or your house, this residential property can be the first cornerstone to building your financial foundation.

What the Three Little Pigs Teach Us About Investment Real Estate

In the fairy tale "The Three Little Pigs," each little pig built their own home, and each had a real attachment to their home. At the beginning of the story, the mother of the three little pigs told them, "You're old enough to build your own houses now. But beware of the big, bad wolf." The mother encouraged her children to go out into the world and gave them some good advice. We soon learn, however, that each little pig ended up with a different skill set, and even though they each knew that they needed to build a house, not all of them were able to recognize a strong foundation. Like the three little pigs, many of us experienced this when our parents sent us out into the world. We each processed the advice we received as young adults differently as we ventured out to begin our adult lives.

Only one of the three little pigs' homes was built on a strong foundation that not only took care of the current little pigs but provided for future generations to come.

The third little pig supported his family and was not critical of his siblings' choices. He gave them a hand-up in their time of need. His strong foundation survived the big, bad wolf, and the experience taught his siblings what a strong foundation looks like. Like the third little pig, I want to help you build a strong financial foundation.

Whether you call it your home or your house, your principal residence reflects who you are in mind, body, and soul. In many ways, how you use your home or house is a statement of your lifestyle or the lifestyle you want to convey to others. Your home should always be about you first. It should reflect your sense of what you want from life, and knowing whether you treat it as a place to hang your hat or as your sanctuary helps you build your foundation.

For most of us, our first or second home purchase is not our forever home. Laying a strong financial foundation might take you time and several home purchases. At the beginning of your journey, have one eye on enjoying your sanctuary and the other eye firmly focused on using the type of home you purchase or the equity you build as a vehicle to drive your Investment Real Estate Way.

If you are not honest with yourself, your foundation won't be built from bricks and mortar. Instead, you will find yourself in the same position as the first two little pigs, always waiting for the big, bad wolf to blow your house down. In today's world, bricks and mortar is more than just the tangible, touchy-feely stuff your home is made from; it is also knowledge and action.

Laying a Strong Knowledge Foundation

There's a lot to learn about investment real estate. You can find information in many different places: websites like vaulttoinvestmentrealestatesuccess.com, online courses, books, classes through private and public learning institutions, local meetups, national learning membership groups like REIN Canada, banking institutions, mortgage brokers, real estate agents, and more. But watch that you don't fall into the rabbit hole and get distracted like Alice in Wonderland.

Today's information-rich society can be a goldmine of knowledge. But how do we effectively mine the information? It's so easy to get sidetracked. How do we stay focused?

This book should help. I've distilled the most important information into a comprehensive guide that will take you step by step through the work and planning to start your investment real estate journey. The book contains all the information you need to purchase and rent your first investment real estate property in just thirty-one days. Use it as your reference guide—I promise I won't send you down too many rabbit holes.

In addition, the workbook and planning guide I created as a companion to this book will be a great resource to keep you on track. The workbook and planning guide is available for purchase in paperback and e-book format on Amazon. You can find more resources in our free Facebook community and our online course. Information about these can be found in the appendix.

I also talk a lot about developing your own Team REAL (or Real Estate Advisory League) to draw on the knowledge of a group of experts. This is one of the most critical elements for success, and I sincerely hope you will invite us to be part of your Team REAL.

Build Your Confidence

In the beginning, you may have little confidence in your ability to become an investment real estate investor; this is reason enough to read this book. In order to build your confidence, you need to get around like-minded people. As I mentioned earlier, a great resource right in your own backyard would be to look for a Meetup.com group in the area of investment real estate. A small fee or no fee gets you access to a meeting of like-minded investment real estate investors offering education to the group. Facebook also offers many investment real estate groups to choose from; I even provide one for readers of my book to connect and interact for support.

 **Ask yourself questions to lay your investment real estate foundation.**

Purchasing your first investment real estate property is the same as starting any business. Being prepared and doing your homework are vital to your success. The questions below will help you build your foundation of knowledge as you begin your real estate journey. Remember, please only use the answers supplied in this chapter as a guideline. You must be able to answer these questions for yourself.

The questions below are designed to get your investment real estate juices flowing.

Honesty is the best policy, and that's how you should handle the following questions. If you are not honest with yourself, who can you be honest with? Record your answers in your notebook or the workbook and planning guide, available for purchase on Amazon.

1. What is investment real estate? What is the difference between residential real estate and investment rental real estate, or home versus house?
2. What percentage of the population in Canada and/or the United States have investment real estate in their financial portfolio?
3. Is investment real estate really what I want? Why do I want it? Am I ready for it?
4. How much money must I set aside to purchase my first investment real estate property? (Don't worry if you don't know the specific amounts yet; use your best estimate. Your answer will become clearer as you read through the book.)

Down payment	$_____
Purchasing costs	$_____
Home inspection	$_____
Closing costs	$_____
Legal costs	$_____

5. Can I support an investment property if it costs me money every month? If so, for how many months?
6. What is the right type of property for me?
7. Is there a demand for investment rental real estate?

It's a lot of questions, but answering them will help you create a strong foundation for your investment real estate journey. If you answered the majority of these questions positively, it is time to move forward. Remember, there is one more coaching challenge for you to complete before you have finished Day 1. The great news is you have taken the first step.

 **Gaze into your investment real estate future. What does it look like? Envision a day in your life five years from now.**

This is an exercise you may want to place under your pillow as you sleep at night or set as a screen saver to refer back to from time to time. For maximum results, keep these words close at hand. Just like great athletes who use visualization to reach their goals, you can use this exercise to set your goals for investment real estate. Reading them again and again is a great way to visualize your future success.

In this coaching challenge, we're going to envision a day in your life, five years from now. Let's get you started by rubbing the crystal ball with the following questions. Get as detailed in your answers as possible. Record them in your notebook or the workbook and planning guide.

- Who are you living this day for? See yourself first, and then imagine your significant others around you.
- Why are you sharing this day with yourself and the others in your life?
- How does this feel?
- How has investment real estate enriched your life and your financial portfolio?

- Where is your investment real estate property?
- Has this created passive income streams? How will you invest these returns?
- Are your relationships with your family, friends, and community supporting your investment real estate decisions?
- What do these relationships look like?

Day 1 Key Recap

Record your key learnings and actionable items in your notebook or the workbook and planning Guide. (Optional)

- ⇧ Investment real estate is a long-term business opportunity and part of the financial portfolio you have decided to take control of and manage.
- ⇧ Just like any investment, there is some risk in purchasing investment real estate.
- ⇧ A strong foundation of knowledge is required for investment real estate success.
- ⇧ The investment real estate journey cannot be taken on your own without help. You need a strong team behind you—your Team REAL.

DAY 2 "READY, SET, GOAL" FOR YOUR INVESTMENT REAL ESTATE AND RENTAL PROPERTY

Use this day to learn the Ready, Set, Goal process, review The Investment Real Estate Way Starter Kit Checklist, and familiarize yourself with your personal income and expense statement and personal net worth statement. At the end of this day, complete the coaching challenges to understand if you are on track to purchase and rent your first investment real estate property.

To reach your goal of purchasing and renting your first investment real estate property in thirty-one days, you need a process to keep you on track. That's why I created Ready, Set, Goal and The Investment Real Estate Way Starter Kit Checklist.

The Ready, Set, Goal process is a training regimen that includes planning, procedures, and strategies. This process is critical to achieving your investment real estate outcome. The thirty-one-day framework is divided into three stages: Ready, Set, and Goal. Using this process, you will put a strong foundation in place, ensuring your investment real estate business will succeed.

A Note on Investment Real Estate Goals

As we learned on Day 1, if you buy more than three properties, you move into a very elite category of the top 2 percent of real estate investors.

My wife and I never set out to become part of the top 2 percent. As our real estate investment plan unfolded over the years, we ended up in the top 2 percent of real estate investors in Canada with twelve doors (income-earning suites or properties), which moved us, ultimately, into the top 20 percent of the wealthiest people in Canada.

Your investment real estate goal should be yours alone. What's right for someone else may not be right for you, and I am not trying to convince you to purchase more than one property. I find that most goals in life change as you get comfortable with each situation and goal you achieve.

Would I love to see you become part of the top 2 percent of real estate investors or in the top 20 percent of the richest people? Yes. By the way, the income threshold is not as high as you might think. This is another reason you should be viewing your net worth statement regularly.

At the end of the day, your status should only be a by-product of you achieving *your* investment real estate goal.

When most of us begin our real estate purchasing journey, we don't have a real estate investment plan because, statistically speaking, most of us will never go on to own more than our principal residence. A lucky few of us may own our principal residence and a vacation property.

The point is it's good to have a plan, but plans change over time. For now, let's focus on purchasing and renting one investment real estate property—your first.

Bang, You're Off and Running!!

Back in elementary school, did you ever compete in a race? If you did, you were probably introduced to the words *ready, set, go*.

The starter of the race would have you line up in your running lanes just before the race began. First, the starter would ask you to get ready (think about the race and get in your correct lane). Then they'd tell you to get set (in elementary school, this was as simple as looking down your running lane and making sure your shoelaces were tied up). Finally, you would focus, waiting for the final word from the starter: go.

As a short-distance and half-marathon runner, I found it effective to apply this simple discipline to investment real estate, where it forms the basis for the knowledge I am going to share.

When I started disciplining myself for investment real estate, I realized I was not in a hundred-yard dash; this process was much more like a marathon. And so, I established a process to get me off and running: Ready, Set, Goal.

The Ready, Set, Goal training regimen is a lifetime commitment to a financial process and an investment real estate starting mechanism.

Ready is your ability to get organized—a willingness and eagerness to embrace investment real estate and do something you never thought possible. The Ready portion of this book spans from Day 3 to Day 18. It's the preparation phase.

Are you ready to take your place on the investment real estate race line and pick your lane?

Once you're there, you can't run your investment real estate race on your own. To succeed, you need the guidance of mentors and experts. The Set stage establishes prearranged and fixed preparations that draw from the coaching and consulting of your Team REAL. This phase lasts from Day 19 to Day 24.

Finally, Goal is your drive and spirit, filled with vigor and enthusiasm to purchase and rent your first investment real estate property. This final phase lasts from Day 25 to Day 31.

The Investment Real Estate Way Starter Kit Checklist

A major component of *31 Days to Purchasing and Renting Your First Investment Real Estate Property* is The Investment Real Estate Way Starter Kit. The kit consists of three pieces: your personal income and expense statement, your personal net worth statement, and The Investment Real Estate Way Starter Kit Checklist.

Don't underestimate the importance of The Investment Real Estate Starter Kit. It's where all the magic happens or where the story ends.

In the contemporary version of the fairy tale "Snow White," the evil queen uses a magic mirror to learn who is "the fairest of them all." Each time the evil queen asks the question, the mystical mirror answers, "My queen, you are the fairest of them all." But one day, the evil queen gets a rude surprise when the mirror states that Snow White is, in fact, fairer. Angry, the evil queen hires a huntsman to kill Snow White.

We may not be evil, but we still need to look in the mirror to understand the reality of our financial situation. Some of us won't like the financial picture we see or won't like the message the mirror delivers, but that's why it's so important to look at our financial reality and know this is our financial base. Once we know our base, we can begin to change things for the better.

Knowledge + Change
= Prosperity for a Wealthy and Healthy Life

Creating prosperity for all aspects of your life forever is connected to the ongoing changes in your life. Whatever we do today must continue to revolve around building a strong foundation in wealth, knowledge, and health. You must commit to unlocking ways to sustain your wealth, knowledge, and health and create a living legacy.

Knowledge's impact on your wealth is evident in the world of investment real estate. Bringing health to your personal finances is a driving force behind my motivation to write this book. Longevity for humankind is at a tipping point. Even though we have been making small, incremental movements in life expectancy, we are on the cusp of taking a leap in extending human life by decades, not just a single year or several years.

In his book *Unretirement: How Baby Boomers Are Changing the Way We Think About Work, Community, and the Good Life*, Chris Farrell says healthy life expectancy, on average, has improved, although at a slower pace than overall life expectancy. Right now, we are living longer but not keeping our health up, and this continues to put more strain on society. This theme of living a longer, healthier life will keep coming up throughout this book. You are going to live longer than you think, so don't fight it. Focus on your financial health; the medical and technological world has your back in the other areas.

Good News through COVID-19

There is some good news for the world's health-care system as a result of COVID-19: new advances in medical technology are being driven faster and further because of the pandemic.

Even though short-term efforts put into curing COVID-19 have taken the focus off of other medical research, there are stories coming out every day about insights into advances in the cure of some types of cancer, Parkinson's, and other diseases that have been around for centuries.

The pandemic has brought two main benefits to the global medical community. First, the amount of medical and health technology innovations being shared is greater than in any time in the past. Second, COVID-19 has made us realize that no country is immune to any disease, and if we want to protect our citizens, we must band together as one world. The medical advances through improving manufacturing techniques and developing a vaccine on the go have been incredible.

I have a lot of confidence that we as humans will defeat this pandemic. We will be even more prepared in the future to combat any disease thrown at us, and we will not allow the world to fall to its knees in the future.

Personal Responsibility

Have you noticed that all of the advice and commentary surrounding staving off the coronavirus relates to taking care of your health and being healthy? Washing your hands, practicing social distancing, and wearing a mask in public are about taking personal responsibility.

You can be the author of your success and have your life play out like a fairy tale.

We all have seen the cruel results of living out your last years in a long-term care facility.

To avoid such a fate, you must be committed to your future. Find a way to stay ahead of the political reality of life. You might think your elected politicians have your best health and financial interests at heart, but we all have seen the devastation of the health-care and economic systems of every nation in the world under the pressure of recent events.

This book is the starting point for purchasing and renting your first investment real estate property. It is a small but critical tool, and if you keep an eye on technological and medical advances, you can ensure you are the keeper of your own finances and health, enabling you to avoid being at the mercy of your political and health-care system.

> *An investment in knowledge pays the best interest.* — Benjamin Franklin

The Investment Real Estate Way Starter Kit Components

The Investment Real Estate Way Starter Kit is composed of three pieces. Together, they make up your personal magic mirror and show you the true reflection of your finances. With the Investment Real Estate Way Starter Kit in place, your investment real estate goals can be realized.

1. Your personal income and expense statement

Let's start with piece number one, the personal income and expense statement. First, we'll learn its definition and look at the breakdown of its parts.

Traditionally, an income statement, or profit and loss account, is one of a company's financial statements. It shows a company's revenues and expenses during a certain period. There is not much difference between your personal income and expense statement and a company's, and when you purchase your first investment real estate property, you become an entrepreneur and small business owner.

Before we get ahead of ourselves, we need to understand what a personal income and expense statement is. Simply put, it is a record of your total personal revenue and total personal expenses that shows your personal total income revenue minus your total expenses, giving you a personal net income. This net income result can be positive or negative.

Later, you will create an income and expense statement as a small business owner that acts as your monthly report on the financial health of your investment real estate property. We will revisit this idea on Day 28, when we review and assemble your first investment real estate property income and expense statement.

There's a fundamental reason for creating a personal income and expense statement. Remember how I spoke to looking in our financial mirror? Well, I first caught my financial reflection in the mirror when my wife and I went to put our first investment real estate purchase together, and the bank not only asked us to summarize our net worth but wanted to know where we were sourcing our funds for the down payment from and if our income could support the purchase.

Supporting the purchase was a critical question that stared us back in our financial face. The bank wanted to ensure that, if a tenant left our rental income home, we could service the mortgage payment and all other operational costs until we secured our next tenant.

This is a theme I will continue to reinforce: the bank or lender is not the evil villain. Don't forget that it is their money they are lending you, and they have every right to protect their investment.

Getting our first look in the financial mirror at the bank caught us off-guard. That's why it's crucial to gaze into the glass in advance. With a sneak peek, you can ensure you're looking presentable and that you reflect what they expect a borrower to be, even before you approach them.

In Coaching Challenge 4, we will work to assemble your personal income and expense statement and gaze into your financial mirror.

2. Your personal net worth statement

Piece number two of The Investment Real Estate Way Starter Kit is the personal net worth statement.

A personal net worth statement is very straightforward: you list all of your assets and all of your liabilities on a form, and then you subtract your liabilities from your assets to get your net worth. You'll find a sample net worth statement form in the appendix.

Creating a net worth statement will help you get a sense of your current foundation and why it's so important. For your personal net worth statement, you need to take stock of everything you own—your assets—and everything you owe—your liabilities. In the appendix section of this book, you will find a sample of a personal net worth statement you can fill in with your assets and liabilities.

The personal net worth statement should contain your current assets, such as cash in your checking accounts and savings accounts; long-term holdings, such as common stocks, bonds, and real estate; current liabilities, such as loan debt, credit card debt, and mortgage debts due (or overdue); and long-term liabilities, such as mortgages and other loan debts. It is important you list your securities and real estate at their current value rather than at past values. Your personal net worth, as mentioned earlier, is what is left over after you subtract your total assets and total liabilities.

This is one of those personal financial reflection moments as you look into your financial mirror: Does everything you own, after you take away everything you owe, give you a positive balance?

Be Honest in Your Assessment

I can give you guidance and a worksheet, but you need to be honest with yourself and list everything you have, just as it is, at this very moment in time. Don't overstate your net worth; the real world will see through this.

The real world I am talking about is the bank or lender who will help you realize your goal of purchasing your first investment real estate property.

The recurring theme of your investment real estate story is that you are looking in the bank's or lender's financial mirror. You must become a reflection of what they expect a borrower to be.

Banks and lenders generally are professionals, and they can see right through any financial information you misrepresent. Therefore, honesty is the best policy. If you are going to make investment real estate part of your financial foundation, let's get you started off on the right foot.

Contrary to what you might think, building your base from an understated position will lead to a strong financial foundation in the future. "Under-promise, over-deliver" is a good adage to live by.

In Coaching Challenge 4, you will put all of your personal information together in your financial mirror and look at the numbers. Remember, as long as you need to source funding to purchase your first investment real estate property, you have to play by the lender's rules, and your financial position must reflect the lender's requirements.

As long as you have not sent anyone out to kill the fairest or shoot the messenger, you will be one day closer to purchasing and renting your first investment real estate property.

Understanding Your Primary Home as Part of Your Net Worth

For more than 20 percent of boomers, 80 percent of their net worth is in their principal residence.

We will refer to your primary home often throughout the book. As you go through life, you will find that most of the houses you own won't be your forever home and more than likely won't be your last home. But this does not mean you should not have pride in your residence or love where you live.

Think of your pathway to your home as a journey through your life. Know that, in many cases, a home becomes one of your most valuable assets, but you can definitely find your home crumbling under your feet if you don't take care of it from a physical maintenance or financial standpoint.

If 80 percent of your net worth is in your home, using it like a personal automated teller and adding financial debt to your home can turn your bank or lender into the big, bad wolf.

The bank or your lender has given you the funds to purchase your home. Remember, and I will repeat this often, it is the bank or lender's money until you make your last payment. If you decide to borrow more funds against the equity you have built in your home and then spend these funds on non-appreciating assets, you will find yourself in a tight squeeze. The bank or lender is expecting their payment on time or they will not advance you any more funds; if this happens, don't be upset, because you are dismantling your brick house.

Your home can be a wonderful part of your investment portfolio if you use the equity to your advantage. Using knowledge about how to create a source of funding and a possible tax deduction can be part of your financial resources and strategies to develop a complete picture of your investment life.

What About Business Net Worth Statements?

The net worth statements for a small business—your first investment real estate property—help bring together expense paydown on your mortgage balance, any positive or negative cash flow, and equity loss or equity growth. Generally, you review these factors at the end of your fiscal year-end. These statements aren't important for us yet; we will spend time reviewing and assembling your business net worth statement later, on Day 29.

3. The Investment Real Estate Way Starter Kit Checklist

The Investment Real Estate Way Starter Kit Checklist is a guide that asks you questions about critical information you need to assemble when you first start to think about purchasing your first investment real estate property.

This checklist focuses primarily on the Ready stage, gathering critical information in one spot. It contains personal information, your goals (the type of investment real estate property, when you plan to purchase, etc.), basic business information (including partnerships, if any), your long-term plan for the property, and information on your core Team REAL members.

The checklist is to be used as the foundational information assembly piece—a way to set your mindset before stepping into the world of investment real estate. Think of the checklist as a primer to your investment real estate journey.

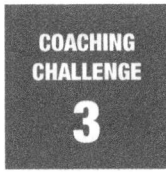

Familiarize yourself with The Investment Real Estate Way Starter Kit Checklist and the Ready, Set, Goal process.

In this day's content, I provided you with a description of The Investment Real Estate Way Starter Kit, what type of information you need to have to get started in the Ready stage, the why, and the when. As you move through the book, you will begin to see how to apply this information.

Take a moment to head to The Investment Real Estate Way Starter Kit Checklist in the appendix, and read through the checklist. Think of this review as priming your investment real estate pump; with it, you will start to collect important information in one spot. This will challenge you to assemble critical personal information, including a projected date to purchase, how you will set up ownership, the type of property, the budget to ready the property, the fees to purchase, and who your core team members will be.

You will also start to get a sense of the Ready, Set, Goal process. You'll be spending far more time in the Ready stage than in any other. As you know, the foundation of my Ready, Set, Goal process was derived from my half-marathon training. The training for a half-marathon starts sixteen to eighteen weeks before the actual race. The bulk of the training is in the Ready stage, and it gets me Set to run a minimum of 20 kilometers before I run the Goal race distance of 21.1 kilometers.

A physical challenge is an easy way to set out your Ready, Set, Goal process to purchasing and renting your first investment real estate property. And an integral part of this is defining your base, better, and best.

Let's start with a simple concept from everyday life and build upon it to get a good understanding of how it works. For example, my wife and I read recently that stair climbing is recommended by doctors and health authorities worldwide because high-quality studies show that climbing just eight flights of stairs a day lowers average early mortality risk by 33 percent. Seven minutes of stair climbing a day can halve the risk of heart attacks over ten years.

Challenge yourself to measure the number of flights of stairs you climb every day for a week. Divide your total flights for the week by seven to get your daily average base. If you average under eight flights, make eight flights as your better, and if you are up for a greater challenge, set a number higher than eight flights and make this your best.

Create your own challenge with the Base, Better, Best process if you are not motivated by our example. Set a challenge you can measure over a week to get your base, then build your better and best objectives, and use the next month to implement your changes and succeed.

Have fun through the rest of your life applying this process to different parts of your life.

Each day, as you work through the coaching challenges, you will be building a solid financial and knowledge base that will get you Ready and Set to achieve your investment real estate Goal.

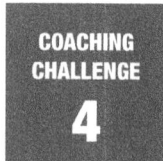

Access your purchasing power through an investor's formula exercise.

For this coaching challenge, you'll complete your personal income and expense statement and your personal net worth statement. In the appendix of this book, you will find a sample of a personal income and expense statement and net worth statement to follow, and a blank copy to fill in. This coaching challenge may take you anywhere from minutes to several hours.

If you already have your own personal income and expense statement and net worth statement, please take the time to match these up to the forms provided and ensure the information is complete.

It is important to remember that everything in our lives is fluid and ever-changing, finances included. I recommend using a pencil with an eraser, as more often than not, something may change, or you will remember things you may have forgotten and need to revise the forms.

Your personal income and expense statement and your personal net worth statement reveal your current situation. They are not only two crucial pieces to securing financing going forward, but they capture the full picture of this starting moment on your investment journey.

Note: Please take the time to complete both statements before you go any further in the book.

Day 2 Key Recap

Record your key learnings and actionable items in your notebook or the workbook and planning guide. (Optional)

- ⇧ When creating your personal income and net worth statements, you must be totally honest with yourself.
- ⇧ It's better to estimate the value of real estate, vehicles, recreational vehicles, furnishings, collectibles, jewelry, and other luxury goods as a little lower than market value.

- For stocks, bonds, mutual funds, certificates of deposit, bullion, trust funds, health savings accounts, and face-value of life insurance policies, assess the value on the day you assemble your net worth statement.
- For total debts, include mortgages, home equity loans, car loans, personal loans, credit cards, student loans, loans against investments, life insurance loans, other installment loans, and other debts.
- Update your net worth statement once a year at the end of the current calendar year.

Stage I:
Ready

Days 3 to 18

STAGE I: READY

CALL OUT YOUR INVESTMENT REAL ESTATE PURCHASING POWER AND MINDSET

Ray Dalio, the billionaire founder of Bridgewater Associates, identifies debt as one of the modern economy's key drivers. He believes debt is not a bad thing; instead, he considers it a powerful engine for economic empowerment and growth. Dalio says the key is to be able to tell the difference between "good debt" and "bad debt."

Good debt is money borrowed for investment purposes to improve your financial well-being, like real estate and education.

Investment real estate has three components that can help your financial well-being: positive cash flow through rent, principal paydown of your mortgage, and appreciation of property value over time.

Although this book mainly focuses on investment real estate, your investment into this book, reading the content and completing the coaching challenges, is also an investment into your overall financial health.

Why Being Ready Is Critical

Earlier, we talked about the "competition anthem" most of us learned in childhood that started any track-and-field race: "ready, set, go."

Each part of the race's starting anthem is important. But it was probably not until you became more competitive in track and field that you realized how important the Ready stage of the race was.

In investment real estate, the race you are involved in is a competition between you and the other people in the race.

I'm not saying that adding investment real estate to your financial portfolio is a competition. You are only competing against those who have entered into the race.

And most of us are building our financial foundation by competing against our own results.

If you haven't already, you will soon notice that the longest and most important stage of the book is Stage I, spanning from Day 3 to Day 18. Why?

It's simple: preparation in life is critical to your success. Look at the base of your academic life. You go through grade school, from kindergarten to Grade 12. Then you choose to attend a trade school, a college, or a university, getting yourself ready to take on your career and adult life.

The Real Payoff of Getting Ready

In his book *Outliers: The Story of Success*, Malcolm Gladwell makes reference to the ten-thousand-hour rule. Gladwell sees this rule as the major component to achieving world-class expertise in any skill.

In an interview with CNN, Gladwell stated, "We see this incredibly consistent pattern that you cannot be good at that (your field) unless you practice for ten thousand hours, which is roughly ten years, if you think about hours a day."

Even though I am not advocating that you spend ten thousand hours practicing getting ready to purchase your first investment real estate property, I have dedicated Days 3 to Day 18—roughly 60 percent of the book—to building a solid foundation of knowledge and concepts for you to follow and practice.

Before we start Day 3, the beginning of Stage I, I would like you to think back to Day 2, when I introduced you to the Ready, Set, Goal process I developed in my area of competitive half-marathon racing and showed you how I spilled this concept over into investment real estate. This process is crucial to your success.

On Days 3 and 4, I introduce you to your purchasing power and talk about how to develop the mindset of an entrepreneur and small business owner.

On Days 7 and 8, we dig deeper into identifying the types of investment real estate and controlling your emotions when purchasing and renting investment real estate.

On Day 12, we introduce you to the concept of FOCUS (Follow One Commitment Until Success), and on Day 18, to the SMART goal-setting framework (Specific, Measurable, Acceptable, Realistic, and Time-Bound).

Days 13, 14, 15, and 16 are dedicated to discussing financing and funding.

Don't sell yourself short. You have already put in some of the ten thousand hours getting ready to purchase your first investment real estate property, and through practicing the concepts and challenges in this book, there is little doubt we will soon be talking to you about your success story.

DAY 3 DEFINING YOUR FINANCIAL BASE AND PURCHASING POWER

Use this day to focus your efforts on your net income and net worth statements, created on Day 2. At the end of the chapter, complete the coaching challenges to understand these completed financial statements and determine your purchasing power to position yourself to enter the world of purchasing investment real estate.

First things first: let's review the Base, Better, Best© process, which we last encountered in the Introduction. (If you need a refresher, revisit the Introduction's "Goal-Setting" subsection.)

Base, Better, Best is useful when creating a current personal income statement. Your net worth statement, which we completed on Day 2, is your base, and it will help you achieve better results on your thirty-one-day journey.

Focusing on your base purchasing power will help you secure the funds required to make your first investment real estate purchase.

Know Thy Measure

What lessons can you learn from reviewing your net income and net worth statements? Many of us are familiar with the ancient Greek aphorism "know thyself"; the literal translation is actually "know thy measure."

> *More than anything else, what differentiates people who live up to their potential from those who don't is a willingness to look at themselves and others objectively.* — Ray Dalio, *Principles: Life and Work*

Many of us were never taught how to manage our finances. Whether you are getting to know yourself or your measure, you can learn many lessons from reviewing your current financial situation. You'll gain self-knowledge and understanding through your spending habits, which will significantly impact your financial foundation. Your spending experience may be either positive or negative.

Unfortunately, this is often the case for our children as well. How often have you heard people discuss the lack of practical money lessons taught in schools and the shame of not teaching our kids the special lessons behind money?

Our kids spend so much time in front of smartphones, computers, TVs, and other electronics, being entertained and getting no educational value. Marketers talk directly to our children almost every minute of every day, trying to convince them to convince you to buy them things they may not need.

Combining our children's lack of financial literacy with our own can be disastrous. These items are often purchased with credit cards, creating bad debt and no type of financial return. And once that money is spent, it's gone forever.

Financial lessons can lead to success, and these lessons often come from work. For example, if you work for a well-run company that takes pride in how they manage their finances, you can learn from how your company handles their income and spending. What observations can you make about how the company you work for operates? What about how you solve real-life issues, such as your management of debt? Are you paying off your credit card balances each month, or are you paying high interest rates? There is nothing like paying your credit card balance off each month to get a handle on your monthly spending.

Reviewing your situation and answering the questions in coaching challenges 5, 6, and 7 can help you identify potential failure or risk and pinpoint possible actions you can take to mitigate the risk.

Your Personal Net Income Statement

As we learned on Day 2, your personal net income statement is essential for getting a glimpse of your financial reflection. It's not only about how much you earn; it's about how much you keep.

When preparing a net income statement, it's important to be totally honest with yourself and ensure you have captured all of your income and all of your expenses.

That way, when you review your net income statement, you can put your understanding of your net income to work.

Many financial advisors recommend tracking your income and expenses over three months to get a longer glimpse into your spending habits. I support this recommendation.

How to Track Your Spending Habits for Three Months

To help you track your spending habits, I've put together a free three-month net income tracking form, which can be found on the Resources page of the Vault to Investment Real Estate Success website. It has been set up for you to track each month and has a recap sheet created to average out your three-month income and expenses.

To best capture your expenses for the next three months, I would strongly suggest you go totally electronic—no cash spending—and consolidate your bank accounts to one primary account for spending. If you have a partner or spouse and don't share your banking, have each person follow these recommendations.

Give the Banks What They Want

The banks are looking for you to meet specific criteria when you apply for a mortgage; that's why it's important to give them what they want right from the get-go. First, go to your bank or primary financial institution and mention you are thinking about purchasing an investment real estate property. Ask them what financial information they will require from you when applying for a mortgage and what format they like to see it in. Many financial institutions have standard forms; request a blank copy. Can you imagine how professional and knowledgeable you will look when you walk into a lender with all of your financial information complete in the format they prefer?

The Importance of Cash Flow

The return on investment for real estate has three components. One component can be immediate return, through positive monthly cash flow, and the other two components, principal paydown and equity appreciation, happen over time. We'll talk about the latter two later in the book, but for now, we'll focus on cash flow.

Cash flow is the amount of money you as an individual have transferred in and out of your personal or business accounts; in simple terms, it's your incoming and outgoing funds. Having more funds coming in than funds going out is good and will leave you financially stable.

Positive cash flow means you have more income than expenses, while negative cash flow means you have more expenses than income.

At the end of the day, positive cash flow sees your bank account growing, and negative cash flow sees your bank account diminishing. This impacts your net worth statement; we will review this more in Coaching Challenge 5.

Being in a positive cash-flow position is great and gives you an excellent starting point. Why? The amount of money you have left over each month will play a large part in determining what type of investment real estate property you might acquire. As we've discussed, when you are borrowing money for a mortgage, you are borrowing money from a bank or a lender. The bank or lender wants to know that, if investment real estate market conditions change, you will have enough positive cash flow to cover not only your personal obligations but your investment real estate should you lose your tenant and have to cover the costs out-of-pocket.

Having a negative cash flow will require you to take a hard look at your income and expenses, and possibly make some adjustments. Some of you in this situation may not be willing to give up your current lifestyle, and you will go no further in reading this book. Is this a tough-love statement? You bet. But if you are someone with negative cash flow who is determined to own your first investment real estate property, awesome—let's see what you can do.

To turn negative cash flow into positive cash flow, you need to either reduce your spending, bring in more income, or—my favorite—do both. The end results are more dramatic and rewarding.

Hammer Time: From Negative Cash Flow to Positive

Reducing expenses is never easy. It will take a concerted effort on your part—a good look in the mirror and tough love.

Let's look at your big picture and then drill it down. Your expenses will likely include the following: housing, groceries, health care, utilities, transportation, dining out, entertainment, recreation, travel and vacation, and debt.

Where to start? Even though the expense categories I mentioned above end with debt, debt should be the first place you start. Look at any payments you are making where a portion of the payment is interest. These are things such as mortgage, home equity or line of credit loans, car loans, personal loans, credit cards, student loans, loans against investments, life insurance loans, other installment loans, and other debts.

I have several recommendations for you to implement. Adopting even one of these suggestions can go a long way to moving you from a negative cash-flow situation to a positive cash-flow position.

First, consolidate any of this interest-bearing debt into one payment that is lower than the combined payments you are currently making. Through this consolidation of debt, you can reduce the higher interest rate debt (e.g., pay off high-interest-rate credit-card balances to a lower-interest-rate loan or line of credit). An essential part of your Team REAL is going to be an accountant. If you are having trouble navigating through your debt and determining the best strategy for debt consolidation as you get ready to purchase your first investment real estate property, I recommend that you get advice from an accountant. The hour or so you might pay them for advice could be easily paid for by having the correct debt restructuring plan and the money you would save in potential high interest payments.

Your work will be all for naught if you run up new spending on your credit cards. If you have multiple credit cards with balances every month, pay off the balances and reduce the number of credit cards to one. Total the credit amounts from all of your credit cards, and with your only credit card remaining, lower the credit available on that card to an amount you can actually pay off every month. You may be shocked at how low this amount might be.

The next big payment could be your vehicle payments and maintenance. It might be time to ditch the ride for a year or two.

Most cities and towns have excellent public transportation. I know the pandemic has caused some concerns, but if you do your research and find safe public transportation, use it. (Your health is paramount; make sure you feel comfortable before adopting this suggestion.)

If your employer allows you to work from home, take advantage of this moment and sell your vehicle. You'll eliminate the cost of payments and maintenance, and can use any extra cash from your vehicle to pay down debt.

Low-Hanging-Fruit Expenditures

Once you have tackled your debt, consolidated it into a manageable payment amount, and ditched the ride, let's pick off the low-hanging-fruit expenditures.

Be aware that I am talking about expenditures you may not be making right now because of the pandemic; this is great if you still have full employment and you never had to use government assistance. Remember, there will be a vaccine, and at some point, government assistance will end.

Restaurants and fast food is a great place to start. It's time to learn how to cook for yourself. The cost of dining out takes a big bite out of your monthly income.

When it comes to entertainment, the monthly subscription to Netflix, Prime, Apple TV, or Disney is much cheaper than a night out at the movies.

And recreational expenditures, like club fees for golf, skiing, boating, or any other type of fee-based recreational membership, can rack up very quickly.

You might think I am asking you to give up your life. I am not. I'm suggesting these changes to get you to realize there is positive cash flow in your future; you just need to make a few spending-habit changes to find it.

As Albert Einstein once said, "The definition of insanity is doing the same thing over and over again and expecting a different result."

Your negative monthly spending will never produce positive cash flow; therefore, you must implement some of the changes listed above.

And, to my Gen Xers, Gen Zers, and millennials, I have one more suggestion.

How committed are you?

The Move-Back-Home Approach

I know you might be thinking, "Are you crazy? I finally got my freedom, and now you want me to move back home?" Yes!

Not all of us have this option, but if you do, it's worth considering. If you move back home, chances are you'll be carrying less debt. You might have student loans, one credit card, maybe a small car loan, and not much else.

Develop a plan where all of your living expenses are gone, and you'll be able to get rid of debt and save.

Convince your parents or in-laws this is temporary. Show them your plan to reduce your debt and save to put yourself (or selves) in the position to purchase an investment property that will include your primary residence. Ensure you have a time frame built in; your parents or in-laws may love you, but don't overstay your welcome.

My son and his future wife had both graduated, gotten jobs, and started their adult lives. They were renting their own residence but had no money left over to save. The solution? They moved in with my wife and me, and within a year, we bought two investment real estate properties as joint venture partners. One of these properties was a bungalow; they lived upstairs and rented the basement suite out.

When my daughter's first relationship ended, she moved in with us temporarily. Using the cost savings, she bought a bungalow and received a non-repayable grant to put an income suite in her new home, all in less than a year. Her mortgage payment was $1,500 a month and the tenants were paying her $1,100 a month in rent—nearly three-quarters of the mortgage!

The significance of my daughter purchasing a bungalow, developing an income suite in the basement, and renting the suite out was more than the long-term benefit of principal paydown, equity growth, and cash flow.

There was also a major psychological benefit. My daughter was raised to be an independent person. Her ability to purchase her own home, fund it herself without any assistance, and raise her daughter in her own home gave her a sense of pride, strength, and confidence.

The "Own Principal Residence" Approach

If you own your own residence and are carrying more debt at higher interest rates than your mortgage interest rate, there might be an opportunity to use your home to consolidate debt and save enormous interest costs.

Where can you start?

As mentioned above, the first place is any payments you are making where a portion of the payment is interest: mortgage, home equity or line of credit loans, car loans, personal loans, credit cards, student loans, loans against investments, life insurance loans, other installment loans, and other debts.

It does not take much to rack up debt and interest payments. Here's another great reason to have a mortgage broker on your side: With their help, it may be possible to consolidate most or all of this debt listed above into a new single mortgage payment. If it is, you are going to be pleasantly surprised—you will end up with a single payment that is much lower than your combined payments, at a much lower interest rate.

A mortgage broker can help you refinance your home. If you can't consolidate all your debt as I have recommended, take a look at the highest interest expenses on your debt. This generally starts with credit cards. Consolidate this debt through a much lower mortgage interest rate; you will end up with a lower overall payment and lower interest rate.

At the end of the day, the goal is to create positive cash flow. Take half of the positive cash flow and put it in a savings account (create a new habit), and take the other half of the positive cash flow and pay down interest-bearing debt.

As you get closer to purchasing your first investment real estate property, the bank or lender will take all your debt and your ability to service this debt into consideration. No debt means nothing to consider.

Adding to Your Cash Flow

There are numerous ways to increase your cash flow. Below, I'll go through a few of my favorite ways that you can start bringing in more money.

Uberize Your Investment

Many people with full-time jobs are taking up driving for rideshare and delivery companies like Uber or Uber Eats to supplement their income.

This is just one of many ways to supplement your income—not to cover your monthly expenses, but to build your financial base of wealth. You can use this additional income to build a down payment for your first investment property or to cover the costs of purchase, such as the cost of borrowing, legal fees, home inspection fees, and repair and renovations costs.

Supplementing your income is short-term pain for long-term gain. Pick part-time work you might enjoy; remember, this is not career employment.

Doubling Down on Uberizing

If I have convinced you of the value of Uberizing your investment, why not double down?

I recently talked to you about my daughter's experience in buying a bungalow, developing an income suite in the basement, and collecting $1,100 in monthly rent from the tenant. My daughter's total mortgage payment was $1,500, meaning she only had to add $400 a month from her own pocket to make her mortgage payment.

Think about the impact on the mortgage principal paydown if my daughter knew she could afford more than $400 a month. Let's say she could afford $900 a month, and she applied the additional $500 a month to her principal paydown. This doubling down on Uberizing would have a significant positive impact on her equity growth.

Could you double down on Uberizing your investment by paying more in rent to yourself?

Why Your Ability to Service Debt Is Important

When considering purchasing investment real estate, your ability to reduce expenses or improve your cash flow is important. Why?

Most people who purchase investment real estate don't have access to the entire purchase price of the real estate and need to rely on banks or lending services.

What you are swapping out to borrow funds to purchase investment real estate is your ability to repay the money you borrowed—the principal and interest amounts.

This ability to service your debt is, in the end, all about your income and your expenses. What you have left over is what you have available to service the debt and play nice in the bank or the lender's sandbox.

Your Personal Net Worth Statement

Recall that, on Day 2, we learned that your personal net worth is your total assets minus your total debts. Reviewing your net worth statement is about understanding what makes up your net worth and putting your understanding of your net income to work.

Your net worth statement puts current market value to all of your assets. People tend to overestimate the value of their assets. An example is the purchase of a new vehicle; most folks assess the value as what they purchased the vehicle for, but the reality is that the moment you take it off the auto dealer's lot, the value drops by several thousand dollars.

I've said it before, but you must be totally honest with yourself when determining your net worth. Remember, lenders have access to information from both auto dealers and the real estate market. With the value of your assets, it's better to estimate them as a little lower than market value because that's what the banks or lenders will do. It allows you to see your financial reflection in the lender's mirror. Vehicles, recreational vehicles, furnishings, and other luxury goods are generally depreciating assets; these assets tend to be items most folks overvalue, while a bank or lender places little value on these items at all.

If you have appreciating items, such as art, jewelry, and collectibles, the lender may require you to have these items appraised if they feel you have overstated the value; don't get caught having to justify your valuations. Why create a negative environment when you are asking to borrow someone else's money?

For stocks, bonds, mutual funds, certificates of deposit, bullion, trust funds, health savings accounts, and face-value of life insurance policies, assess the value on the day you assemble your net worth statement.

For total debts, include mortgages, home equity loans, car loans, personal loans, credit cards, student loans, loans against investments, life insurance loans, other installment loans, and other debts.

Many financial advisors will ask you to update your net worth statement once a year at the end of the current calendar year, a recommendation I support.

Action is the foundational key to all success. — Pablo Picasso

Your Purchasing Power Base

Your net worth could be in great shape, and maybe you could even use some of your assets as collateral for the purchase of investment real estate. Most banks and lenders really don't want your collateral in exchange for a mortgage. These lenders are not in the business of taking over and liquidating your assets if you can't pay back a mortgage.

The bank and lenders are more interested in your ability to service the mortgage payment for the funds they are lending you.

The best way for the bank or lender to assess this is to view your purchasing power base. Your purchasing power base is the amount of positive cash flow you have left over at the end of each month that can service debt or mortgage payments.

The amount of surplus debt you can service will also help determine your down payment amount for a mortgage.

Working with your mortgage broker or lender, you can identify how much you will need for a down payment and what mortgage amount you qualify for. Your down payment can range from 5 to 20 percent of the purchase price of the home. This 5 to 20 percent is a general rule, but if you are self-employed, you may find that this number could go as high as 35 percent. This is, again, a great reason to have a mortgage broker as part of your team; they'll get you clarification on lending rules before you even approach a lender.

On Days 13 to 17, we will examine other aspects of your purchasing power, including the down payment amount; all costs to purchase; the funding of the down payment beyond your ability, if necessary; financing institutions; and purchase price.

Listing Price vs. Purchase Price

When considering the price of real estate, it is important to remember that the purchase price and the listing price are two different things.

The listing price is what the owner of the home would like to sell the home for.

The purchase price is the price that you, as a buyer, are willing to pay for the property.

Many times, the price difference between what the owner is willing to sell the home for and what the buyer is willing to pay is too far apart, and the deal doesn't get done. This is where your real estate agent comes in handy, as they have access to what the comparable properties in the area are selling for. These comparable properties can be used to negotiate a better or market-value price, or sometimes even increase the price.

Late Blooming: Especially for Boomers

This book is meant for anyone interested in buying their first investment real estate property: millennials, Gen Zers, Gen Xers, and boomers.

Millennial, Generation Z, and Generation X readers, feel free to skip the next section. Or, if you have boomers in your life whom you think might benefit from this information, please read on. Remember, if you are looking for excellent joint venture partners, it might be boomer time.

You are never too old to set another goal or to dream a new dream. — C.S. Lewis

Boomer or Bust

In his book <u>The Five Secrets You Must Discover Before You Die,</u> Dr. John Izzo wrote, "By planting a new tree today, the legacy of your life would change. It is not too late."

My life has been filled with late blooming, including earning a university degree and purchasing my first investment real estate property in my late forties, starting half-marathon training and competitive racing in my early fifties, and earning my certification in real estate investment coaching (REIA) recently.

Like Dr. Izzo, I believe that once you take a new path, your life changes, and you start creating a legacy you never thought possible. It is not too late, and my story is proof of that.

Part of my coaching technique is to share guidance and lessons I have learned along the way. In the "Welcome" chapter of the book under the subheading "Value," I refer to the guidance and lessons as value bricks. Over their lifetime, boomers have collected many value bricks to share. These value bricks may be our own thoughts or those of people who have influenced our lives.

Boomers are living longer. Please recognize and embrace this good news and know you may have lots of time left on Earth. Purchasing investment real estate can help you with income and a place to live through the years you didn't think you would have.

A 2016 article from everythingzoomer.com titled "Keep Slaving Away at Work — It's Good for You" discussed a study that found retiring after age sixty-five may help people live longer, reduce the risk of chronic illness, and delay age-related decline in physical, cognitive, and mental functioning. The study, conducted by Oregon State University, was published online in the *Journal of Epidemiology and Community Health*. The report said that even among people with health issues, the risk of dying from any cause over the study period was 11 percent lower among people who delayed retirement for one year, until age sixty-six. The risk of dying fell even further among people who retired between the ages of sixty-six and seventy-two.

What's more, the benefits of remaining in the workforce past sixty-five occurred irrespective of gender, lifestyle, education, income, and occupation.

I know you are thinking, "Come on, Rick, I've given my employer thirty to forty years of my life, and now you want me to give them more?" Well, maybe not your current employer. Investment real estate is a way for you to run your own business, provide you with an income, and give you time to give back to your community.

The youngest boomers are now starting their last decade before they turn sixty-five in 2030. If you are one of them, it is time to buy real estate investment properties while you still have a job. As I mentioned, the banks love to lend money to people who can easily service the debt and may not even need the money.

You need to look at your individual financial and health circumstances and decide if you are going to be in a strong enough financial position to fully retire or healthy enough to live independently on your own.

If you are in your mid-fifties and have no investment real estate and no system in place to buy and manage investment real estate, then stay working for your health and start buying real estate investment properties. In the future, as you purchase investment real estate and your portfolio grows, you might discover this is your second calling, and you can put on your entrepreneur hat and work for yourself.

If your retirement streams of income put you in a position to buy investment real estate, evaluate whether or not investment real estate is right for you as a way to keep you engaged in the workforce to reduce the risk of chronic illness and delay age-related physical, cognitive, and mental decline. Building your own real estate investment business can be engaging, social, fun, challenging, different, and manageable on your own terms.

How Many Doors Is Ideal?

The advice on how many doors you should own is endless; to me, it's as easy as one, two, three ... four doors. First of all, four doors puts you in the top 2 percent of real estate investors in Canada—pretty neat bragging rights. Second, these four doors can do wonders in helping you build a strong financial foundation, unlock sustainable wealth, and create a living legacy. Four doors of additional investment real estate income added to your 401K, IRA, or Roth, if you are American, or to your Canada Pension Plan, OAS seniors' benefit, pension, or RRSP earnings, if you're Canadian, can be a nice supplement. In many cases, the revenue from the four doors could generate even more revenue than your government-sponsored retirement funds. Whoever thought you could get a raise in your retirement years?

Amortization is a critical factor for boomer investment real estate investors. We will talk more about amortization on Day 14. To give you a brief description of amortization, it is the length of time to pay off a loan or mortgage. In many cases, the time of repayment is a locked-in number of years, for example ten, fifteen, twenty-five, or thirty years.

In my example below, I am speaking directly to the youngest boomers of their generation; for the Gen Xers, Gen Zers, and millennials, it's a thought-provoker.

If you feel you still have a decade of employment ahead of you, you might consider looking to make your amortization period over ten years, knowing you will have one or maybe even several investment properties paid off as you turn sixty-five.

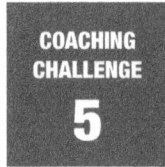

Review your personal net income statement and personal net worth statement.

On Day 2, you reviewed and completed your personal income and expense statement and net worth statement. As a recap, the template can be found in the appendix section of this book. Now, let's dig deeper into these important documents.

Have you ever noticed that when you take a step back and reflect on the information you have assembled or take time to think through issues without rushing into a situation, you tend to make better decisions?

In this challenge, check in on your work from Day 2. Make sure all is accurate, and that you have captured everything you need to. These numbers are your current base.

Most folks don't like talking about their personal finances, and in many cases, will not even share this information with their own family members.

I have asked you to bravely look in the mirror and be honest with what you see. If you are going to borrow money from other people, honesty is the best policy. In today's digital age of finance, it only takes a few minutes for a financial institution to check your credit through credit bureaus. There are credit bureau organizations like Equifax and TransUnion, which track your personal financial information and even give your credit rating a score. Your credit score is what financial lenders use to see if you are deemed creditworthy and a safe risk to lend money to.

You need to make sure your net income statement is current and accurate, and the same with your net worth statement. If your information is not correct, it could affect your ability to receive any funding. You may be forced to pay a higher borrowing interest rate or only borrow a certain amount.

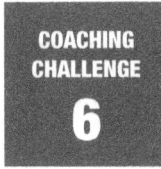 **Track your spending habits for three months.**

There's no better time to get started tracking your spending habits so you can see where you're leaking money and put a stop to it.

Download the three-month net income tracking form from the Resources page of the Vault to Investment Real Estate Success website. (This is in Microsoft Excel format; please feel free to convert to any other format that works for you.) It has been set up for you to track each month and has a recap sheet created to average out your three-month income and expenses.

Remember, it's best to go fully electronic for this exercise—no cash payments—and it'll be easiest if you spend from one account. If you have a spouse or partner and don't share banking, have them do this, too.

Seeing all your spending in one place will help you identify areas where you can cut back, ultimately reducing your negative cash flow and increasing your positive cash flow.

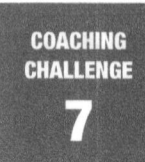

COACHING CHALLENGE 7

Identify your purchasing power base.

With the financial information you identified from your net worth statement and your net income statement, you can start to understand your purchasing power. From your net worth statement, the financial lender can see signs of how you manage your funds. Seeing an accumulation of positive net assets gives the lender a story on your ability to create personal wealth.

Your net income is the biggest factor in your purchasing power because each month, after all of your income and spending activity, you have positive cash flow; this underscores your ability to handle additional expense payments.

I am not suggesting you take on any additional debt. By purchasing an investment real estate property and receiving monthly revenue income (rent), you can cover the monthly expense obligations. Remember, the financial institution is only trying to ensure you can cover this debt if you lose your tenant for a while.

This is an area where a good mortgage broker can help you. Each lender is different, and their lending rules are different. Not all lenders need your monthly positive cash flow to cover the entire costs of the investment real estate; some lenders are happy to see your ability to cover half of the costs. These lenders realize vacancies happen; they want to feel comfortable that a short-term vacancy will not be a financial issue for you.

Phone a couple of mortgage brokers and tell them you are a potential client. Ask them:

1. to identify a minimum of three lenders who will lend to first-time real estate investors, and
2. to identify what percentage of the rent each lender will allow you to add to your income for debt servicing.

Take note of their responses. When it comes time to choose a mortgage broker for your Team REAL, you'll already have a sense of who you might like to work with.

Day 3 Key Recap

Record your key learnings and actionable items in your notebook or the workbook and planning guide. (Optional)

- ⇧ Positive cash flow means you have more income than expenses, while negative cash flow means you have more expenses than income.
- ⇧ Tracking your income and expenses over a three-month period can give you a glimpse into your spending habits, ultimately helping you increase positive cash flow and reduce negative cash flow.
- ⇧ Positive cash flow can be improved by consolidating debt, reducing expenditures, Uberizing your investment, moving back home, and other methods.
- ⇧ Your down payment can range from 5 to 35 percent of the purchase price of the home.
- ⇧ The listing price is what the owner of the home would like to sell the home for.
- ⇧ The purchase price is the price you as a buyer are willing to pay for the property.
- ⇧ It's never too late to enjoy the benefits of investment real estate.

DAY 4 ENTREPRENEURIAL AND SMALL BUSINESS MINDSET

Use this day to discover if you have the mindset of an entrepreneur and to develop the skills you need to operate a small business. At the end of the chapter, complete the coaching challenges to decide if this is a mindset you feel comfortable with, and determine what your investment real estate success will look like.

Purchasing investment real estate is not a hobby; it is a business and needs to be treated like one. To do that, you need to tap into the mindset of an entrepreneur and small business owner, and learn the business skills that will lead you to success.

In decision theory and general systems theory, a **mindset** is a set of assumptions, methods, or notions held by one or more people or groups of people. A mindset can also arise out of a person's worldview or philosophy of life.

Entrepreneurship is a system of crafting, starting, and operating a new business. More often than not, this starts out as a small business.

Small businesses are usually privately owned corporations, partnerships, or sole proprietorships. Industry Canada considers a small business one with fewer than one hundred employees.

According to an August 20, 2020 Success Harbor article, eight out of ten new employer firms—businesses with one or more employees—survive at least two years, half at least five years, and a third at least ten years.

The reasons why some small businesses survive and others fade away are numerous. Our investment real estate company, Vault to Real Estate Success Corporation, celebrated its twelfth anniversary on March 20, 2020. I am very proud of this fact, and it's one of the reasons we wanted to give back through this book.

We wouldn't have been able to succeed without an entrepreneurial mindset, strong business skills, and a well-crafted business plan. I'll touch on these and many other aspects of entrepreneurship as it relates to investment real estate throughout this chapter.

The Entrepreneurial Mindset

The biggest part of being ready for investment real estate is your mindset. With an entrepreneurial mindset, you will be able to make the right decisions for your investments. As I mentioned earlier in the book, only 4 percent of Canadians and 8 percent of Americans own investment real estate. This means the relationship most North Americans have with real estate is with their own principal residence, and they don't view their home as a business.

However, investment real estate is a business, and as an owner of investment real estate, you need to develop the mindset of an entrepreneur. A business has revenue and expenses, and to be a viable business, your revenue must be higher than your expenses. You must make the correct choices, track your finances in an income and expense statement, and understand the revenue and expense factors that drive your decisions.

The Oxford English Dictionary defines an entrepreneur as a person who organizes and operates a business or businesses, taking on greater than normal financial risks to do so. Does this sound like you? Remember, if you have the mindset of an entrepreneur, this is an excellent start.

Through this book, your own research, your planning, and your Team REAL, you can acquire the knowledge and skills needed to be an entrepreneur. You'll learn to be a good organizer and operator of your own investment real estate business.

Build Your Business Skills

Purchasing investment property has never been easier than it is today. But as an investment real estate owner, you are running a small business, so you need to have business skills.

I first started to develop my business skills by taking business courses through a community college. Many community colleges offer standalone classes that teach you how to start a business and the financial fundamentals needed to sustain it.

Later, a friend (who became a joint venture partner) introduced me to an investment group. The group is a resource for investment real estate education, analysis, research, and strategic leadership. Joining this group gave me a network of like-minded people to share ideas with and learn from. This group helped me a lot in the beginning of my journey, and finding a group of your own might benefit you, too.

In many cases, you can source these groups right in your area through sites like Meetup.com, where you can search for meetup groups for small business, entrepreneurship, or investment real estate. My goal is to also provide my Facebook community as an investment real estate resource of investment real estate content for readers of this book.

But colleges and groups aren't the only way you can build business skills. Today, you can access many different websites, podcasts, YouTube videos, books, and online courses to hone your abilities. Investing a little time can help you on your financial journey and give you the small business skill set needed to present your proposal to your financial community, secure their support, and find success in investment real estate.

Craft Your Business Plan

Successful small business owners understand the need for a strong business plan. A business plan is an in-depth business document that lays out a pathway to achieving your goals and sets a time frame in which the business objectives are to be accomplished. In the appendix of this book, you will find a worksheet entitled "Craft Your Business Plan." This worksheet helps you do just that by laying out seven distinct areas that outline the scope of your investment real estate business. In each area, you will find several points regarding your business, its financial projections, and the steps along your pathway to achieving your investment real estate goals. This worksheet details the concrete steps you'll take to get to your goal: the purchase and rental of your first investment real estate property.

Keep your plan simple. Stay focused on the nature of your business: the purchase and rental of your first investment real estate property.

In the appendix, you'll also find a sample business plan. The business plan is specially tailored to the purchase and rental of investment real estate, and I'm confident you'll find it valuable as a template and reference for creating your own business plan.

Remember, your business is investment real estate, and purchasing and renting investment real estate is the plan. Part of good planning is to expect the unexpected, and this is why, throughout the book, we talk about building a contingency fund for unexpected repairs. We also deeply encourage you to form your own Team REAL to be a resource for unexpected circumstances—those times when you need reliable answers and expert guidance.

Why Make Investment Real Estate Business Your Business?

Investment real estate is a true brick-and-mortar business in the most literal sense. When you think of brick-and-mortar businesses, you may think of businesses you visit in person, like a shopping center or a free-standing box store, but many brick-and-mortar businesses also have a digital arm of their business. For example, you can visit BestBuy in person, or shop on BestBuy.com. Investment real estate, on the other hand, is a piece of property that you as a business owner rent to a tenant.

There's no limit to where your investment real estate business can take you. I know many investment real estate owners who don't own in the city or town in which they live. They are purchasing in towns or cities that are more financially viable than their own. Despite owning multiple investment properties, my wife and I have never owned any investment properties in the city we live in; also, we have owned investment real estate in up to three different cities at one time.

The great thing about building your investment real estate business is you have a ton of folks who are trained professionals—your Team REAL—helping to support your small business. The guidance you get from your team is like no other. These trained professionals only get paid upon your successful purchase of investment real estate. If you keep them engaged and they believe you will use their services again down the road, they are a go-to resource at any time. What other small business gives you access to a team of experts, all invested in helping you succeed?

Our Small Business

The core of our small business started with two investment real estate properties and grew to a double-digit portfolio. My wife and I became part of the top 2 percent of investment real estate investors, and we were able to achieve this success through the principles I am sharing with you in this book.

Our investment real estate investments have included homes (some of which have been converted with income suites), condo-style apartments, and vacation rental homes (we owned a thriving vacation rental business).

We have used various financing methods to purchase our investment real estate: family; other people's money; trading our investment real estate expertise for equity in properties; trading our creditworthiness for property; and purchasing foreclosures, then renovating to make these incredible rental properties.

Once you decide to start down the path to purchasing investment real estate, the opportunities that present themselves will astound you. To this day, we are still frequently approached by folks with investment real estate opportunities. I'm confident this will happen to you, too; you just need to get started in the investment real estate business.

Part of our investment real estate portfolio includes joint venture partners, whom I have provided with investment real estate coaching. On Day 15 of the book, we will discuss the funding of investment real estate and introduce you to joint venture thinking.

Over the years, we have retooled our company to include more than just investment real estate. My ability to coach others led people to ask if they could hire my services to help them build a small investment real estate business. We added one-on-one coaching, and today, we aim to reach a larger audience through our website full of investment resources and rich information, a blog, a podcast show, books, and online courses.

Shifting Mindsets: From Residential Real Estate Owner to Real Estate Investor

Many of us experience a real estate life cycle that looks something like this: Early in life, you look to purchase your first home, and as your life and work life unfold and you start to move up the proverbial residential real estate ladder, buying bigger and better to deal with your growing family's needs. Then, you put the family homestead up for sale and move to a smaller lifestyle-driven home, but you still want all the bells and whistles. Sometimes the emotional attachment to the family homestead is so strong because of all the special occasions celebrated there. The memories of holiday meals, birthdays, anniversaries, graduations, and other special family moments can mean you have a hard time pulling the switch and moving to a home that makes more sense for you.

My wife and I delayed our decision to sell for almost ten years because grandkids came into our life and we thought we would still need three extra bedrooms and three extra bathrooms. The only thing we did not calculate is that our families live their lives, and even though we would get visitors and guests once in a while, it did not happen as frequently as we thought it would.

Also, grandchildren are often registered in activities and start school quicker than you can imagine and you never have the number of sleepovers you had envisioned. I am not asking you to be selfish, but you need to do what works best for you, not others. And yes, that means even your family. It's all part of shifting our mindset from residential real estate owner to real estate investor—the mindset of an entrepreneur.

There are different strategies to building your real estate investment portfolio; this could include staying in your own home and accessing equity to invest, or downsizing, balancing the purchase of a new home with funds set aside to invest. We will discuss these strategies once we start to understand what our real estate investment team looks like and how to assemble this team. Back in the Introduction, I talked about strategies for all generations. Please note that what I describe is a generalization and each of us is different; what I am suggesting is a guideline.

Many of our friends started their families ten to fifteen years after us. Think about how having your family later in life can impact your financial plans.

The Role of Coaching in Cultivating Mindset

Whenever I watch interviews with a person who has reached incredible heights, they talk about taking personal responsibility. One of the ways to do that is through working with a coach. Coaching can be a great tool for developing your entrepreneurial mindset and preparing to make your first investment real estate purchase—and many more, if you choose. It pushes you to take personal responsibility.

Over the years, I have worked with many different coaches and I strongly believe in the importance of having a great coach to guide you. Even the greatest athletes, including Michael Jordan, Wayne Gretzky, Serena Williams, and Tom Brady, talk about the significance of having great coaches in their lives.

Through this book, my goal is to help coach you in the area of purchasing and renting your first investment real estate property. Unfortunately, I can't be with you every minute of the day. But by introducing you to self-coaching methods, I can give you a greater chance of success.

When cultivating your mindset, let's also get you started in learning to develop a personal coaching system and to recognize when you may need a personal level of coaching in your investment real estate journey. Just like athletes, businesspeople, actors, and performers have benefited from great coaches, you'll discover there are many great investment real estate coaches available to help you, too; later, on Day 19, we will outline where to find them and how to bring them on board to your Team REAL.

For now, here is the self-coaching method I use. I hope it will benefit you, too.

COACH: Clarify, Outcome, Apply, Commit, Help

Hugh Phillips, one of my business training coaches, introduced me to an acronym I would like to share with you: COACH—Clarify, Outcome, Apply, Commit, Help. I use this coaching technique for myself and for my joint venture partners and clients in investment real estate.

The wealth of information on the Vault to Investment Real Estate Success website will help you to **Clarify** how investment real estate will be part of your financial base.

You have already decided that your **Outcome** is to purchase and rent your first real estate investment property in thirty-one days.

Now, it is time to **Apply** the investment principles in this book. Identifying your team members and applying the Ready stage's coaching challenges will put the Goal stage of your investment real estate quest within reach.

Staying **Committed** to investment real estate is where I and others on your Team REAL will help. This book and the many resources mentioned within are here to keep you committed to carrying out your first investment real estate purchase and rental.

Finally, don't be afraid to ask for Help. Click on the word *help* and it will give you access to my email address. If you need answers in your investment real estate journey, remember, I'm just an email away. (Please ensure you give me as much detail about your question as possible.)

By opening your mind to coaching, embracing the COACH acronym, and completing the coaching challenges in this book, you'll be able to develop your entrepreneurial mindset, experience personal growth, and position yourself for investment real estate success.

The Qualities of Successful Entrepreneurs

Most successful entrepreneurs have a few things in common: they are disciplined, confident, open-minded, competitive, creative, and determined self-starters. They have strong people skills, a strong work ethic, and passion. When it comes to investment real estate, the good news is you don't have to possess every one of these qualities or excel in all of them. Instead, you need to determine the qualities you believe you show strength in, work those qualities, and then turn to your Team REAL to help you in the areas you need it.

Let's start with discipline. You have heard our story of purchasing and renting our first investment real estate property in thirty-one days, and it took discipline. Do you have this type of discipline? Can you think of a specific time-bound goal you set and accomplished? What makes you think you can apply this same discipline to purchase and rent your first investment real estate property in thirty-one days? How can your team members keep you focused on this goal?

I am so happy that I had an open mind and gave investment real estate a hard look. Investment real estate today is a vital part of our financial portfolio. That fact that you're taking the time to read this book demonstrates a willingness to open your mind to other investment alternatives.

The nearly two decades I've spent in the investment real estate business demonstrates my discipline and determination. Can you think of something you have been engaged in for a number of years, and can you carry this level of discipline and determination into an investment real estate business?

Working with joint venture partners and family requires strong people skills. Are you involved with people in certain areas of your life, and can you transfer these skills to involving others in your investment real estate business?

I find myself sometimes needing a little nudge to get a project underway. This is where accountability can help. Talk to a team member, let them know what you are trying to accomplish, and ask them to check in on you and your goal every once in a while.

Characteristics of Investment Real Estate Investors

In addition to the basic qualities of entrepreneurship, the successful investment real estate investor needs good management skills. Management is a theme that runs through every area of your investment real estate journey.

First, you need to be able to manage the purchasing process of buying an investment real estate property.

Second, you need to manage your personal finances. Learning to run your own finances effectively will lead to you managing your investment property's income statement well, and will ensure you have a property with positive cash flow.

Third, you need to manage the entire rental process. For your first rental, this will include ensuring condition and function of the property; finding a tenant; qualifying a tenant; completing a walk-through checklist with the tenant; reviewing and signing the lease with the tenant; finding and hiring a property management company that reflects your purpose, values, and mission; investing in marketing your rental and focusing on the tenant; and reaching out to the tenant from time to time.

Cultivating an Entrepreneurial Mindset with Base, Better, Best

No one ever earned a gold medal in the Olympics by getting up the day of the race and running for the first time. Growing and developing as an entrepreneur and small business owner is progressive. Just like runners train, making incremental improvements, you need to pace your learning through action.

Cultivating an entrepreneurial mindset is a journey. In Coaching Challenge 8, I ask you to identify your entrepreneurial qualities and those qualities you may need help with.

Preparing and planning is an important area of cultivating one's mind. When you take time to develop a personal income and net worth statement, you are engaging your mind to have an entrepreneurial mindset. Being engaged in the basics of finance can go a long way to growing a small business mindset.

In Coaching Challenge 11, you can use the Base, Better, Best process to develop your entrepreneurial mindset. Below, I also apply this process to help you progress through the purchase of investment real estate. You may recognize you are not a very disciplined person and you succumb to resistance through fear or self-doubt, get distracted easily, are a perfectionist, or have a tendency to beat yourself up. Base, Better, Best is a great way to move through these challenges.

We first talked about this system in the Introduction. To refresh your memory, the Base, Better, Best system is starting at ground zero with a skill, developing that skill, and recognizing that your base for that skill has developed a level; then, this new level becomes your base and you go into development mode to build upon your new base.

And remember when I talked to you about "done is better than perfect"?

In his book *Do the Work*, Steven Pressfield outlines one of his key principals: "Don't think, act." Pressfield supports this thinking by writing, "We can always revise and revisit once we've acted."

This ability to act can be attached to entrepreneurial qualities, such as discipline, self-starting ability, and determination.

Let's look at one of these qualities and see how we can start with your base. We'll start with discipline. In your investment real estate journey, your first base might be as simple as developing an interest in finding an investment opportunity to add to your financial portfolio but having no idea what that is.

You then decide to get better by reading and researching numerous types of investment vehicles you could stick your money into. You identify a host of investments, like stocks, bonds, commodities, investment real estate, and many others.

Finally, after careful consideration, you decide on your best. The best is to actually define investment real estate as your investment vehicle of choice.

Using the Base, Better, Best process, you continue to develop your entrepreneurial mindset and take the process to the next level.

You decide the new base in your entrepreneurial journey is to read *31 Days to Purchasing and Renting Your First Investment Real Estate Property*.

The road to success takes all of the qualities you'll outline in Coaching Challenge 8.

The goal of the book is clear, and you may be sensing these first thirty-one days of purchasing and renting your first investment real estate property are the biggest part of your learning curve. You are correct.

I am not trying to minimize the process or make it look easy. There are too many misleading get-rich ideas out there that try and convince you that you can do it with little time, effort, or resources. That's simply not true. It does take time, effort, and resources.

Investment real estate is a big decision and a lifelong commitment. If it were effortless, everyone would be doing it. As I mentioned in Coaching Challenge 1, only 4 to 8 percent of North Americans own investment real estate, and just half of those folks own three or more properties. Clearly, very few people are doing it.

The process isn't easy, but it's made much easier when you follow the guidance I lay out in this book. And, speaking from personal experience, I can tell you the journey is worth it.

A Warning: Don't Chase Doors

As I have mentioned before, my goal is to get you to purchase investment real estate as part of your financial portfolio. Before we get further into the business side of investment real estate, I want to caution you not to chase doors. A door refers to each rental unit you own; a duplex is two doors, a triplex is three doors, and so forth. For now, we're focusing on our first investment real estate door.

The person who introduced me to adding investment real estate education as part of my development didn't listen to the advice being taught at the educational organization we both were members of.

My friend thought that the more properties he purchased, the better off he would be, and so he chased doors. We became partners in a couple of investment properties, and within a year, he had purchased twenty-six doors.

Unfortunately, a year later, he had overextended himself and was not taking care of the basics we will talk about throughout this book. He ended up selling all of his properties and we had to buy him out of the joint ventures we had purchased together. He was such a great guy and joint venture partner, but he made a fundamental mistake that ultimately led to his downfall: he never took the time to review each investment property he was purchasing.

The lessons my wife and I were able to learn from other people's mistakes have become part of our small business mindset.

Your Investment Real Estate Business, Business Structure, and Taxation

Small businesses are critical to most of the world's economies. Such businesses account for the largest percentage of businesses in most countries. In Canada, entrepreneurs running small businesses make up 98 percent of the businesses across the nation and employ over 7.7 million people, according to Statistics Canada. When making investment real estate part of your financial portfolio, understanding small business mechanics is therefore critical to your entrepreneurial success.

The specifics will vary based on local laws, but generally speaking, you can choose to operate your investment real estate business as a sole proprietorship, a partnership, or a limited corporation.

Small Business Structuring

There are varying ways to structure your small business.

A **sole proprietorship** is an entrepreneurial business owned and run by one individual and in which there is no legal distinction between the owner and the business entity. A sole entrepreneur does not necessarily work "alone"—it is possible for this individual businessperson to employ other people. Many times, in today's digital world, sole proprietors use third-party companies to handle things like bookkeeping, marketing, and other busines functions. As a sole proprietor, you can often hire folks as a one-off charge or on a limited contract term.

A **partnership** is a business run by two or more individuals who decided to combine their resources in the interest of creating a profit. Throughout the book, we will refer to joint venture strategies involving family, friends, and acquaintances that also can be described as partnerships. I discuss joint venture agreement paperwork and recommend using a joint venture agreement, which legally protects all parties. This is especially true in a partnership because it is an unincorporated business, meaning the partners are personally responsible for any liabilities.

Finally, a **limited corporation** is a common method of incorporating a business. In most cases, incorporation protects the owners (shareholders) of the corporation from the majority of liabilities; however, as I mention later in the book, not all lenders will allow you to purchase investment real estate without having personal guarantees attached. There are also some downsides to incorporating: the cost can be expensive and you'll have to pay yearly fees. For example, you are required to pay for an annual report, prepared by your legal team, which can cost from $250 to $400. Also, you are required to file a yearly corporate tax return, and these fees can add up to nearly a thousand dollars.

For the most part, I believe investment real estate should be a part of your financial portfolio, not your entire portfolio. Therefore, at this stage, where you are adding one investment real estate property to your financial portfolio, registering your business as a sole proprietorship or partnership is the most straightforward way to proceed. Use a legal joint venture agreement should you decide to create a partnership on some of your investment real estate purchases. Later, if you decide to grow your investment real estate business like we did, restructuring your business as a corporation can have some great advantages.

Deciding on a Business Structure

When it comes to choosing a business structure, do your homework. As part of your initial discussions with your lawyer and your accountant, ask if you should incorporate or leave everything in your own name.

The initial and annual cost may help give you clarity on your decision.

My advice comes from experience. We incorporated because I intended to accomplish two major tasks: to own numerous investment real estate properties and to build a coaching and consulting business after my corporate career.

However, if you are going to keep your investment real estate portfolio small, or you aren't sure yet, I would suggest that you not incorporate. Here are a few reasons why:

- The purchases and deductions associated with an investment real estate business can really help you at tax time.
- Even for corporations, most lenders will require you to sign personal guarantees when financing, and you get no personal protection from your lenders for investment real estate.
- It's possible to buy foreclosures as a sole proprietor well under market-value pricing. In our experience, the lender would not sell these properties to our corporation and we needed to secure financing in our personal names.
- The annual costs as a corporation can get expensive. I have found if you have your properties in your name and include them in your personal tax return, your accounting bill tends to be lower.

Am I a tax expert? No, but I can talk from personal experience.

When my wife and I started out purchasing investment real estate, we incorporated. It was not only because of the number of doors we planned to purchase;

it was more about having a vision where I saw myself helping others to purchase investment real estate and envisioned having multiple revenue streams down the road. As of today, we have half our portfolio in our business and half our portfolio under our corporation. In the next section, I will share why. It is important to know life gets in the way and takes you in directions you do not expect.

Later in the book, on Day 19, we will discuss assembling your Team REAL, but right now it's more important to discuss real life.

If you see investment real estate as a side hustle, this is where you need to use the team you'll build later and talk to them about what your investment real estate business might look like in the future.

Life Can Get in the Way: Reasons to Wait to Incorporate

As I mentioned, I had bigger plans for our corporation than simply investment real estate; at the time of writing, it has been over ten years since we incorporated. I loved the idea of coaching and writing and added these items to our incorporation. I knew that, someday, we would generate revenue that would be outside of the rental income from our brick-and-mortar investment real estate portfolio. That revenue comes from the coaching services, courses, and other products I have gathered under the umbrella of the Vault to Real Estate Success Corporation.

Incorporation comes at a cost. To stay incorporated, there is an annual registration fee in the neighborhood of one thousand dollars, and we must file an annual corporate return, which is more complicated than for other business structures. There are also incidentals of a couple of hundred dollars.

You have to ask yourself if you are going to generate enough positive cash flow to cover these costs should you be shelling out over $1,500 a year.

If you had no legal costs to keep your company incorporated and the accounting bill would be much lower than a thousand dollars, would you be richer in the long run?

You might be reasoning that you are protected from personal liability by being incorporated. In truth, it's not so straightforward. The banks or lenders are happy to lend to your corporation, but they are looking for signed personal guarantees.

I advised my children in the beginning to incorporate, as we started to purchase real estate through joint ventures together and they had full adult lives in front of them with their partners. Their aspirations have changed, as children and life got in the way and they are no longer with the same partners. With the average annual cost of their corporation's annual return and corporate accounting fees, it did not take long to realize this thousand dollars a year could be better invested.

Starting out as a sole proprietorship or partnership ensures you aren't faced with the high costs associated with incorporating. You can always incorporate when you're ready.

Base, Better, Best – The Process

The Base, Better, Best process to purchasing power is a progression of levels through your investment real estate purchasing journey. Your base should be etched in stone; it is your first investment real estate property, and the reason you purchased this book. Your better and best should not be etched in stone; living through lessons learned through your base will give you so much insight into how investment real estate can work for you and your investment portfolio.

For example:

> **Base**: Purchase first investment real estate property
> **Better**: Purchase second, third, and multiple investment doors
> > **Best**: Purchase multiple investment doors (attached to a long-term plan and exit strategy)

Dreams are illustrations from the book your soul is writing about you. — Marsha Norman

I can't think of a more appropriate way to describe dreaming what your investment real estate portfolio might look like for you in the future—your better or best.

I had a dream to have more than one investment real estate property. This might not be your dream, and I support whatever investment real estate path you follow. This book is all about getting you to take your first step to purchasing your first investment real estate property, no matter what your dream looks like.

Risk and Reward

Investment real estate is no different than any other investment you decide to make. Whether it's stocks, bonds, mutual funds, or index funds, there is always some degree of risk.

You may have heard financial folks say "the lower the risk, the lower the reward," and "the higher the risk, the higher the reward."

Investment real estate is an area of my financial portfolio I have always believed is more hands-on, and I feel this helps me to lower the risk. With a strong financial foundation, I believe I am in a better position to make wise investments. Let me explain: Over time, the rental income has lowered my exposure to debt with mortgage paydown. We have seen our income rise with rental income increases, and we have sold a few properties and used the equity growth to pay down some of our mortgages. By paying down some of our mortgage balances early, we will have a few no-mortgage investment properties in the next several years, which is a nice benefit that lowers our risk with an increase in revenue.

It is not about how much you earn; it is about how much you keep. Riches come from your capital—your wealth in the form of money or other assets—working to earn more capital. And by putting your capital to work with an entrepreneurial mindset, strong business skills, and a firm plan in place, you'll position yourself to keep more and thereby build a strong financial foundation.

Tap into the mindset of an entrepreneur and small business owner.

In this chapter, we talked about the qualities of an entrepreneur and a small business owner. These are the qualities that are essential to business success—and, therefore, investment real estate success. How many of these qualities can you remember?

⇧ List the qualities of an entrepreneur and small business mindset. At the very least, say them to yourself out loud. It's okay—no one is around. Then, go back and review them. Which did you miss? Are there any we didn't include that you would add? Use your notebook or the workbook and planning guide to keep on track.

Does your mindset match up?

In Coaching Challenge 8, you created a list of the qualities of an entrepreneurial and small business mindset. For this challenge, make sure to have that list handy.

When you look in the magic mirror and judge the person standing in front of it, what do you see? You, and only you, can judge yourself and see if you have what it takes to be a successful entrepreneur and small business owner.

⇧ How many of the qualities that you listed in Coaching Challenge 8 reflect you?

- ⇧ Only through your actions will people judge you as essential, respectful, productive, and ambitious. What types of actions can you take as an entrepreneur and investment real estate investor that will inspire these types of positive judgments from others?
- ⇧ Being an entrepreneur and small business owner takes work and action. Are you able and willing to make the commitment?

Grow and develop your entrepreneurial mindset.

In Coaching Challenge 9, I asked you if you were willing and able to commit to entrepreneurship. If your answer was yes, great—now we're going to work on developing that entrepreneurial mindset that will lead you to investment real estate success. Answer the following questions in your notebook or the workbook and planning guide.

- ⇧ How do you see yourself growing and developing the qualities of an entrepreneurial and small business mindset?
- ⇧ Are there any areas of entrepreneurship that you are already strong in? In which areas could you use some improvement?
- ⇧ What specific resources will you use to strengthen your mindset and develop new business skills?

Coaching Challenge 11: Define your base, better, and best.

In this coaching challenge, we will define your base, better, and best for your investment real estate portfolio. For right now, think about what type of investment property you can see yourself owning. We will review your thinking on Day 7 and help you identify which investment real estate property type is right for you.

- ⇧ Take a few minutes to think about your initial investment real estate base. What type of property might you purchase as your first investment real estate property?
- ⇧ Going further, let's consider your better. What would be a step up from your base?
- ⇧ Finally, let's think about your best. In an ideal world, what would your investment real estate business look like?

Day 4 Key Recap

Record your key learnings and actionable items in your notebook or the workbook and planning guide. (Optional)

- ⇧ Prepare and plan for your investment real estate business with an entrepreneurial mindset.
- ⇧ Build your small business skills through developing an income and net worth statement.
- ⇧ Use coaching as a tool for your investment real estate success.
- ⇧ Recognize your personal characteristics of being an investment real estate investor.
- ⇧ Repeat the Base, Better, Best process for your investment real estate education.

DAY 5 DON'T GIVE UP YOUR DAY JOB, AND OTHER INCOME ADVICE

Use this chapter to discover why you need to maintain your day job, why diversifying your income is essential, and how to use your income to get your first investment real estate mortgage. At the end of the chapter, complete the coaching challenges to brainstorm ways to enhance your income and strengthen your ability to service debt.

Your motivation to read this book may be as simple as purchasing and renting your first investment real estate property. Or, you might be thinking ahead and have your eye on entrepreneurship, with the goal of building an extensive investment real estate portfolio that enables you to work for yourself.

Whatever your goals, having a day job or career is important when purchasing your first investment real estate property. Building sustainable wealth comes over time, and in many cases, it will come from many different sources—including your employment.

Why You Should Keep Your Day Job

Who hasn't heard the saying "Money makes the world go round"? Surprisingly enough, the mere fact that you're earning money might be more important than having the money itself. Even if you have a ton of money as security, many lenders see your employment as more significant to help maintain your equity without spending it away. Employment—having a regular source of income—gives you greater purchasing power.

All riches need to be protected against inflation and costs, and the revenue to cover these expenses is often obtained through a job. When you purchase an investment property, there are costs to maintain it, and the first question a lender asks you is if you have employment. As a first-time investment real estate investor, borrowing gets a whole lot easier if your answer is yes. Let's dive a little deeper into why it's essential that you have a day job—and that you keep it.

Keeping your job and purchasing your first investment real estate property allows you to have your cake and eat it too. The following are key advantages to remaining employed while launching your investment real estate business.

Please understand I am not discouraging you from eventually following your passion to be self-employed. However, it is important to know that many lenders have different rules for self-employed folks, including the percentage of down payment required, which could go as high as 35 percent.

I will continue to remind you that you are playing in someone else's sandbox and it is their money they are lending you. Don't get mad or upset; instead, understand the rules and learn to play nice.

Below, you'll find three great reasons for keeping your day job:

1. You Have Guaranteed Income

As you build an investment real estate portfolio, you will be borrowing money, and lenders like to know you have stable employment with a good income.

That's why, in the early years of building your financial foundation, I would encourage you to keep your day job.

While you are working and earning, you can use part of your earnings to purchase investment real estate and rent this investment real estate to bring in monthly revenue. You have given yourself a raise and didn't even have to talk to the boss about more money.

2. You Can Earn While You Learn

Building your investment real estate business can be a very educational experience. Basically, you are getting paid to learn the ins and outs of entrepreneurship and small business while maintaining your regular employment. In contrast, going to an Ivy League business school is expensive, harder to do while holding down a job, and the time you spend earning a degree is generally unpaid. Plus, keeping your job gives you income that may enable you to hire a coach; whether it's a personal development coach or an entrepreneurial coach, having a coach to help you understand your business can be instrumental in your success. We talked about coaching in the previous chapter, Day 4.

3. Stay with Your Professional Passion

Many folks acquire a skill they are great at and go on to become experts in their field. Rest assured that you don't have to give up your true calling to become an investment real estate investor; it doesn't have to take up all of your work time or leisure time. You may have designs on your future and dream of practicing your professional passion while being self-employed; through investment real estate, you learn to become an entrepreneur, and over the years, you can create substantial income from rental real estate that will provide the financial means for you to transition from your employed professional career to a self-employed professional career in your field of expertise.

By sticking with a career and job you love, you have a stable financial foundation that gives you the luxury of providing for your family and leisure activities.

4. Uberize Your Investment – Crush Your Interest

I described this concept I call "Uberizing" your investment on Day 3, and I hope that you can see how this idea can make a difference in your life. It is a simple method to speed up your wealth creation. In today's digital world, you can easily supplement your income simply by accessing an app. But you don't have to drive for Uber; there are multiple ways to earn part-time income. My point is that earning additional income and applying everything you earn to principal paydown in the early stages of your mortgage can make a big dent in your interest payments. Many financial lenders allow you to pay down your mortgage between an additional 10 to 20 percent per year. You will be shocked at how even an additional ten part-time hours a week at minimum wage can positively impact your mortgage principal paydown.

Minimum wage is different in all parts of North America. Use ten hours at your jurisdiction's minimum wage and set a plan for one year, two years, and five years, then calculate the wages and use the mortgage refinancing calculator I have provided as a free resource on our website, vaulttoinvestmentrealestatesuccess.com, under the [Resources tab – House Loans – Calculators](#).

More details about this on Day 14.

Diversifying Your Income Builds Financial Stability

While having a job is extremely important, it's not the only piece to the diversification puzzle. You may also find yourself in the awesome position of building other income sources as you develop your investment real estate portfolio. Some great examples of this are funding a company pension and registered retirement funds (401K, RRSP), purchasing stock in other companies, and funding government pension programs.

Diversifying your sources of income is a prudent idea, as most of the investments you will make over time will be cyclical. This means everything you invest in will go through the highs and lows of the economy.

Some of your investments may be healthy at any given time, while others may experience a low. The health of the investments in your financial portfolio will support one another and act as a solid financial foundation—which, in turn, will support your investment real estate investments.

Is there a chance your investments might not be a safety net? Could you lose your employment at the same time as your investments drop in value? Can these dangers impact investment real estate as well? The answer to all of these questions is yes.

COVID-19: An Economic Low

During the recent pandemic, many people lost their jobs. I don't want to minimize this; we saw unemployment rates hit over 10 percent.

Many governments mobilized to financially protect their citizens—both those who were working and those who lost their jobs. The governments instituted financial support programs, mortgage deferral programs, and programs to protect tenants from being forced from their rental homes.

During this pandemic, we only lost one tenant and had a new tenant within a week. We had to hold our rental rates, and we forgave one tenant half their rent for a couple of months. After six months of the pandemic, only one of our tenants has lost their employment. The one tenant who asked for our assistance directly has met her rental obligations and has not asked us for any further assistance. We didn't receive any government funding for the rental amount we forgave, nor did we ask.

The one program we took advantage of was the mortgage deferral program, just in case. This program allowed us to put off making our mortgage payments until a later date. Not knowing how many of our tenants might lose their jobs, we asked for the maximum deferral, six months. In this way, we were able to proactively protect our properties by deferring our mortgage payments, but we had the majority of our rents coming in.

We had enough income being generated to cover our property taxes, insurance, property management, and condominium fees. We could have had our property taxes deferred as well, but this is an area we didn't have to use.

Being firm believers in diversifying our investments, my wife and I have numerous income sources, including investments and salary. When the COVID-19 pandemic hit, having this other income in place ensured we had the resources to help our tenants. Having finances from other sources during a crisis was necessary, and our lenders were more at ease knowing we had money coming in during the coronavirus.

Unforeseen Benefits of the Rental Deferral Program

Unexpected issues happen in life; we've seen that with COVID-19. But no matter what's going on, your property will still age and experience wear and tear. Deferring an issue means just that: you're putting something off that will still need to be addressed later.

While we weren't impacted the way we had anticipated—for example, losing our tenants or tenants being unable to make rent—we decided to take a calculated risk and address capital work projects in our building that we knew needed to be done. As a group of owners, we proceeded with major upgrades that had been planned before the pandemic. Taking the funds we had saved over the six months from the mortgage deferral program, we invested into the capital work projects. We repainted the entire interior and added new flooring; we also did some landscaping work and a few other minor repairs. We received rave reviews from our existing tenants.

I recently returned from reviewing and taking pictures of the upgrades to our buildings. We painted and recarpeted all the common areas of the building. We also did some other minor upgrades, and our tenants have been raving about all of this work.

The pandemic is ongoing at the time of writing, but as owners, we have shown our tenants we still care in tough times. We will likely all benefit as owners, with the building holding or increasing in value; only time will tell. We also have heard that family members who have visited the buildings are spreading the word about how well managed our buildings are; you can't put a value on this type of PR.

The Risks of Not Diversifying

In her September 2020 article on the stock market and retirement, personal finance columnist for the *Washington Post* Michelle Singletary said, "You can't time the market." I love this quote, but it is also a life lesson. All of us have lived through COVID-19. There is no way the world saw this pandemic coming, and Michelle's quote is further-reaching, as it can speak to everything in life.

The coronavirus proves you can't time life.

While some income sources may remain healthy through a catastrophe, others may be severely impacted. That's why it's so important to diversify your income streams and investments. That way, you aren't putting all your eggs in one basket, and a single disastrous event won't have the power to make or break your financial health.

But no matter what happens, nothing is forever.

Over the last hundred years, there have been many other financial disasters; as an investor, you may have lived through a couple of these. You can think about the stock market in 1929 and 2009 and the collapse, but there's more to consider than just the financial markets. What were the reasons behind the downturn in the economy and the market? Think about the 2020 coronavirus, SARS in the early 2000s, 9/11, and the subprime real estate crisis in 2007–2008. All of these events had economic consequences, and every time, life went on and the world bounced back.

Through COVID-19, we were all encouraged to practice social distancing and wear masks as the financial world restarted. The story of COVID-19 may take years to unfold completely, but the world again will continue on. We humans are a very resilient bunch and will manage our way through this pandemic.

We will find a vaccine—multiple vaccines—and the world will return to a new normal.

The Stock Market and Why It Matters

Not everyone reading this book understands the stock market, and I don't profess to be an expert. But regardless, many of your income sources will be tied in some way to the health of the stock market.

If you are paying into a government pension, a company pension, any registered retirement funds, or purchasing mutual funds, stocks, commodities, and other financial investment vehicles, you are invested in the stock market.

Major countries have their own stock markets, and as an investor, you can trade in most of them.

In Canada, the major stock market is known as the Toronto Stock Exchange (TSX), and in the United States, the major stock markets are the New York Stock Exchange (NYSE) and the Nasdaq (NASDAQ). The health of the U.S. markets is measured by an index called the Dow Jones Industrial Average, which tracks select stocks traded on the NYSE and the NASDAQ and is commonly taken as a representation of the performance of the economy as a whole.

You might be saying, why does the stock market matter to me? In the simplest terms, it is a way for you to understand your country's economic health. If you are invested in any retirement or financial vehicles, it gives you a big-picture view of your investments' returns.

A Peek into Your Financial Health

Did you notice that, with the impact of forcing everyone to stay home, all the technology stocks took off in value, and the NASDAQ went to record highs? For those of you who are not right on top of the stock markets around the world, here's a basic explanation. The stock markets are where folks go to buy and sell shares in public companies, for example, bank stocks like Bank of America and Bank of Montreal; technology stocks like Apple and IBM; pharmaceutical stocks like Pfizer, Moderna, and Johnson & Johnson; and an endless list of others. The NASDAQ is tied into technology companies, and during the pandemic, because of the stay-at-home orders, tech companies like Zoom, Apple, and Google rose in value.

In life, there are losers and winners. Life in the stock markets is no different. Have you noticed that now, as the COVID-19 vaccines roll out, the technology stocks are not as strong as they were earlier in the pandemic?

As mentioned earlier, the NYSE and the TSX are where most common stocks are bought and sold. Indexes like the Dow Jones Industrial Average and the TSX Composite Index, which measures the performance of the TSX, give us a snapshot of the health of the stock market. As I wrote this book, I looked at the highest value of the stock market in 2020: the Dow Jones was at its highest point on February 12, 2020, at 29,551, and the TSX Composite, on February 20, 2020, was at 17,994.

Then the pandemic arrived and many folks exited the stock market, causing values to drop because of all the uncertainty.

Then North America began to shut down in areas like retail, transportation, and hospitality, and on March 23, 2020, the Dow dropped to 18,541, and the TSX dropped to 11,228.

The Worldwide Vaccine Roll-Out's Positive Impact on Stock Markets

As of March 12, 2021, at market close, the Dow is at 32,778.24 and the TSX Composite is at 18,851.32. Have you noticed the major stock markets are well above pre-pandemic levels?

Timing the real estate market is no different than the stock market, and the chance to buy at the bottom of both the stock market and the real estate market due to the coronavirus has already passed.

The Side Benefits of Financial Return

Building a business while learning the nuances of business fundamentals is what I call the side benefits of financial return. You grow, learn, and develop as you invest your money in a live business situation.

You not only develop your skills as an entrepreneur and small business owner, but you will also find that these skills are transferable to your personal life and the lives of family and friends.

Power to the People

Whatever investment vehicle you purchase, you cannot purchase investments—or anything, for that matter—without having funds left over after you have received your income and paid your monthly expenses.

You can buy things on credit, but, as we discussed earlier, interest on your purchases and a negative cash flow has a way of restricting your ability to buy. In short, it eliminates your purchasing power—your financial ability to buy products and services.

I believe that, through investment real estate, your purchasing power allows you to use your income to purchase income. Diversifying your income streams gives you a more stable income, which provides you with greater purchasing power.

 **Understand the relationship between your employment and your purchasing power.**

We have talked about the importance of employment. While employment is only one step to securing funds to purchase investment real estate or any type of investment, it's one of the most important.

As we have discussed several times already, if you are self-employed, you will be treated differently by lenders. Lenders want more of a down payment amount from someone who's self-employed, up to 35 percent of the purchase amount of the home.

If you are already self-employed, I am not asking you to give up your self-employment; rather, just understand the lenders' rules so you will be prepared and won't encounter any surprises.

Lenders want to observe how you manage the money you earn—are you a carefree spender that continually spends more than you earn, or are you someone who knows how to manage the money you earn and have funds left over at the end of the month to save or invest? Unless you have funds available at the end of each month or pay period, a lender may deem you not creditworthy and decide against lending you mortgage funds.

- If you are employed, write down in your notebook or the workbook and planning guide a few ways you can bring more value to your employer. Within the next week, set up a meeting with the boss and see if you can get a raise to help increase your purchasing power for investment real estate.
- Write a list of outstanding debt you can eliminate from your net worth statement before you look for mortgage financing. For example, if you are continually carrying a credit card balance, yet you have money in your savings account that you could use to easily pay off the balance, do so, and don't carry a credit card balance you can't pay off every month.
- If you are self-employed, get a part-time job that pays you a regular income that you can use with the lender to help lower your need for a high down payment amount. It's short-term pain for long-term gain.
- Brainstorm a list of "Uberizing" opportunities you may be able to add to your income base to strengthen your ability to service debt.

Day 5 Key Recap

Record your key learnings and actionable items in your notebook or the workbook and planning guide. (Optional)

- Employment is the most important factor to most lenders.
- Understand the lenders' rules for self-employed folks and what you can do to put yourself in an better position short-term.

- ⇧ Financial diversification plays an important role in your financial picture.
- ⇧ Don't be surprised by the unexpected.
- ⇧ Make the most of other sources of income.

 # DAY 6 ALL IN THE FAMILY

Use this day to determine who in your family will influence your investment real estate decisions. At the end of the chapter, complete the coaching challenges to define the role each friend and family member will play.

Your family is an essential part of your life, through good times and bad. But what is your family's role in your investment real estate journey? What role will your parents, children, and moral support team—other family members and friends—play? Can any offer you a place to stay as you build funds to purchase your first investment real estate property, or are they good candidates for joint venture partners?

Enlist the Support of Friends and Family

We all have family and friends who influence and pressure us, and the purchase of investment real estate should never go unsupported by our loved ones. How we handle our investments can be very disruptive to our household. Your financial lenders will often be looking at your household's financial health to determine if they are going to lend you the funds to purchase an investment property.

If you can't adequately explain to your spouse, family, and friends the important role investment real estate will play in your life and financial portfolio, how are you going to convincingly present your proposal for lending support to your bank?

I suggest that you and your spouse or partner read *31 Days to Purchasing and Renting Your First Investment Real Estate Property* at the same time so that you share an understanding of this big decision in your life. Each of you should use a different-colored highlighter as you go through the book and have conversations around each coaching challenge. Each person's interpretation of the material might be a little different.

Recently, a coaching client approached me to help their family purchase a property together—a sister and her spouse and her brother and his spouse. At the end of the day, I helped each couple to realize they were not on the same page regarding the type of property, the rental strategy, how to finance, and the overall buy-and-hold strategy. In the end, the sister and her husband decided not to proceed, and I worked with the brother and his spouse to purchase and rent this investment property on their own.

The sister and spouse were happy for the brother and sister-in-law and went on to purchase their own investment properties more in line with their investment philosophy. The family relationship was preserved.

It's important to plan this out in detail early in your investment real estate journey because your parents, children, and other family members and friends will be with you for years to come.

You will share many of your life's journeys with your parents, children, other family members, and friends. Similarly, your investment real estate purchases have a very good chance of coming up in your discussions with them.

At the end of the day, whether parents, children, other family members, and friends become part of your investment circle or not, they will always have opinions and influence your decisions. That's why it's best to be upfront and prevent your investment decisions from creating a rift in the family.

This happens more often than you might think. And sharing and discussing with friends and family sometimes ends up with a positive result. For example, I worked with a coaching client who received an inheritance from her mother early because the mother saw the benefit to her daughter (my client) and granddaughters of purchasing investment real estate now instead of waiting until her death.

The family stories about investment real estate could be a whole chapter in itself. Before discussing the ways your family might be involved in your investment real estate journey, I would like to share one more client story with you and the lessons learned from it.

An Investment Real Estate Story Unreleased

I recently worked with a client—a great young guy starting out in life who wanted to purchase his first investment real estate property. The first thing I ask all my clients is if there is anyone else who will be involved in the purchase, and he said no.

He had been living at home, saved up a considerable down payment, and after a couple of false starts on employment, he secured a great job and was ready to purchase his first investment property.

We found him a real estate agent, and out they ventured to find the ideal property. After months of searching for the right home at the right price in a great rental area and neighborhood, he settled on a bungalow property that would allow him to live upstairs and create an income suite in the basement. He asked me to review the property with him. It ticked all the boxes and was the perfect choice for his first investment real estate property.

Although he'd spent months working with me, getting ready and getting qualified for the purchase, he decided to take his parents along for one final look before making the offer. I'm not sure exactly what happened on that tour of the home, but I'll never forget the result: his parents talked him out of the purchase.

This story illustrates something I've learned over the years: no matter how much a person says they aren't involving anyone else in the decision, there is always someone.

As you work through the initial search for an investment property, make sure you talk to anyone you might involve in the purchasing process, even if you think you only want this person to see the property. Parents, children, and other family members and friends may ask to come along and give their opinion of the property and the location, but make sure they understand the role this property will play in your life (i.e., investment real estate with the goal of renting). These folks should know why this type of property is right for a rental, and why the location is great for the type of tenant you have decided on. Remind anyone that comes along to view it that this may not be where they would live with their family, but it is perfect for your ideal tenant profile. (We will go into further depth on your ideal tenant on Day 7.)

Remember, the people in your life can have strong opinions.

Don't get me wrong; I am not saying that you shouldn't involve the folks you love and respect in your life. Instead, simply make sure these people understand what you are trying to achieve, identify their role, and make sure they agree to and understand that role.

Understanding Ownership Terminology Before Talking to Family Members

When you are investing in property owned by more than one person, there are only two possible ways to do it: joint tenancy or tenancy in common. I have a strong opinion regarding which method you should use when purchasing a property with a person other than your spouse or partner, and I will explain this to you. But first, let's get clear on what joint tenancy and tenants in common are.

Joint Tenancy and Tenants in Common

A property owned by more than one person must be owned in one of two ways: either as joint tenancy or tenants in common. In both these scenarios, the owners hold an undivided portion in the property.

In easy terms, the main difference between joint tenancy and tenancy in common is the right of survivorship. In other words, it determines what happens to the property when one partner dies.

Only a joint tenancy relation enjoys the right of survivorship. Right of survivorship occurs when only the living survivor (or survivors) continues to have legal claim to the property.

If property is held as tenants in common, the interest in the property passes down to the estate of the deceased and is transferred to beneficiaries by the estate.

Please seek legal counsel to discuss which option is best for you and your circumstances.

My opinion is that you should use the tenants in common method most of the time. I recommend you use tenants in common with partners outside of your spouse, such as children and other joint venture partners, because relationships can be unpredictable.

Joint Venture Agreements

Property purchases with anyone other than your spouse or partner should have a joint venture agreement in place.

For example, we have joint ventures with both our children, and both their relationships and marriages have ended. We are partners with our daughter's ex-partner and were previously partners with my son's ex-spouse. Having tenants in common protects our wishes that we are not passing on major assets to people who are no longer part of our family.

You just never know when a partnership or marriage will dissolve, and that's why all parties must have a way out of the agreement.

Remember, life is ever-changing. Make sure you are prepared for all changes.

In the appendix, there is an outline of a joint venture agreement. My wife and I have multiple joint venture partnerships, and we have spent thousands of dollars developing a standard joint venture agreement to use in our business.

The standard length of a joint venture agreement is over fifteen pages; ours has six articles and one schedule. On the first page and in the first paragraph of the joint venture is the following statement:

"Any investment is speculative; real estate is no different. Every investor should consult independent advisors with experience in real estate investment."

Determining Your Family's Role

A role is a set of behaviors, rights, obligations, beliefs, and standards. It is important to remember that your family members' and friends' roles in your life have developed over the course of years, sometimes since you were born, and will be different than the roles of professionals you pay for advice, services, and coaching.

As I mentioned earlier, your family and friends may be aggressive in giving you advice, or they may be passive. Many times, family and friends will share your behaviors, beliefs, and standards. Some friends and family may be less concerned about giving you their opinions and just want to see you happy. Your feelings may be a concern to some but not to others; just as friends and family can be benign in their advice, not wishing to hurt you, they can also be brutally honest.

It is important to remember there may not be anyone in your circle of family or friends who have purchased and rented investment real estate, yet most of these people will still have an opinion. That opinion may be based on hearsay, and you should weigh their advice carefully. In contrast, some of your family and friends will own residential real estate, and use this firsthand experience as their basis and bias for their comments and opinions on your investment real estate venture.

However, just because your family and friends own personal residential real estate, it does not make them experts on owning investment real estate. One piece of advice you will continually hear from me is not to hire a member of your Team REAL who has never purchased or owned investment real estate (more on that on Day 19). If you have family or friends who own their own homes, awesome, but homeownership is not a business investment venture, and residential homeowners aren't necessarily qualified to give you business advice.

On Day 19, I will expand on other roles of your family members and friends, from being an investment partner to playing a professional role on your Team REAL.

Conversation Is Key

It is important to talk to family and friends who are part of your everyday life about what you are doing. These folks generally don't have a vested interest in your success, other than your well-being. With less than 90 percent of North Americans owning investment real estate, most family members and friends will know very little about the topic. If you want to involve them or have their support, you should be able to explain your interest in investment real estate. Doing a great job of explaining the importance of investment real estate in your life to them has an added side benefit: it can go a long way in attracting lenders or joint venture partners to your investment real estate pursuit.

Ask your friends and family members if they own any investment real estate property or know of anyone who owns investment real estate. You might be surprised how many of these folks can be part of your Team REAL.

> **COACHING CHALLENGE 13**
>
> Define the roles of your friends and family in your investment real estate journey. Who among them are your raving fans?

We've all seen raving fans. You know the ones—they're devoted to their team or star of choice, cheering them on through thick and thin. In a way, they can be loosely be construed as an integral part of the team. If not for the fans, especially ones that purchase tickets, sportswear, trinkets, and memorabilia, there would be no revenue, and without revenue, there is a good chance there would be no team.

If you don't think fans are important, then you are not a sports fan. Think about the opera or Broadway—any type of entertainment, for that matter. Every athlete or performer during this pandemic has mentioned how much they miss their fans. Fans provide positive reinforcement, and it has been shown time and time again how positive reinforcement contributes to success.

Sit down with family and friends and explain what you are trying to accomplish through investment real estate. Think about what it would take for them to be your raving fans. What do they need in order to believe in what you are trying to accomplish, and think you're a good bet for people they know to invest in you as a joint partner or live in one of your rental real estate properties?

- Write down the names and roles of each person in your notebook or the workbook and planning guide.
- Identify each family member's role: mom, dad, spouse, siblings, children, cousins, and friends you view as part of your extended family.
- Now, who among these are your raving fans? Not everyone in your family or among your close friends will be a fan or support you in your investment real estate journey. Many of us have family and friends who don't have the same political, religious, or other beliefs we do, but this does not stop those folks from being close to us. You don't need everyone to buy in to your investment beliefs; this never even has to be a discussion.
- Where possible, try and convert folks to your way of investment thinking. But that said, should they be totally opposed or very negative, don't even bring the subject up. Why destroy a relationship when you don't have to?

> **COACHING CHALLENGE 14**
> **Determine which friends and family, if any, will join your Team REAL. Who is experienced and knowledgeable enough to become a full-fledged member of your team?**

Some friends and family may be great choices to add to your Team REAL, while others are best left sitting in the bleachers, cheering you on as raving fans, or even outside the stadium if all they're going to do is boo. Look at your list of family members and friends and the roles you defined for them in Coaching Challenge 13. Think about each person and decide if you will involve them in the purchase of your investment real estate property, even as an observer.

You will need to look at each person's professional skill set and see if anyone you are close to can help you. Do they have investment real estate experience? Your sister-in-law may be a real estate agent, but does that mean she has any experience in investment real estate? Be careful you don't default to people's opinions just because they are close to you; skill set is important, as you are running a business.

- ⇧ Are there any family members who can play a part in your investment real estate journey? Do they have the professional skill set to play a role on your Team REAL?
- ⇧ Your raving fans support what you do. If you can't include them on your team, you can still share your journey with them for support and encouragement. Similarly, avoid sharing about your investment real estate goals with those who don't share your outlook or who have a negative opinion that brings you down.

On Day 20, we will talk more about your Team REAL and their role in the purchase and rental of your first investment real estate property.

Day 6 Key Recap

Record your key learnings and actionable items in your notebook or the workbook and planning guide. (Optional)

- ⇧ Have family and friends join and support your investment real estate journey.
- ⇧ Don't take advice from those who are not experienced in investment real estate.
- ⇧ Cultivate raving fans, and avoid discussing the topic with the naysayers.
- ⇧ There are different options for ownership; decide which one is right for you.

⇧ Creating a joint venture agreement is a must when investing in real estate with partners.

⇧ The positive societal and financial benefits of investment real estate are tremendous. Use your knowledge to communicate this to your personal community.

DAY 7 THE TYPES OF INVESTMENT REAL ESTATE PROPERTY AND TENANTS THAT MATCH

Use this day to learn about the different types of investment real estate property and discover the different types of tenants. At the end of the chapter, complete the coaching challenges to identify the right type of property for you and create your ideal tenant profile.

As a first-time real estate investor, your first investment real estate property is your most important one. It sets you on a path to the type of property you might find yourself most drawn to if you decide to expand your business. However, just because you're drawn to a certain type of property does not make it the right choice for you. You may find yourself giving up valuable credit options for borrowing more money in the future. That's why, before purchasing your first investment real estate property, it's essential to do some research.

By understanding each property type below, you can make the right choice about your investment property right from the get-go.

It is important to remember this property is not about you and your tastes. The type of property you want to purchase to live in as your principal residence doesn't matter here. There's a big difference when building an investment real estate business.

Types of Investment Residential Real Estate

Single-Family Residence – These properties don't have any shared walls with neighboring properties and should have land between all sides of the property.

Multi-Unit Properties – These are generally up to five units in a building. Starting at six units, properties tend to be classified as apartment blocks (for more information on this, refer to the zoning in each municipality).

Condominiums – These properties are classified as individual ownership of a suite in a building with access to common areas owned by all condo owners. There are condo fees that must be paid to maintain, repair, and improve the common areas. There could be common amenities like tennis courts, hot tubs, exercise rooms, pools, and spas, and the upkeep of these facilities is covered in the condo fees.

Apartment Buildings – These are similar to condominiums but tend to have one owner who has a property management team to maintain and rent the building units.

Townhouses – These are single-family homes, usually on two or three floors, that share walls with similar properties. They differ from condominiums in that there are no neighboring units above or below, and they tend to have outdoor space in the front and back of the property. Similar to condominiums, there are fees for shared facilities, areas, and maintenance.

Manufactured Homes – Sometimes referred to as mobile homes, these are manufactured in a non-removable steel chassis, which allows them to be moved. You find these homes most often on leased land.

Modular Homes – These are similar to mobile homes but adhere to specific building codes required by state, provincial, county, and municipal jurisdictions. These don't have an axle or frame and are transported on a flat-bed truck.

Vacation Homes – Sometimes referred to as second homes, these can be single-family homes, condominiums, townhouses, mobile homes, or cottages. What makes these properties popular is they are close to beaches, ski resorts, or other recreational activities. Over the last decade, services like Airbnb and VRBO have added a different dimension to owning and renting this type of property, with a global reach. We won't get into vacation homes in this book, but I'll talk about them in a future book.

All these properties come with different financing rules—another strong reason to have a mortgage broker on your Team REAL who can advise you on each property type. The cost of borrowing (interest rates) could vary, as can term and amortization lengths. We'll talk more about these things on Day 15.

Finding the Right Type of First Investment Property

After reviewing the above types of investment properties, you probably get the point: there are many options for properties that a first-time investment real estate investor can purchase.

I have lived through a few first-time investment property scenarios. In my personal experience with lenders, I've found that bungalows can be easier to finance, but do your homework with your mortgage broker and get a feel for the lenders' mood. If the real estate market is good, lenders tend to loosen their way of thinking.

Below are two success stories related to duplexes and bungalows.

Duplex: Residence and Rental

If you don't already own a principal residence, I recommend looking for a bungalow with a separate entrance to the basement, or for a side-by-side (duplex). The idea is to lower your risk by having two doors. One door is your personal residential or primary residence upstairs in a bungalow, and the other door is the entrance to an income suite in your basement; or, you have a side-by-side with one half as your primary residence and the other half rented out.

Our first investment property was a joint investment with my mom and dad. They bought a duplex and lived in one side, and my wife and I joined them in purchasing the other side. We rented out half of the duplex in a joint venture partnership. We did extremely well on this property from a cash flow and equity growth standpoint, but it was short-term success. I will share the failure to grow our investment real estate portfolio later in the book. It took us ten years to realize our mistake of exiting investment real estate too early.

Bungalow: A Bump in the Road Turns to Opportunity

My daughter had a personal relationship that ended. She had shared a home with her partner, and this home was sold and the proceeds were split in half. My daughter was now a single mother with no home, and a single household wage-earner.

During this time, the city she lived in was trying to address the lack of affordable rentals and offered a $15,000 grant to go toward renovations to create legal suites in single-family homes. The income suite had to remain in the program—being rented out to a long-term tenant at an affordable rate—for five years. I remember my daughter saying, "Five years seems like an awfully long time." How quickly that went by.

My daughter bought a bungalow with a separate entrance to the basement. Part of the suite in the basement had been developed. For $33,000, my daughter completed the renovations on a legal suite, including two new egressed windows to conform to the city bylaws for the bedrooms, a new washer and dryer, two new furnaces, and a kitchen, including appliances.

She had to keep the rent capped at $1,100 a month plus part of the utilities. But incredibly, my daughter's mortgage payment was $1,500. Subtract the $1,100 in rental income and my daughter's home with an income suite was costing her $400 a month plus part of the utilities.

As a single mother with an income suite in her principal residence, my daughter did not have to endure the financial pressure felt by many single mothers. The tenants were making a significant portion of her mortgage payment plus principal paydown on the home.

Of course, duplexes and bungalows are not your only options. You can also purchase other types of investment real estate properties: condominiums, townhouses, single-family homes, and multifamily homes. As I mentioned above, make sure to assess the rental marketplace, find out the mood of the lenders, and determine what works best for you in the area you are looking to purchase. You must buy from the head, not the heart.

Your Ideal Client-Tenant

In addition to deciding what type of property is best for you, think about what type of client-tenant you want to work with.

Each tenant profile is different, and their need for rental housing is different, too. Often, the stages of life dictate one's housing needs. Imagine the following life stages:

Student: You're about to attend a trade school, college, or university and need to move away from your parents' home to be close to school. The property you rent may only be for the duration of your school year, or you may decide to work nearby in the months you do not attend school and stay in the rental home for the entire year. Your diploma or degree program is two to four years in length. After you graduate, you move on in life, and the residence you lived in during school is not going to work for you as you pursue employment. In many cases, this housing is close to the college or university, or close to great transit.

Early Career: You've graduated and decide to get a job or start a career. Your initial employment is not paying you a ton of money, but you have your work life. You are concerned about your spending and will look for a studio apartment or a one-bedroom, or you may realize sharing a two-bedroom apartment could lower your costs even further. You may not have enough money for a vehicle, so being close to a great transit system and services is key.

Serious Relationship: You have now met the love of your life, and you move in together; the "bath towel as drapes" may no longer work because your significant other would like a home you can be proud to live in. You still can't afford the down payment on your own home, but the area and type of property become more important to you.

Family: Now you decide to start a family. You have not been able to save for a down payment, but the type of housing you need for your young family is beginning to take on more significance.

Now you're getting the idea of what possible tenants look like based on their needs in the stage of life they are in.

Are you starting to picture the type of tenant you would like to attract to your property? Why is the tenant profile so important? You might find that you can get higher rents for student housing, but it takes extra time, effort, and higher tenant turnover to manage; is this for you? Or do you like the idea of sustainability and tenants staying longer? The cash flow could be lower but consistent. Or, perhaps you love the idea of helping young families, and the area you bought in has great parks.

You need to understand yourself and your financial resources. Now, your tenant needs a closer look.

Understanding the Tenant

A tenant is someone renting a property from a landlord, and a client is a person receiving services.

REIN, one of the real estate educational groups I belong to, has been in business for over twenty-five years. About four years ago, REIN asked us as members to pivot from calling ourselves landlords and rebrand ourselves as rental housing providers. At first, many of us thought this was a cute marketing ploy, but for REIN, the change ran much deeper.

Moving from landlord to rental housing provider takes a mindset shift. You may have started as a renter and had a landlord. This landlord's behavior, or that of several landlords, may have created your impression of what a landlord should sound like and how they should behave. Many people have had negative experiences with landlords at some point in their lives, and REIN's decision to rebrand helped to distance its members from the negative connotations often associated with the word *landlord* and create new, positive associations for *rental housing providers*.

As a first-time investment real estate investor, think back on how you were treated as a tenant. Was the experience positive, negative, or neutral? If it was negative or neutral, ask yourself what you would have done differently as the property owner to make the rental experience more enjoyable.

What would a good landlord have looked like in your eyes?

By viewing your renter as a client and thinking of yourself as a rental housing provider who is providing your renter a service, expectations rise from not only your renter's standpoint but from your perspective. If you use a property management service, you would expect them to provide a level of service to keep your renters happy. Why would you not expect this of yourself?

On Day 25, we will examine how to market to your renters. Shifting your mindset from landlord to rental housing provider is going to be critical in this process.

Creating Your Ideal Client-Tenant Profile

If you listen to many entrepreneurial podcasts or read many books about small business, they discuss how you should identify your ideal avatar.

What is an avatar, and what does your look like? Let's dig a little deeper.

An avatar is simply your ideal image of your customer. Your ideal tenant avatar has a customer profile that is a best-case scenario for your investment real estate property. Your property type has an influence on your avatar. Perhaps you own a one-bedroom apartment condo near the financial downtown core of a city; in this case, you might consider your ideal avatar a single, business-educated professional who earns a good salary and likes to live downtown to be close to work because they don't own a vehicle. They might also love to dine out, and are looking for a great selection of restaurants; things like entertainment and a good gym might also be important to them.

Think about your parents, friends, or other family members. Talk to them about their rental experiences. Dig deeper and find out when and why they rented. Ask them what type of properties they rented in and favored, and why.

Draw upon your real estate agent's expertise. Get introduced to property managers you can talk to and find out about their experience. Again, if your real estate agent or the property managers see you as a potential client, they are apt to provide you with excellent information.

Then, use all this information to create your ideal client-tenant profile, persona, or avatar, as described in this chapter.

By creating personas or avatars for your target renter, you'll know their characteristics, preferences, desires, pains, and ideals. Having clarity around who your target renter is before you even purchase your first investment real estate property could be your secret sauce to making investment real estate ownership more enjoyable and rewarding.

Creating a target renter avatar can help you leap ahead of your competition because you have given the acquisition of a renter real thought and effort. You are dealing with real people with real-life issues, and understanding your target renter makes your life easier.

Below, in Coaching Challenge 16, we will encourage you to think this process through and identify your ideal tenant avatar.

Matching Your Client-Tenant Profile to the Property Type

Matching up your client-tenant qualities to equal your property type's qualities is not an exact science, but there are clues and cues. Examining certain areas of the client's needs can help you develop your client-tenant profile.

Many of you may be familiar with Maslow's hierarchy of needs. I don't want to get too psychological, but there are some common undertones that people who rent are looking for.

Maslow's hierarchy of needs has five levels. For our purposes, we'll focus on Maslow's second level, safety. Maslow saw safety broken up into seven areas: employment, resources, property, health, body, family, and morality. Even though I don't think all these areas will help develop the client-tenant profile, most renters are looking for a safe and secure place to call home. Part of your responsibility as an owner of investment rental real estate is to provide some of these needs. Below, we'll see how some areas of Maslow's second level, safety, match up with your job as a rental housing provider.

Employment

As your tenants enter the rental market, their financial resources dictate the funds available to them for rent. You may find that if you purchase your investment property close to shopping centers, big-box retailers, or fast-food restaurants, these folks will earn minimum wage or slightly higher. Are first-time renters and folks making lower incomes the tenants you wish to attract, and can you purchase a property that earns you positive cash flow even when renting to people at the lower end of the income scale?

A location close to an educational institution will attract students who don't have large incomes for rent. In many cases, you may find yourself renting housing by the room, with common areas, including washrooms, to make this type of rental property make sense.

In downtown cores, you might attract higher rents because many of the folks living in the downtown core are working professionals with a higher disposable income.

Resources

The resources tenants might be looking for include things like shopping and services. How close are they to your property? How accessible is transportation, such as public transit, including bus or rapid transit? Your rental property may be out of the downtown or educational district, but its proximity to great shopping, services, and transit, can mean it commands higher rents because of the resources surrounding it.

Property

Many tenants starting out will rent in a condo or apartment-style property. These tenants don't want any property responsibility. They expect all maintenance and repairs to be taken care of by the landlord.

We talked about the closeness to shopping, services, and transit. Now the tenants are going to view the property's safety and curb appeal. When the tenants drive up, are the grounds well maintained? Is the outside of the building in good shape? Are there well-lit entranceways and common areas, including hallways and laundry room? How secure is the entrance?

Health and Body

The building's sports amenities may not be necessary, as tenants know these come with a higher cost, but being located close to recreational facilities might be important.

Family

Most new tenants like to get their family's opinion on their first rental property, and these folks will be very critical. They will be looking at the property through their own eyes, and they may not have rented in years. They will be more concerned about the cleanliness and safety of the building and the parking situation for when they come to visit; be aware that the whole family may have a say when you rent to someone. In some cases, the parents may be footing part or all of the rent, especially for student housing.

The Client-Tenant Relationship

On Day 4, we talked about how investment real estate requires an entrepreneur's mindset, and we discussed the fundamentals of operating a small business.

To operate as an entrepreneur and small business, you need to have revenue, and in the area of investment real estate, the revenue comes from your client-tenant. Without a client-tenant relationship, there is no business to operate.

Knowing that all your revenue will be sourced from your client-tenant, you can start to see why understanding the interconnection between tenant and property is essential. The type of property you purchase will influence the kind of rental income you will receive.

Revenue is one of two key ingredients of your investment real estate business. (The other ingredient is costs to operate. Starting on Day 13, we'll review the financial side of your property type decision.)

Therefore, it's essential to make smart decisions surrounding your client-tenant choice. What type of client-tenant are you looking for? Why is this client-tenant important to you? And how do you put your client-tenant profile together?

How to Put Together Your Ideal Client-Tenant Profile

Putting together your ideal client-tenant profile takes some effort, but it's worth it.

You need to sit down and think about who you are trying to attract. Students, working service people, young professionals, single couples, couples with preschool families, couples with school-aged children, empty-nesters, active seniors, or seniors who require some services—the list of potential client-tenants is endless.

There are a few strategies that can help you. To determine the tenant profile, you could spend some time in the neighborhood and sit outside the building for a couple of hours in the morning watching the tenants' comings and goings. Or, get your real estate agent to ask the building's property manager if they know the primary tenant profile makeup.

If you are going to purchase in a multifamily complex, do your homework on the current tenants living in the building. For example, if you are trying to attract single professionals in their late twenties or thirties and the complex is full of retired seniors, this will not work. Or, think of this situation in reverse—what if you have decided on a client-tenant profile of retired seniors?

In coaching challenges 15 and 16, I would like you to think about what is more important to you: the type of property you would like to purchase, or the type of client-tenant you would like to cater to? Once you have decided if you care more about the building type or the client-tenant type, do the coaching challenge that aligns with your needs first.

Determine which type of investment real estate property is right for you.

Many factors can influence the type of investment real estate property that is right for you. Your *why* might be as simple as that it's the type of investment real estate you are familiar with or experienced with.

In this challenge, try and think outside the four walls of making your decision. The beautiful thing is that the choice you make can change later in the process; don't become a prisoner to your thinking. Open the door to different types of investment real estate alternatives and do what's best for your business.

⇧ With the different types of investment residential real estate identified in the readings today, which property type might you consider for your first investment property and why? Record your answer in your notebook or the workbook and planning guide.

Create your ideal client-tenant profile.

Using the information you learned today, it's time to start creating your ideal client-tenant profile. Get out your notebook or workbook and planning guide and write down traits you believe should be included in your tenant profile. Why did you choose this type of person? Your own experience can influence who you think would be your ideal client-tenant. Don't be afraid to choose a type of client-tenant whose life experience has been different than your own. Because you have probably not lived every client-tenant profile personally, putting yourself in their shoes can help.

- ⇧ Create your client-tenant profile or avatar. Who do you want to work with, and why?

Day 7 Key Recap

Record your key learnings and actionable items in your notebook or the workbook and planning guide. (Optional)

- ⇧ When choosing your ideal type of investment real estate, consider why this investment real estate type works for you and your circumstances.
- ⇧ Put time into developing a client-tenant relationship and the qualities of this relationship.
- ⇧ Creating an ideal client-tenant profile could be the secret sauce to your investment real estate success.

DAY 8 HOME MAY NOT BE WHERE THE INVESTMENT HEART IS

Use this day to identify your ideal marketplace for investment real estate investment and why. At the end of the chapter, complete the coaching challenges to choose a real estate marketplace for your first investment real estate property.

Now that you've identified the type of property you want to invest in and determined your ideal client-tenant profile, it's time to understand your marketplace and where to invest. It may not be in your neighborhood, city or town, or even your state or province. Today's coaching challenge will help you identify the right marketplace and highlight why this location is right for you. You'll find some ideas for choosing the neighborhood, town or city, and state or province. Staying closer to home could be a great idea for your first investment property, but let's make sure the economic fundamentals make sense and learn how to recognize these fundamentals in your own backyard.

Choosing Your Desired Location

When it comes to real estate, there is a cliché: "location, location, location."

Its purpose? To underscore that real estate experts consider the location to be the most important factor in determining a property's desirability.

The Three ROI Sweet Spots

A great location supports the three return-on-investment (ROI) sweet spots of your investment real estate. These three sweet spots are the equity growth, the positive cash flow (the rent), and the principal paydown.

Equity growth is the property's increasing value in relation to your original purchase price. Real estate values can fluctuate. Equity growth can be the foundation of a buy-and-hold strategy. Many factors can influence value increases, including scarcity of land, new housing, labor and labor costs, and materials. These factors can influence prices to move up or down. Time is the one variable that tends to work in the owner's favor over a long period.

One-off events can also influence equity growth. For example, in many places, the current pandemic has driven single-family homes up in price considerably because people don't want to be crowded into the high-density core of towns and cities anymore.

The values can also drop, like we saw with the subprime crisis of 2007–2008. It is important to remember that price drops rebound over time and that values have reached and, in many cases, surpassed the values from those difficult years.

Positive cash flow is the return on investment for real estate investing. Cash flow can be simply described as the funds left over after you take the revenue of the rental property and subtract all the costs to operate the property. If you have funds left over, you have positive cash flow. If you are in the red, you have negative cash flow. Positive cash flow is critical to a successful investment property. You must be continually asking if there are ways to increase revenue or reduce costs. Decreasing revenue and increasing costs can spell disaster and can't be maintained for long. This is a reminder that you are operating a small business, and a profit is essential to financial success. We'll cover positive cash flow in more detail on Day 29.

And, finally, principal paydown is the reduction of the principal amount of the mortgage or loan—the amount you borrowed and have to pay back. This doesn't include any payments toward interest.

The Significance of Your Sweet Spots

The importance of the ROI sweet spots varies. Although equity growth is wonderful, you should not count on it every single year. As I mentioned earlier, the real estate market can be cyclical; values will inevitably go through up and downs.

Positive cash flow is important, but as long as you can generate enough revenue to cover all operations costs, this is not an absolutely necessary area. In our strategy, we'll ensure you have built in a contingency fund to cover all unexpected expenses for those times when positive cash flow is temporarily interrupted. (I recommend this to be between 5 and 10 percent of your rental income.)

The one area you need to protect as your holy grail is principal paydown. I ask you to protect your principal paydown at all costs because it is where all the magic begins on the return on your investment.

In most cases, when people purchase an investment in stocks, bonds, mutual funds, ETFs, and other financial vehicles, they have been advised to look at dollar-cost averaging—in other words, to have funds deposited each month into an account that supports the purchase of more stocks, bonds, mutual funds, ETFs, and other financial vehicles. These funds you invest are generally from after-tax dollars and right out of your own pocket.

That's why, even though value growth and positive cash flow are great features of your return on purchasing investment real estate, the most critical ROI sweet spot is your principal paydown. It is important because once you have rental income from a client-tenant each month, part of the rental income is going to principal paydown of your mortgage. Your client-tenant is funding this value growth for you; these funds are not coming out of your pocket. Even though you as an owner have made the initial down payment, this generally is the only money you invest going forward. The client-tenant pays all future costs, including the principal paydown. You have someone else funding the equity in your property.

All the Benefits with No Commitment

Every year the tenant continues to make the principal paydown payments, more of the payment funds add value and equity. Each year, the percentage of return on your initial investment amount grows as someone else makes the investment for you. You get all the benefits with no commitment beyond providing a nice rental home.

Things to Consider When Choosing the Location

When choosing the location of your first investment real estate property, there are many different attributes to consider. On Day 9, we will discuss the big picture of factors to consider when purchasing your first investment real estate property. For the purchase of your first investment real estate property, the preference should be in your own neck of the woods, a location you can drive to in less than an hour. This property can be the fertile ground for your learning about investment real estate. In many large metropolitan areas, there are surrounding communities that could fit this bill.

At the end of the day, it is my hope that you can find an investment real estate property close to where you reside that makes economic sense and is right for you. Don't force the property to fit—your first property should be one you can manage directly, but don't get hung up on this.

Having options outside your immediate area can make a big difference in both the affordability of the property and the affordability of the rental. Rental rates in the area you purchase in will be key to supporting your purchase and the long-term financial health of your investment property.

We discussed property types on Day 7; choosing the rental property type connects to the rental marketplace. You might find the ideal location only to find out the zoning bylaws don't allow rental properties, or you can't develop the type of rental property you desire. For example, you might settle on purchasing a bungalow to develop an income suite in the basement, but the city or town zoning bylaws prohibit this type of rental property.

Don't assume that just because there is multiple-family housing in the neighborhood, you can develop a rental income suite. Instead, contact the town or city administrative office and ask to speak with someone on staff who handles the rental housing zoning. These folks are knowledgeable, they love to share this information, and it's free to use their services.

Having the Three Sweet Spots and Eating Them, Too

As I mentioned above, it would be nice to find an investment property within your own living proximity, but if you can't, it's not a dealbreaker. Using a real estate agent's services at this point is helpful (and you won't have to pay for their services until the actual purchase of your property), but if you have done your research on the three sweet spots, you can venture out on your own without one.

How much work do you want to do in the beginning to identify the right location? If you have identified the property type to purchase, what is the value of this property type? Do the prices fit within the economic profile of your property type? Have you been able to identify the equity growth for your type of property in various neighborhoods over the last several years? Do you have firsthand knowledge of the rental zoning restrictions? Are you aware of the rental rates and their variability? It's a lot of questions, but they're important ones. Can you access all of this information on your own? Yes, and you could think of this as part of your investment real estate education.

Could you teach yourself to become a teacher, doctor, lawyer, or any other profession? Yes, but would it be accredited? And if you are not doing these professions as your primary working role, why would you?

An accredited real estate agent must work hard to earn their accreditation and constantly refresh their skills to keep their license. That's why I recommend working with one. The only caveat is that you should make sure that they own investment real estate when hiring anyone on your team. I would rather see you well-armed with the right questions to purchase the right property than watch you chase price.

Your real estate agent has access to all of this information. When you make your offer, it should be because the property fits your property type profile, including potential equity growth, positive cash flow, and principal paydown.

Don't forget that the real estate marketplace prices are dictated by the comparable sales in the area you are looking to purchase in.

When planning your purchase, have your real estate agent source an area for you to purchase in that includes all three elements. If your first property does not meet all three of these elements, is this a dealbreaker? Yes. Getting you started on the right investment real estate property is part of the goal of this book. The percentage of investment real estate investors is small, and the right property is out there for you.

You may have heard the old saying, "Another bus will come along." This is also true in investment real estate—the right property for you will come along.

Remember, if you have the right questions in hand and you are working with a real estate agent who owns investment real estate, then they will know the complete metropolitan area in terms of zoning laws, property types, value appreciation, rental rate increases, etc. They are a valuable resource to have on your Team REAL when choosing a location.

COACHING CHALLENGE 17: Identify and research your ideal marketplace.

Your ideal investment real estate marketplace is where your investment real estate property type meets the three sweet spots of return on investment. This is important because such a marketplace will deliver a competitive purchase price, with the best opportunity for an increase in property values and rents. It gives you the best chance that the rental marketplace's changing demands will fit your long-term buy-and-hold strategy. Your research today will help you find that ideal marketplace. Write your notes in your notebook or the workbook and planning guide.

- ⇧ Choose your desired location. What is the average selling price of your investment real estate property now? What have the property value growth and rental rate growth been in the past five years? (You can use any MLS service in the United States or Canada; find one via a Google search. Also, this should be information your real estate agent is publishing on their website every month.)
- ⇧ Do some research using PadMapper.com. What is the current average rental amount for your type of investment real estate property of choice, and what has been the average rental rate increase on this property over the last five years?

Day 8 Key Recap

Record your key learnings and actionable items in your notebook or the workbook and planning guide. (Optional)

- ⇧ When pinpointing a great investment real estate location, use solid market information.
- ⇧ Review the numbers on potential properties in the market area and review the equity growth, the positive cash flow (the rent), and the principal paydown to find your sweet spot.
- ⇧ Have your real estate agent help you identify several properties that can meet the criteria of a successful investment property.

DAY 9 GOING FURTHER: GROSS DOMESTIC PRODUCT, JOB GROWTH, AND POPULATION GROWTH

Use this day to discover the impact of gross domestic product, job growth, and population growth on purchasing your first investment real estate property in your marketplace. At the end of the chapter, complete the coaching challenges to learn about the local area and build your own top ten GDP list.

According to Investopedia, gross domestic product (GDP) is the monetary value of all finished goods and services made within a country during a specific period.

Are you wondering why you should learn about GDP, job growth, and population growth, and how these things impact your first investment real estate property? It's simple: not understanding the economy has driven many entrepreneurs and small businesses out of business. Working hard to earn money and then investing that money into a business without doing your economic homework can be a cruel teacher.

That's why GDP can have a surprising effect on your investment real estate business. Here's how.

GDP ties into the economic health of a country. It can be broken into the economic health of states or provinces, right down to cities and towns.

If your area has a solid positive GDP growth, this can help give you an excellent pool of client-tenants to draw from. The client-tenants are the revenue source to your investment real estate. These client-tenants must have a stable or growing job market in which to source employment. Population growth is critical because client-tenants come and go, so having a new source of people to draw from is also vital.

When researching GDP, the first thing to look for is the demand for finished goods and services; if there is strong demand, it signifies a strong labor market. Living in an area of strong GDP not only gives you client-tenants to draw from, but they will often be making higher wages, and if you see higher wages, this allows you to increase your rental rates. Remember, the opposite is true when the GDP growth is negative. A declining GDP can push people and jobs out of your area, contribute to lower wages, and force you to lower your rental rates. If you don't have strong GDP growth in your area of interest, you should look instead for an area with a good GDP.

Luckily, you don't have to have a degree in economics to understand GDP growth. There is plenty of information available if you simply do a web search on your locale's GDP.

You should constantly be scanning the news and social media for announcements of new employers moving into your chosen area; this could be anything from businesses to governments. Look for any manufacturers setting up facilities to produce their goods, companies like Amazon or Walmart adding to their distribution centers, or major retailers opening a new store. Also, governments tend to be large, high-paying employers—are there any new departments opening up to serve the public? Governments also like to stimulate growth in tougher times to ease the impact of an economic downturn; review any announcements about capital work projects, such as new roads.

Do you know your town, city, state, or province? Do you know who the largest employers in your area are and what types of paying jobs they are supplying? Is there a rotation of employees into your area? What kind of housing do they need? These are all excellent questions to keep in mind to keep an eye on prospective client-tenants in your area.

Get to understand what factors drive economic growth now, and what will be driving it five years in the future. As an investment real estate investor, you need to keep one eye on the now and the other eye on the future. Remember, if you are going to lock into financial arrangements to finance your investment, certainty can help your business regarding revenue and expenses.

All this economic information is available for free; employers and governments love to share goods news about growth and future plans.

The Top Ten GDP Method

Once you have done some research about GDP, it's time to start using the Top Ten Method of GDP in your area. This method can help you pinpoint the best area for your first investment real estate property.

The Top Ten Method of GDP is fairly simple. Just list out the top ten local manufacturing industries, employers, services, transportation routes (air, road, water, rail), government agencies, and forms of entertainment. If there are areas you know about that are not mentioned in the documents you consult, please feel free to add them.

Using these lists, you can identify where most of these top ten are located; this will help guide you to find a great area in which to purchase your first investment real estate property.

For example, your ideal tenants might be folks who have a secure job and want to live close to work. Knowing this, you could create a top ten list based on employers who pay higher monthly salaries. Purchasing in an area with higher-paid employees can help influence your rental rates.

Or, perhaps your ideal tenants are students. In that case, put together a top ten list of the higher learning facilities, universities, colleges, trade schools, and other educational institutions that attract students. Remember, these students can be a large source of your client base during and after their pursuit of higher learning. Student housing has its challenges and can be a great source of return on your investment if done correctly.

GDP Matters

I hope you now understand how GDP can influence your chances of success in investment real estate. Purchasing in an area with declining GDP can make your life far more difficult, while an area that's growing can mean higher rents and a better chance of securing your ideal client-tenants for your property. Keep it in mind while searching for your first investment real estate property.

COACHING CHALLENGE 18

Learn about the local area.

Knowledge is power. Asking questions protects your investment and increases your knowledge base. With that in mind, it's time to call your local city or town's business and economy department. Ask them the following questions, and take note of their answers. Remember, answering these questions is their job, and no question is out of bounds when it comes to investing.

- ⇧ Can you tell me the town/city's gross domestic product?
- ⇧ Can you tell me the town/city's job growth?
- ⇧ Can you tell me the town/city's population growth?
- ⇧ Is there neighborhood-level information available on these topics? If yes, where do I access this information? If no, do you know where I could access this information? (The trick is to get people you are gathering information from to be a great resource for other areas you might not have thought about.)

Even though I have talked about the importance of building your Team REAL and assembling a team of experts to draw upon, self-education is also a critical component of your success. If you have found an area that potentially has all the characteristics to fit your property type profile, move on to the next coaching challenge, where you'll assemble your own top ten list.

Build your own top ten list.

As we learned in this chapter, a top ten list can help you to identify the best area for your investment real estate property purchase. Using the area you identified in Coaching Challenge 18 as fitting all your criteria for your investment real estate purchase, list out the following:

- ⇧ Top Ten Local Manufacturers
- ⇧ Top Ten Employers
- ⇧ Top Ten Service Providers
- ⇧ Top Ten Government Agencies
- ⇧ Top Ten Entertainment Venues

Remember, your top ten doesn't have to be limited to the list I have provided above. Make your own observations and build your own list; for example, you could live in a city known for its indoor and outdoor sports activities and the top ten recreational facilities could be an essential industry. Think about this for a moment. If you are purchasing an investment property in an area where physical activity is important to the residents, you might think about having storage closets set up for recreational equipment; it's great feature to attract tenants.

Also, access to all major forms of transportation is important. Listing the distances to the airport, train station, bus station, rapid transit, public transportation, and car rentals can be useful information to have and share with potential client-tenants.

This list will help you understand where exactly is the ideal location within your target area to make your investment real estate purchase. Being one step ahead with your knowledge of the area can only improve the choices you make, and it'll be a great asset when it's time to market your property.

Day 9 Key Recap

Record your key learnings and actionable items in your notebook or the workbook and planning guide. (Optional)

- ⇧ Look into the gross domestic product (GDP) for your area and find the visible signs that indicate this would be a great market for investment real estate.
- ⇧ When recognizing your top ten GDP factors, create your own top ten list for your particular area.
- ⇧ Know your area. Drive it, walk it, bicycle it, and take the time to look around.

 # DAY 10 TRENDS AND TIMING

Use this day to identify trends and timing. At the end of the chapter, the coaching challenges will help you focus your efforts and prepare you to recognize trends and timing related to investment real estate property and the rental real estate market.

Trends and timing can mean the difference between success and failure. In both business and real estate, trends and timing are cyclical, and it is important that you can quickly observe the ups and downs of the investment real estate market.

Remember, by purchasing and renting your first investment real estate property, you'll be running a small business, and all businesses need to be aware of trends. Why?

Trends will give you insight into and an awareness of both the status quo and changes in the real estate market. With this understanding, you'll be able to position yourself for success.

Trends

Managing a small business and being on trend in your business field can help you forecast better. You'll be able to look at what is happening now and in the future, have a chance to get out in front and not be a follower, create better business ideas, sense or see early signs of issues, and improve your business.

Timing

There is a Chinese proverb that says: "The best time to plant a tree was twenty years ago. The second-best time is now."

This is how I feel about investment real estate. The best time to buy and rent investment real estate was twenty years ago. The second-best time is now.

Trends in the Real Estate Market

Trends are, as the word suggests, a direction in which something goes. Just like other areas of life, the real estate market experiences trends. These trends can be influenced by many different factors, such as technology, population growth, entertainment, sports, employment, and more.

With the recent coronavirus pandemic throwing the world into serious lockdown, having a safe and secure place to live has become more important than ever. The impact of this situation on the rental market is not yet clear; how folks think of their rental homes may take on a different feel and look.

Here are my thoughts on the current and forthcoming trends in the real estate market.

- In the past, community-driven spaces were important to renters. Until the pandemic is over, folks may not be comfortable with sharing common spaces.
- Rental rates in less densely populated urban areas may increase.
- Short-term rentals such as Airbnb may experience a setback as people may not feel comfortable renting places with a high turnover of tenants.
- Shared tenant living, such as two-bedroom units, may not be as attractive.
- On the flipside, people working from home may be more attracted to two-bedroom units, where they could turn one bedroom into an office space.
- Smaller living. You may have noticed on TV there are shows dedicated to people building tiny homes to live in. Some people like to keep their global footprint smaller and may be looking for a well-designed home to rent that has a smaller area for living. Can you fill this need?

- ⇧ New tenant protection legislation adding pandemic clauses. Governments are always looking for ways to protect their citizens. With the recent pandemic, you never know if there will be bylaws or laws developed around social distancing in the common areas of a building or the need for sanitizer at the entranceways of each complex. This could happen if the government feels owners have neglected this. This could also be a good way for you to step it up a notch as an owner and install, for example, hand sanitizer at the entrances and exits of your building. It could convince a potential client-tenant you care about their health.
- ⇧ More people may become real estate investors, seeing the opportunity to create safer living spaces for tenants. Millennials may become more serious about entering the investment real estate market.
- ⇧ No-contact access to rental homes; there may be a movement toward swipe keys to enter buildings and living units. Apps may be developed and added to smartphones and smartwatches to allow entrance to buildings and homes.
- ⇧ Municipalities may become more tenant-friendly; more secondary suites will be added in private homes, and more alternative rental suites over the garage.
- ⇧ Free Wi-Fi as a standard rental feature.

The items on the list above are only a few current and future trends; there are many more we have not even thought of. Remember, the coronavirus has taken the world from total lockdown to a movement to open back up. How the new world swings back to a new normal is anyone's guess, and it presents an opportunity for many investment real estate investors.

Timing Your Investment Real Estate Purchase

The lyrics to the song "Timing Is Everything," sung by Garrett Hedlund and written by Natalie Nicole Hemby and Troy Jones, take us on a journey that many of us can relate to.

As a real estate investor, the words resonate with me. Just like the song says, timing is everything.

As a first-time investment real estate investor, it's essential to do your homework. Understand that the real estate market is not perfect, and the timing is never going to be just right, but a good investment real estate property will come along just in time, if you are ready. (In fact, this is why the majority of the learning and knowledge in this book is part of the Ready stage.)

Earlier in the book, we talked about how you can't time the stock market. Timing the real estate market is a lot like timing the stock market. You can never predict the future with 100 percent accuracy, but you can look for signs.

On Day 9, we talked about understanding GDP in your area, which can contribute to your understanding of how to time the market. There are real estate cycles, too. For example, I live in an area that depends heavily on oil and natural gas to drive the economy. When oil prices were at an all-time high for some time, our economy was booming. When oil prices started to drop in price and the overreliance on one customer to buy our product became evident, the economy took a ten-year hit.

You should try and time when to buy investment real estate and buy when you think the timing is right. Many folks have missed out on opportunities by trying to time the real estate market or the stock market, so it's important to do your research.

Sure, if you bought real estate or invested in the stock market twenty years ago, you might look like a genius today. Twenty years ago might have been the best time to buy, and the second-best time is now.

If you are following the recommendations in my book, you are developing an acute sense of the type of property to buy and the market to buy in.

When researching investment real estate, it's important to realize that the various factors that affect real estate trends and timing are not only local but global in nature. The importance of thinking outside your own real estate bubble can be easily seen during COVID-19. Many countries and industries scoffed at the pandemic initially. Think of how much better some industries, like the hospitality and travel industries, would have fared had they gotten out in front of this disease. The industries and governments would not have stopped the coronavirus in its tracks, but they could have saved themselves millions, perhaps billions of dollars in expenses rather than let the disease control their delayed decisions. Think about things like population migration, employment levels, affordability of rental housing, real estate listings and sales, working from home, and other factors. Working from home has a good chance of being a major factor in how people live going forward; therefore, rental homes will need to have well-thought-out home office layouts or provisions. How many investment real estate investors are pivoting to this trend?

Will we see the end of the COVID-19 pandemic? Yes, maybe before my book enters the market. Eventually, the real estate market will settle down to a norm, but it will be a new norm.

Even though the world has seen a vaccine in early 2021, how long before it is available and administered to the entire world? How many people will embrace the vaccine, how many people will take a wait-and-see attitude before receiving it, and how many people will totally resist taking it at all? Do your homework, and watch the trends of how countries whose people embrace the vaccine first are acting. Are there any lessons to be learned? People will always need a place to live, but this place to live might include an area to work from. What are you doing as a real estate investor to follow this trend? Are you going to get ahead of the curve and use working from home as your specialty? I mentioned earlier about free Wi-Fi—this may be one of several work-at-home features you offer.

Don't Neglect Timing and Trends

Whether you embrace something like work-at-home to set you apart from other investment real estate investors or time your purchase in accordance with market trends, keeping an eye on trends and timing can help position you for investment real estate success and place you ahead of the curve.

Identify current market trends.

In this coaching challenge, it's time to identify current market trends, including generational shifts, smart home technology advances, single-family homes, and low lending rates. Try to identify which of these are long-term trends versus short-term trends and why.

If we are seeing work-at-home becoming a permanent segment of the real estate market, what else are we seeing as trends? For example, folks are not returning to the gym or health clubs, people are not traveling and are having staycations instead, more people are buying vehicles and not taking public transportation, and fewer people are dining out, with most opting to stay home to eat.

Also, you need to look at short-term trends. Currently, with the COVID-19 scare, there has been a movement back to single-family homes, where people feel more secure. Once there is a vaccine, will this trend continue, or will we see people return to higher-density living?

The list is much larger than the areas I have just outlined. Let's think about the components of trends. What are we seeing now? Even if there is a vaccine, how long will it take for the entire world to embrace it? And what can you learn and profit from in your world of investment real estate? Write down your thoughts in your notebook or the workbook and planning guide.

- ⇧ What major trends are you seeing in your real estate market?
- ⇧ What trends do you think will last several years?

⇧ Are the trends you see areas you can develop into your investment real estate plan?

 **Consider your timing.**

Timing the real estate market is not easy.

When you review the timing of your first investment real estate property purchase and rental, think about the different elements of success through investment real estate. On Day 8, we discussed the three key elements: equity growth, positive rental income, and mortgage principal paydown.

⇧ Is there any reason not to purchase your first investment real estate property now? Why or why not?
⇧ Which elements do you feel may not work for you at this time in purchasing and renting your first investment real estate property within thirty-one days? Why?

Day 10 Key Recap

Record your key learnings and actionable items in your notebook or the workbook and planning guide. (Optional)

- ⇧ Keep your eyes open and your ear to the ground when watching media (social or traditional), reading newspapers or blogs, and listening to radio or podcasts on housing and rental trends.
- ⇧ Review lending information and join several lenders' newsletters, email lists, or social media platforms showing lending and interest rate trends.
- ⇧ Look for shifts in the types of real estate people are gravitating toward.

DAY 11 DECREASED VACANCIES AND INCREASED RENTAL DEMAND

Use this day to learn to recognize the signs and stages of decreased vacancies and increased rents. Today's coaching challenges will help you find the best rental marketplace that will deliver these two key factors for investment real estate success.

American entrepreneur Julian Hall once said, "When opportunity knocks, make sure your door isn't locked."

Halls's words are very important to your investment real estate business.

As you learned on Day 10, there are going to be moments in your investment real estate journey when trends will start, and if you are paying attention to slight changes in the decrease in vacancies and the increase in rental demand, you can ride the moment. Hall's advice is sound: listen for the knock of positive trends in the investment real estate marketplace. If you are watchful of the trends, you should be able to purchase a great property and rent when the market is starting to move up. Timing can make a big difference in your success.

We have discussed revenue and expenses that result from operating your business. I talked earlier in the book about Uberizing your investment and working an additional job to pay down your mortgage. But there's more to it than that.

Think about the importance of decreased vacancies and increased rents. If you have locked into a long-term mortgage interest rate, you have secured one of your biggest business operating costs. By holding costs steady and using your increased revenue—the result of raises in rental rates—to pay down your mortgage principal, think of the impact it will have on your equity growth, even if this equity growth only comes from mortgage paydown.

Decreased vacancies are a critical sign the rental market is improving. There's a definite upside of increased rental demand: it leads to higher rental rates.

Increasing rental rates by the amount permitted by your local government annually and getting access to additional funds to pay down your mortgage principal more quickly is good. Banks allow you to increase your mortgage payments, and what is cool about this feature is that if the market takes a downturn, you can return to your lower mortgage payments; we have done this several times. In this way, we have taken years off our mortgage amortization length.

Investment real estate success is attainable by using the Uberizing technique and increasing your mortgage payment through increased rents.

Taking the time to research the area in which you purchase your investment real estate and noticing, through GDP markers, if you are purchasing and renting on the verge of decreased vacancies and increased rents can have real impact on your success.

Look for positive economic ripples. Know you are not going to get the timing of strong economic growth perfect, so start to ride the wave, even if it is a slow build.

How to Identify Decreased Vacancies and Increased Rents

One of the best tools for identifying areas of decreased vacancies and increased rates is doing several drive-throughs and, more importantly, a walk-through of the area, town, city, subdivision, or neighborhood. The main reason to do several drive-throughs is to visit at different times of the day. Arrive early in the morning so you can get a feel for the amount of traffic exiting the area with residents on their way to work, and do another drive-through around the supper hour, so you can observe how many vehicles are parked on the streets and reconfirm the number of residents working outside the home.

In addition, checking out the area in mid-morning and mid-afternoon is critical during this time of the pandemic because if you notice spouses out together, it could mean both spouses are working from home.

Lastly, driving through the area on the weekend can give you a sense of the demographics and types of families living in the area. For example, you may see people out with strollers, young kids out with bikes or skateboards, adults out for a run, or older adults out for a walk.

After driving around, make sure you park the vehicle, walk the neighborhood, and, if you are really adventurous, take a run through the area. Make sure that, as you walk, you have questions about the area in your mind.

Take notes, talk into your smartphone to record your observations, and take pictures. Look specifically for the following and record your insights:

- New chain stores, local retailers, restaurants, and services being constructed.
- Signs of women, seniors, and children in the area. Are they out playing and walking?
- Tenant vacancies in shopping centers. A large number of vacancies can be a bad sign.
- Visible signs of new public transportation routes being added. Many cities are expanding their light rail transit (LRT) systems and are supporting LRT with new bus routes created as short rides to an LRT station. Public transit growth is one of the signs of higher population densities.
- Health-care providers, hospitals, doctors, dentists, or optometrists' offices nearby.
- Parks, playgrounds, and clean city trash cans. Look at the age of the park benches, trash cans, and playground equipment. Many cities are now upgrading such infrastructure to compostable materials.
- Pet-friendly—watch for dog parks, dog poop dispenser bags, folks out walking their dogs, or the park trash can smell test: smell for dog poop. (My wife covers her nose whenever she walks past a park trash can!)
- New schools, or new additions or renovations to the existing schools. Many towns and cities encourage infill building (new housing development in older neighborhoods) and allow higher population densities in older communities. While doing a drive-through, look for older elementary schools being renovated or new additions being made; this is a sign of families moving into the area. One advantage of the older neighborhoods is the lots are bigger, and the local governments are often allowing owners to tear down older homes and build a duplex or multifamily home on the same lot.

During your drive-through and walkabout of the area, look for rental signs. Are there a lot of places for rent, or just a few? If the area ticks all the boxes on the list above, there is a good chance there will be increased rental demand from prospective tenants looking to take advantage of all the area has to offer.

While checking out the neighborhood, if you see a property for sale that could be the one, take a picture with the house number and the street sign.

Later, once you own an investment real estate property, it's essential to ensure all the boxes continue to get checked. You should never be taken by surprise that your rental market has changed. If the area is getting busier and there are very few vacancies, it may be time for a rent increase the next time your place is vacant. If you notice signs, you can quickly scan the rental websites to see if your rates are on par with what's available or if you can increase your rent.

In this way, performing a drive-through and walkabout each year will maximize the return on your investment.

If you don't have time to do an annual drive-through or walkabout, find out if there is a community center and get on their newsletter email list. The newsletter may contain great information about the benefits of the area, and it's free.

The Demand for Rental Properties

Earlier, I talked about the growth rate in North America and the need to invite folks from other parts of the world to immigrate to the United States and Canada to help offset our population declines and labor shortages. These people will need rental accommodations, as often they will not be in a financial position to buy their own homes when they first enter the country. Thus, it's clear the demand for rental properties will not be shrinking anytime soon.

In Canada, over half of the country's population growth is from immigration, and in the United States, over the last several decades, immigration has ranged from a third to half of the population growth. In fact, the North American economies have outpaced the growth of Europe and Japan because of immigration.

Remember, when immigrants first enter North America, they generally can't qualify for residential mortgages and must rent. That creates demand.

Demand comes from other factors as well. The recent pandemic is an excellent example of folks needing stable homes to live in as they waited out this virus.

Another opportunity for rentals lies in the millennial segment and a segment of the boomer generation. According to a *Huffington Post* article titled "Half of Canada's Millennial Homeowners Have Buyer's Remorse," dated April 10, 2017, 52 percent of millennials believe they will never purchase a home. This means a large segment of the current labor market needs safe and secure housing, and their demand is creating shortages in the rental market. The segment of the boomer generation we discussed earlier was left out of the housing ownership market and will also continue to need rental units.

There is undoubtedly a high demand for rental housing now, and it's projected to continue.

Digging Deeper: Visiting the Local Administration Office

Once you have made your drive-throughs and walked through the targeted neighborhood as well, visit the local city administration office and ask to speak to someone who knows the area you are looking to purchase in. Don't forget that it is not only the visual clues in the neighborhoods that are important, but also what is on the drawing board for the future. What does the town or city have planned for the area? These administrative folks are happy to share information about any service and growth expansions coming up.

Find out if the town or city is rental-friendly, and if there are grant programs the city might have in place to encourage the development of rental units.

Many cities and towns are trying to revitalize the aging residential areas just off the downtown core and encourage higher population growth. There is a program known as infill; infill is where cities and towns allow for higher housing densities on residential land. All you have to do is drive through many older areas and see that developers are now allowed to build duplexes, townhouses, four-plexes, and even six-plexes where a single-family home was once zoned. If you were able to buy an older home with a good-sized lot near the downtown core of a city or town, and you were then allowed to build a multi-housing unit, you could collect excellent rents because of its proximity to services and being new in construction. Ask the local city administration offices about the rules and possible grants for the development of infill. It's truly a great opportunity.

Mapping Rental Rates in Real Time

Earlier, I mentioned the website PadMapper.com, a location-based apartment rental search engine with real-time filtering. It's an amazing tool for understanding the rental rates and demand in your target neighborhood. Using a map as its browsing interface, it loads listings as the user moves around the map.

PadMapper.com works for most towns and cities in North America. I love this tool, as it is free to search the information, and you can do research in advance of purchasing investment real estate in any neighborhood, town, or city you might be considering.

PadMapper gives you access to the rental information for each unit, as shown online. You can drill down to the size (square footage), number of bedrooms, number of bathrooms, other rooms in the rental unit, and multiple pictures of the unit. By reviewing the pictures, you get a feel for how each home presents to potential clients and what you need to do to stand out from your competition.

Why Research Rental Rates?

I use an excellent property management company, but I still review the area's rental market each time we have a vacancy to see current rental rates. It is a great way to keep your property management team honest. Really, for me, it reconfirms the great job my property management company is doing.

Knowing rental rates for the type of investment real estate property you are looking to purchase is a great way to source financial information to anticipate the financial results of your investment real estate through your projections.

On Day 3, we challenged you to review your income and expense statement and your net worth and use these two financial vehicles to see if you are ready to purchase and rent your first investment real estate property.

Working with a mortgage broker as part of your Team REAL will let you know what each lender will allow you to use as revenue to help secure your mortgage. Providing reliable financial revenue information can go a long way to securing financing. In addition, mortgage brokers know their lenders' tendencies, and if the lender is aware of a trend toward higher rental demand and increased rental rates, they may be more flexible on their lending rules.

The information on PadMapper can often give you a sense of what costs are covered by tenants in this neighborhood, such as if they pay their own power bill and cable or internet.

Remember, the more accurate the information you can provide to your lender, the easier it makes their job ... and their ability to say yes.

A lender is all about your ability to repay your loan on time. As an investment real estate professional, you should be able to discuss signs you are seeing in the area of reduced vacancies and increased rents. Don't ever assume lenders are aware of real estate market conditions, especially regarding investment real estate. As I stated earlier, in North America and Australia, a low percentage of the population owns investment real estate, and many lenders have no experience with this type of investor.

COACHING CHALLENGE 22 Do a drive-through and walkabout to search for signs of decreased vacancies.

As a potential investment real estate purchaser and renter, a lot of opportunities can be noticed by simply driving slowly or walking through the neighborhoods you are interested in.

When you drive slowly or walk through these neighborhoods, take the time to write down or audio- or video-record the walk; don't drive if you are by yourself and make these observations. Use this checklist below, and add items that are important to you.

Neighborhood Walkabout Checklist: (If you are recording audio or video, start by mentioning what neighborhood you are walking and observing; the higher the number of items on the neighborhood checklist below, the better. These are all signs of attraction to this area and can lead to decreased or low vacancies.)

Neighborhood Checklist

1) Approximate age of area
2) Duplex or multi-family housing in area
3) Any signs in the windows for basement suites
4) Playgrounds and what type of facilities (e.g., ice rinks, interactives, etc.)
5) Local services (e.g., daycare, nail and hair salons, etc.)
6) Schools
7) Street parking
8) Parks and pathways
9) Other

Research your desired area on PadMapper.com.

Today's technology and free online resources make researching rental rates and vacancies easier than ever. In this coaching challenge, I'll walk you through a free vacancy and rental rate app you can use anywhere in North America: PadMapper.com. PadMapper is not the only app of its kind, but it is the one I have used for years. Don't be afraid to search for other resources on your own. Follow the steps below to research your desired area using PadMapper.

How to Use PadMapper:

- Enter PadMapper.com in your web browser.
- At the top of PadMapper's webpage, click the search box in the top left-hand side of the homepage. It asks you, "Where to?" Type in the name of the town or city and press enter.
- The town or city will pop up as a map with all of the available rentals.
- Each property on the map looks like a red dot or pinhead. You can focus on each dot and drill down to the details of the property.
- On the right-hand side of the PadMapper map of the town or the city are several tools. First is a rent slider; you can pull a dot across the bar, from zero up to $5,000 a month for rent.
- You can check a box for Long-Term or Short-Term Rentals.
- You can also check a box for studio, one, two, three, or four-plus bedrooms.

- ⇧ The last box on the page on the bottom right-hand side is a picture of a featured property; you can click on the word Featured and get directed to the property's site.

Day 11 Key Recap

Record your key learnings and actionable items in your notebook or the workbook and planning guide. (Optional)

- ⇧ A slow drive or walk through an area is a great way to observe whether it has demand for rentals over other areas and see if there are signs of a decreased vacancy rate.
- ⇧ High demand and low vacancy rates might be worth considering paying a little more for the property.
- ⇧ Use free services like PadMapper to help determine rental demand and vacancy rates.

DAY 12 FOCUS (FOLLOW ONE COMMITMENT UNTIL SUCCESS)

Use this day to get to know your real estate business strategy. At the end of the chapter, complete the coaching challenges to focus your efforts and prepare for your investment real estate purchase by confirming your target property type and developing your expertise in this area of real estate.

Getting distracted is one of the easiest things to happen in life. With so many distractions afoot, many of us never get around to doing the one most important thing. In our business lives, we can quickly find ourselves moving on to the next thing. It's a common problem today, especially in our fast-paced world, where different technologies compete for our attention.

What's more, all of these distractions can lead to analysis paralysis, which compounds our lack of focus.

Analysis Paralysis

First, let's examine where most people get bogged down.

The phrases *analysis paralysis* or *paralysis by analysis* are often used to describe one person, but it can also refer to a group.

Whether it is on your own or as a team (in investment real estate, this means you and your spouse or joint venture partners), you become paralyzed to move forward toward your One Investment Real Estate Thing.

By now, you have a basic understanding of investment real estate, the mindset required, what investment real estate is, the different roles of people in this journey, the types of investment real estate, the economy, trends and timing, and some terminology around renting.

All this information could have you running in all different directions, which wouldn't get you any closer to purchasing and renting your first investment real estate property.

I don't want you to get stuck in a rut and think investment real estate is too complicated. I don't want you to be held back from deciding to purchase and rent due to your fear that other potential problems may arise.

The journey of the perfect investment doesn't exist. There is no superior financial product. The ups and downs of the financial world are legendary, and they have made their mark through history.

Analysis paralysis can give you an overload of options and stop you in your tracks. So how do we overcome it?

Let's FOCUS

That's where the acronym FOCUS comes into play. We lack focus, and it directly leads to analysis paralysis.

I love this acronym. I see *focus* as being a word of present and future tense. Although slightly different versions exist, many using the word *course* for the letter C, the word that works for me is *commitment*: Follow One Commitment Until Success.

A commitment is lifelong, and if you are truly committed or believe in your cause, it is lasting and stays with you forever. It is a lifelong journey to success. Success never ends; success always begets success. If you are going to create a living legacy, it is a commitment for life—success upon success.

Creating your Vault to Investment Real Estate Success will take focus. When we lack focus, we tend to get the numbers, processes, and strategies in the combination for our vault out of order. If your vault does not open, you need to adjust your combination of numbers, processes, and strategies by adjusting your focus. Adjusting your focus will keep you on track with your commitments.

Alexander Graham Bell once said, "Concentrate all your thoughts on the task at hand. The sun's rays do not burn until brought into focus."

Bringing Things into Focus

I am an avid reader, and I also love listening to podcasts. While I enjoy all things business, it sometimes gets me distracted. There is always one more great idea around the corner, so I need to ensure I am keeping my commitments and not simply moving on to the next flavor of the day.

Luckily, I found a simple exercise that helps me concentrate my thoughts and bring everything into focus.

Try it for yourself. Write your distractions down on a piece of paper and the words "not again" after each distraction. Make several copies of this list. Each day or each week, depending on how distracted you continue to be, put this list through your paper shredder and pledge that you will be focused on your investment real estate goal. Each time you review this list, remove any item that you have overcome as a distraction.

I ask you to take a breath and learn that investment real estate can be a realistic expectation in your wealth portfolio. Not only that, it has the potential for financial success.

But there's one catch: moving from fear to gain takes focusing on one thing.

Why Focusing on One Goal Is Important

What is the importance of having just one goal to solidify your base?

In their book *The One Thing*, authors Gary Keller and Jay Papasan state there can only be one. Keller and Papasan's rationale behind the idea of the one thing and their process about focus is their belief in how hard it is to avoid puzzling distractions that come our way. By focusing, we can direct our attention on the one thing that is critical at that point in time. The book says we should aim for fewer intrusions on our daily life, whether business-related or personal, so that we can pay attention to the most important thing.

Identifying Your "One Investment Real Estate Thing"

Keller and Papasan's recommendation applies to what we're doing as well. When it comes to investment real estate, you should choose one area of focus and stick to it. We'll call it your One Investment Real Estate Thing.

When I first started in investment real estate, my goal was first to understand if investment real estate, as a side hustle or part-time business, was right for us—my wife, my family, and me.

Earlier in the book, I mentioned I had this desire to control at least part of my financial future rather than allow others to control it all. For example, government retirement programs such as Social Security (United States) or Old Age Security (Canada), company pension plans, and funds I gave to others to administer into mutual funds were all controlled by others. I wanted one hands-on investing thing.

Once we decided investment real estate was our hands-on investing thing, we started on our path to purchasing investment real estate. But it took us a while to determine what our One Investment Real Estate Thing would be, and that caused us a lot of challenges we could have otherwise avoided.

This book drills our years of twists and turns down into thirty-one days. Since you're reading this book, you can skip years of twists and turns. Instead of taking on various types of investment real estate, investing hundreds of thousands of dollars before settling on the investment real estate type that is right for you, you can focus right from the get-go.

If you are this far into the book, you have decided investment real estate is going to be your one hands-on investing thing. And you're likely one step ahead of where we were: you know the importance of focusing on one thing, and you've at least given thought to what type of property might work best for you.

Your One Investment Real Estate Thing leads us to the challenge proposed by Keller and Papasan: "What can you do right now that will help you achieve what matters most to you?"

How to FOCUS

You need to take time and give some thought to many different factors that might underlie your thinking and help mold your decision. You may have already thought out the type of real estate property you are interested in purchasing, but making your choice may not be as simple as it seems. Understanding the factors to consider prior to your initial search can have a lasting effect as you move through your investment real estate life.

What to Consider When Choosing Your "One Investment Real Estate Thing"

In Coaching Challenge 15, we discussed the types of investment real estate properties. Each of these property types has its pros and cons.

On Day 9, we talked in-depth about gross domestic product (GDP). GDP helps you see the bigger picture in terms of the economic conditions surrounding you, on multiple levels: your municipality, your state, your province, or your country.

Below are some more factors to consider that can have a tremendous impact on your investment real estate choice.

Capital Investment – Property is a capital investment, and towns, cities, states, provinces, and countries make their own capital investment—infrastructure—to support your capital investment in real estate with schools, recreation centers, libraries, police services, fire stations, hospitals, and much more. This great capital investment into your community of choice can have a massive impact on your ROI and your investment's longevity.

Smart Communities – Changes in technology are happening rapidly, and we are hearing more and more about artificial intelligence, or AI. If your community does not support technology, you will end up in a vacuum. Think about something as simple as Wi-Fi. To gain a competitive advantage, large chains like Starbucks offered free Wi-Fi to attract customers, while many independent coffee shops resisted. These coffee shops disappeared, replaced by smarter independent owners who embraced technology by adding little things like more charging outlets and USB ports.

Changes Due to Technology – The way new real estate is built is changing. Technology affects the way we lock our homes, cover our windows, turn the lights off and on, check our home security, heat and cool our homes, and more. Smart technology can range from our thermostat learning our habits and adjusting the temperature and power based on when we are home and away, to watering our lawns automatically on a schedule. Emerging technology is now being taken into consideration as builders, developers, and engineers develop communities.

Market Forecast – Market growth could be a sign of new jobs, new industries, new services, and new people entering your area and creating growth.

Innovation in the area and improvements to technology, transportation, recreation, and services can change the dynamic of residential areas. Recently, where I live, a major communications company was updating to fiber optics; these infrastructure upgrades can draw more people into the area, but are renters willing to pay for these services? Can you attract a clientele interested in these service upgrades?

Remember, more people come with costs to the community. How your community handles its tax revenue can impact your costs to operate. If a city has developed a heavier reliance on its residential tax base, you could see your property taxes and utility rates take an increase you were not planning for.

Fiscal Incentives – Communities try to attract people to live in them and will develop incentives toward that. For example, over the last several years, we have seen towns and cities offer secondary income suite incentives in the form of non-repayable loans to develop a suite in your current home and create lower-cost housing for others to move into. These non-repayable loans are totally forgiven once you have met the criteria of keeping your secondary income suite rented over a fixed number of years at a certain rental rate.

Cash Flow and Alternatives – Communities, towns, cities, states, provinces, and countries are always competing to attract businesses and industries into their communities as a form of employment and revenue. For example, Amazon Distribution Centers have been a big attraction to communities in recent years.

Many communities are trying hard to attract new industries to ensure they do not rely on one business or industry to drive their economy. Consider what the auto industry did to Detroit. When many of the auto manufacturers left Detroit, it took years to draw new industries back to the area. There have been multiple similar examples over the years as North American companies moved their factories to Asia.

Non-Financial Factors – This category of factors can include safety, security, public transportation, ease of walking, running and biking paths, lower population density, parks and recreation within walking distance, and more. In the current pandemic, many people will want to practice social distancing but still want to be part of a community.

Health Concerns – With COVID-19 and people working from home becoming more common than ever before, there is a movement shifting away from high-density residential areas to the suburbs and single-family homes. Will this trend reverse once circumstances change?

Digging Deeper into Fiscal Incentives

Fiscal incentives offered by communities should be a significant factor in your decision-making when it comes to choosing your One Investment Real Estate Thing.

As mentioned above, first-time homeowners' grants, income suite development grants, home improvement grants, and other housing incentives are vehicles used to drive many different aspects of the economy and contribute to communities.

From the standpoint of economic stimulation, this is a smart strategy. The jobs created by these incentives tend to be higher-paying jobs, as you're dealing with tradespeople with specific skills; the materials purchased to build these homes support many different retailers; the taxes generated for goods and services benefit the state or province and country; land is required to build these homes; services are required to support the families moving into new areas of construction; and the list goes on.

Creating these housing incentives jump-starts and supports economic impact almost immediately, and the cost to governments is low compared to the sustainable economic return to government coffers.

First-Time Home-Buyer Incentives

First-time home-buyer grants, sometimes referred to as first-time home-buyers' boosts, are typically awarded based on a few criteria, primarily financial need and income qualifications. These grants or boosts are available in the United States and Canada and have had a long history of usage in Australia. Make sure you do your research with your Team REAL, including your lender. The governments tend to use this incentive as an economic stimulus mechanism, and the amounts offered fluctuate from time to time. Also, like many programs, restrictions apply, so read the small print.

In the United States, many states have initiated grant programs to help lower-income residents purchase their first home. The United States Department of Housing and Urban Development (HUD) also provides grants to first-time home buyers.

Canada's First-Time Home Buyer Incentive can help you purchase your first home. This incentive aims to help first-time home buyers without adding to their financial burdens. There are no additional monthly payments. Participants must meet minimum insured mortgage down payment requirements.

Income Suite Development Grants

I am a big fan of secondary suites, and developing a secondary suite in your home can have a huge positive impact on your life. Secondary suites are a way to give yourself a hand-up in difficult financial or personal times and can provide long-term lasting income as you work your way through life.

A prime example is my daughter's story, which I covered earlier in the book. Using a secondary suite in her home made a huge impact on her and her daughter's lives. My daughter was able to secure a secondary suite grant for her home from her city.

We found out about this program through our primary bank; it's pretty neat when your financial institution puts on a free seminar to train you on how to secure funding to help you with owning your home. (Remember that, in addition to contacting your municipality about secondary suite programs, your financial institution is another great resource. Banks and lending companies are here to help.)

In a 2018 blog post, *Show Me the Green* talked about how over 75 percent of Canadian municipalities allow secondary suites in primary residences. At the time of posting their blog, *Show Me the Green* indicated there were nineteen secondary suite grant programs in Canada.

The grant program my daughter received from her city funded a non-repayable grant of $15,000 for a total renovation cost of $37,000. The renovation spending included bringing window egresses up to city building codes, purchasing a new washer and dryer, putting in new flooring, creating a new access to the secondary suite, putting in a kitchen and appliances, and painting. The secondary suite already had the basic layout in place—two bedrooms, office, and laundry room—but everything had to be upgraded or built new to code.

There were two main caveats in securing the city secondary suite grant. One, it had to comply with building codes (the final inspection was to be done by the city before a tenant could take possession), and two, the secondary suite had to be kept in a rental program for five years. In positive news, the specified rates were competitive in the rental marketplace.

My daughter's mortgage payment was $1,500 a month and she was receiving $1,100 in rental income. For a single mother, this income was critical to her livelihood.

The five years in the city program went by quickly, and my daughter has gone on to marry a great guy. They live in the same home and have since renovated most of their upstairs. The home continues to go up in value, and with a secondary suite, the income potential will always be available. There are many different grant programs and renovation tips available in many municipal areas. This great article offers information about secondary suites, renovation tips, and grants for Canada.

Home Improvement Grants

When you purchase any capital asset, it will require upkeep over time, and maintenance is critical to the asset holding its value and appreciating. But purchasing an investment property or a home doesn't always require you to go it alone on regular maintenance.

As mentioned earlier, governments are always looking to find ways to stimulate the economy in slow times or when a disaster hits an area hard. Governments will step in to bring an area back, contributing to economic relief or area revitalization.

Make sure you check into all the different programs; you might be surprised at what's offered. I would recommend you look online first. Start with the municipal websites, and then go to the state or provincial and federal websites, searching under "home improvement grants." Don't be afraid to do a general web search under "home improvement grants," either. The seminar I attended that was put on by one of Canada's major banks was very helpful. Major banks or lenders have been known to support the state, provincial, or federal government programs because the governments, in some cases, will guarantee the loans for the banks or lenders when you borrow money for these programs.

Saving You from a Death Sentence

Governments know keeping seniors in their homes is a great way to keep the strain off of public facilities, senior care homes, and long-term care homes. Senior care homes and long-term care homes can be expensive to maintain and are very labor-intensive.

Many states and provinces have grants to help maintain seniors' own homes and improve accessibility. I have written several blog posts over the years encouraging seniors to look at keeping their homes and adding a secondary income suite to offset costs, including the May 2020 article "OK Boomer: How to Get in the Now or Be Society's Roadkill."

Staying in your own home not only gives you a sense of independence as you age, but as the recent coronavirus pandemic has sadly made clear, staying in your own home can give you a safe and secure place to live. We've watched as COVID-19 runs rampant through senior long-term care facilities, and it's fair to say that staying in your own home can perhaps save you from a death sentence.

When it comes to fiscal incentives for homeowners in the USA or Canada, it is important to remember you are dealing with different levels of government, and patience is a good rule of thumb. You will have your home for a long time, so keeping your cool as you access free money is worth every minute.

Other Housing Incentives – Many municipalities, states, provinces, and countries have different programs committed to affordable and safe housing in their communities. Affordable housing is always an election hot button, and you'll find that all three levels of government tend to step up with funding.

Even though affordable housing incentives may not fit into your investment real estate strategy, it gives you a lot of insight into politicians' minds. With so much information only a click away, type "housing incentives (name of your community)" into a search engine and do some research.

These incentive and funding programs are a healthy hand-up when it comes to housing. So, give yourself a hand.

Government Financing Options

Before we get deeper into the financial end of your first investment real estate property, make sure you also check into government financing options. There are usually lots of hoops to jump through to borrow funds from the government, but it is an alternative funding option. On Days 15, 16, and 17 we will look at all your financing options.

 **Complete a focus challenge.**

Life is full of distractions. My wife and I grappled with many distractions, too, before we embraced investment real estate as part of our financial portfolio.

I am happy to take you through the FOCUS method, which we used to eliminate distractions when we decided to strengthen our financial foundation.

Below is a list of our distractions. These lasted almost a decade, undermining our efforts, before we got focused and committed to improving our financial foundation. It is my sincere wish that you learn from our experiences and don't take a full decade to drill down on your life's distractions. Let's get at it.

Rick's Distractions

- ⇧ Work
- ⇧ Family activities
- ⇧ Spending everything we earned, plus more
- ⇧ Purchasing depreciating assets

⇧   No budgeting technique

⇧   Travel

Now it's your turn. In your notebook or using the lines below, make a list of what is distracting you. It is okay to borrow any items that are on my list if they're a distraction to you, too.

⇧

⇧

⇧

Identify your "One Investment Real Estate Thing."

Once you have identified your distractions in Coaching Challenge 24 and decided to eliminate as many from your daily life as possible to make room to focus on investment real estate, you're one step closer to your goal of purchasing and renting your first investment real estate property in thirty-one days.

And now that you are ready to have investment real estate as part of your investment real estate portfolio, it's time to make a big decision. Do you remember, back on Day 7, when you decided what type of investment real estate best fits your needs?

Let's take action and make this type of real estate your focus and your One Investment Real Estate Thing. In your notebook, the workbook and planning guide, or using the line below, write the type of investment real estate you want to acquire.

My One Investment Real Estate Thing

 **Research the grants, subsidies, and other incentive programs available in your target area.**

Federal, state/provincial, and municipal governments offer grant or subsidy programs for first-time real estate home buyers, as well as other real estate incentive programs. In this challenge, we're going to identify and list any programs available in your area. Who knows—there might be a perfect option to take advantage of for your investment real estate purchase. By doing your research, you can unearth opportunities right in your own backyard!

List the federal/state/provincial/municipal grant/subsidy programs in your target area:

⇧

Day 12 Key Recap

Record your key learnings and actionable items in your notebook or the workbook and planning guide. (Optional)

- ⇧ FOCUS: Follow One Commitment Until Success. Remember this acronym and execute its meaning often.
- ⇧ When you decide on your target property type, you must select one that ticks the boxes for you. Consider working capital, cash flow, smart communities, technology, non-financial factors (e.g., public transportation, parks, walkways, etc.), market conditions, and health factors.
- ⇧ Researching and using incentives, including first-time buyer programs, income-suite development grants, home improvement grants, and government financing options, allows you access to capital, much of which you never have to repay.

 # DAY 13 FINANCING: WHAT IS BEST FOR YOU?

Use this day to focus your efforts and prepare for financing your first investment real estate property. At the end of the chapter, complete the coaching challenges to identify the different areas of financing and decide what type of financing is best for you. Creating a great financial vehicle is a major element of the financial phase.

Part of the magic of investing in investment real estate is your ability to get someone else to pay for the entire purchase price of your investment real estate property by paying rent over the years.

To purchase an investment real estate property, you will still need to put some skin in the game. You will be required to invest anywhere from 5 to 20 percent of the purchase price. This is your down payment. Remember that 5 to 20 percent is the norm for people who have regular employment, but should you be self-employed, your down payment percentage could be as high as 35 percent. The difference between your invested funds and the purchase price is the mortgage amount.

The mortgage amount is the funds you will access from lenders. Over the next couple of days, we will focus on mortgages and discuss how you will approach the lenders and access the funds.

The funds you will borrow and the interest on those funds will be covered by the tenant and their rent check.

First, let's start with the basics: What is a mortgage?

Mortgages Defined

Many folks break the most important aspects of a mortgage down to two parts: the principal and the interest. I think of the mortgage in three important parts: the principal, the interest, and your down payment portion or amount.

The financial experts might disagree with my definition, and that is okay. I include the down payment portion or amount because your down payment influences your interest rate, your mortgage insurance, your amortization period, your term, your payment strategy, and your ability to fund another investment real estate property should you want to continue adding to your investment real estate portfolio.

Even though many of the same banks operate in the United States and Canada, the taxation laws and mortgage rules are different.

Not only are there different rules in the United States and Canada, but there are different rules and regulations in different states, provinces, and municipalities. This is why your Team REAL is so important. To get a true understanding of your local rules, consult the experts in the geographic area in which you wish to purchase your investment real estate.

What Is the Prime Rate?

Before we get into the types of mortgages, it's essential to understand the concept of the prime rate. The prime rate is the lowest interest rate available for non-banks, including bank loans for preferred consumers of mortgages, loans, and credit cards. This rate represents the best rate a customer could access.

Strive for Prime

On Day 15, we will talk about the importance of your credit score; as you will learn, not all credit scores are treated equally. A top credit score can make you a bank or lender's preferred consumer. They will work hard to get you as a customer and will work hard to keep you, too.

The other reason I talk about the down payment amount is because it can also have a bearing on your return. When I discussed higher costs to borrow, interest, and insurance, I may have made it sound all bad. This is not true. You should be able to put down a lower down payment than the conventional 20 percent, like 5, 10, or 15 percent, and still have a positive cash flow. A lower down payment can lead to higher returns on your investment. How can this be? Remember, your investment is the amount of funds you invest, not the full price you paid for the property.

Let's look at the example below.

If you purchase an investment property for $200,000 and you put down 20 percent, this means you require $40,000 of your own funds.

However, if you can put down 5 percent and still see a positive cash flow to cover all operating costs, you only have to invest $10,000 to purchase the property! The rest will be covered by rental costs, saving you money.

Purchase Price of Investment Property	$200,000	$200,000
Down Payment Amount	$10,000 (5%)	$40,000 (20%)
Principal Mortgage Amount	$190,000	$160,000
Default Insurance	$7,600	$0
Total Mortgage Amount	$197,600	$160,000
Principal Paydown $ (Over 5 Years)	$32,922	$26,557
Interest	$44,987	$36,427
Total Principal Paydown and Interest	$77,909	$63,084
Remaining Balance	$164,678	$133,343
Monthly Mortgage Payment	$1,298	$1,051

When determining your down payment size, you need to decide how volatile the real estate market is. I talk about the volatility of the real estate market because you don't want to be caught at the top of a hot market and see your equity shrink as the prices move down. A 5 percent fluctuation in pricing downward could eat up all your equity. A real estate agent, part of your Team REAL, can supply information about how real estate prices have performed over various periods of time: six months, a year, or several years. Ask your agent what has been the average value increase yearly over the last five years, and if they have noticed any value changes out of the ordinary, up or down.

Remember, I am recommending a long-term buy-and-hold strategy. If you are in this investment for the long haul, a 5 percent downwards change over one year may not be meaningful. Like any investment, do you have the patience to stay the course?

With a 5 percent down payment, your monthly mortgage payment will be higher, and it will include the cost of default mortgage insurance.

Use this information to your advantage when creating your mortgage. You need to consider your risk tolerance level. Are you able to invest only 5 percent down and purchase two doors in one property, creating two income streams?

Sweat Equity

On Day 15, we will discuss further how sweat equity can become a significant part of refinancing down the road. It can give you access to additional funds because of equity growth.

Sweat equity through your own skills can help add value to a property when you perform work to the house that adds value, but you don't get compensated until you refinance, sell, or have an appraisal done to reflect the new value. The new value can be added to your net worth statement, reflecting a strong picture of your wealth.

I am not recommending you flip your investment property; flipping is a unique skill and strategy. Flippers are constantly looking for fixer-uppers, and they do the work themselves or hire a general contractor. Flippers make their living by purchasing and renovating in a short time frame. Flippers know what they are looking for; long-term buy-and-hold is not in their vocabulary.

Mortgage Cash Account vs. Mortgage Vacation

The challenge regarding your principal residence or investment real estate is deciding whether you should have a mortgage cash account or a mortgage payment vacation process.

I'll explain what these are below. My wife and I deal with two major banks for our investment real estate mortgages. One of these banks has a mortgage cash account component, and the other bank has a mortgage payment vacation competent.

We have used both the mortgage cash account and the mortgage vacation process over the twenty years we've had our investment real estate portfolio. We have used these methods several times, and both have worked great.

First, please review the explanation of both the mortgage cash account and mortgage payment vacation.

After the explanation, I will give you actual examples of how we used these methods, their purpose, and their benefits and drawbacks.

Mortgage Cash Account (MCA)

At one of our major banks, once you have a standard mortgage, you automatically have an MCA. Initially, when your mortgage opens, the balance in your MCA is zero. Funds get deposited to your MCA whenever you go above and beyond your mortgage payment plan and pay more than your regular amortized payments. This extra amount is a critical point to understand because it carries multiple meanings.

1. Your MCA represents money you've put toward accelerating your mortgage payments. This means any additional funds or additional principal payments contribute to your MCA. For example, our bank calculates our repayment plan based on semi-monthly payments, but we chose a bi-weekly plan to match our pay schedule. This payment option means that every year, we are making two additional payments (52 weeks + biweekly = 26 payments vs. 24

semi-monthly payments), and these additional funds are allocated to the MCA account.

2. Your MCA isn't a real account in the sense that there is no separate account number associated with it. It is merely a virtual account that keeps track of how much you've overcontributed (based on the original amortization plan) to your mortgage.

Mortgage Payment Vacation

With the mortgage payment vacation option, you can make lump-sum payments or pre-pay a little more each month toward the opportunity to take up to four months off from making your mortgage payment when it benefits you the most.

Flexible mortgage payment features will result in interest capitalization. That means the interest adds back to the principal outstanding on your mortgage.

- ⇧ Interest is added back to each mortgage payment due date.
- ⇧ The amount of interest capitalized cannot cause your mortgage to exceed the lesser of a 90 percent loan-to-value (LTV) ratio or your original principal balance.
- ⇧ The LTV ratio expresses the amount of a mortgage as a percentage of a property's total appraised value.
- ⇧ With a mortgage payment vacation, you are only deferring principal and interest; all other costs need to be covered.
- ⇧ If necessary, adjust the amortization period remaining at renewal so that the mortgage does not exceed the original amortization period remaining. This variation may increase the number of your regular payments after the renewal.

The Purpose of a Mortgage Cash Account or Mortgage Vacation

Both of these methods should be viewed like a rainy-day fund. It's financial protection in case of an issue with tenants, the property, the employment market, and other economic factors.

Funds Versus Time

The mortgage cash account gives you access to funds, while the mortgage vacation gives you access to time.

Your bank or lender set these methods up because they make money from you as a client as long as you have a mortgage. If you pay off the mortgage, they lose their revenue. The lenders love real estate as an asset because it is tangible, and if they know you are using the funds to add value to the property or keep the property afloat during an economic downturn, they are willing to help, as it protects their investment.

Benefits to You

Even though your tenants may sign a lease for six months to a year, you can never be sure they will renew their lease. And you never know how long you might have a vacancy for, either.

We have lived through multiple vacancies with our properties a few times in our twenty years of owning investment real estate.

No Strain, No Pain

Thanks to these two options, we were able to take a deep breath and analyze the situation without any undue financial strain. We have utilized both the mortgage cash account and mortgage vacation strategy to lower our financial risk until we could find new tenants. Knowing you can defer mortgage payments up to four months can relieve a lot of stress, not to mention provide financial relief.

With a mortgage cash account, you can borrow up to the amount posted on your year-end mortgage statement plus whatever has been accumulated over the time frame since your last mortgage statement. You don't need to withdraw all of the funds, but some banks have a minimum; for example, our bank has a minimum of $2,500 you can access.

You can use the MCA or mortgage vacation for more than mortgage relief for vacancies; for example, you might want to update your investment property, and accessing the MCA or deferring mortgage payments could give you the funds to do some upgrades, adding value to your property and keeping tenants happy. By adding value, you may even be able to set a higher rent.

Remember, with the mortgage cash account, you still need to make all operational payments, and with the mortgage vacation, you are not making your monthly mortgage payments. However, you still need to cover all other costs (e.g., property taxes, condo fees, electricity, etc.).

Drawbacks of These Deferral Programs

By using the funds you already paid down on your mortgage, part of your equity is now added back to your mortgage balance, and it will now take longer to pay off your mortgage than you first planned.

Or, if you have taken time off from your mortgage payments, they get added back on to your mortgage, and it will now take longer to pay off your investment.

Which Is Better: Mortgage Cash Account or Mortgage Payment Vacation?

Between the mortgage cash account and mortgage payment vacation, I consider the mortgage cash account to be a better option for the following reasons:

- ⇧ You have instant access to cash even if you have received no rent.
- ⇧ With the cash, you can cover all monthly expenses, including renovations to make the property more attractive.
- ⇧ If you can promptly rent the property, any additional money left over can be applied back to the mortgage principal, which helps build funds back into your mortgage cash account.
- ⇧ Having no rental income puts a ton of pressure on you, and you may need to add personal funds to the investment property's bank account.

Make sure you have discussed your options with your mortgage broker. Banks can differ in their policies, and some banks may not offer any of these options.

A slightly higher interest rate may be worth managing if you have more flexibility when tenant issues arise.

Understanding lenders' rules about how to defer payment amounts is important. But along with that, how the lender will lend you funds can be interesting as well.

Someone Else's Sandbox, Their Rules

Earlier in the book, I talked about whether or not to incorporate. We faced this decision with the best two investment properties we had purchased to date.

I got a lead on two properties in bankruptcy that were controlled by one of Canada's major banks. We put an offer in on both properties simultaneously, and the bank said they would accept our offers on the condition that we buy them in our personal names and not in our corporation. This opportunity to buy these two properties at once, at a price too good to pass up, was irresistible. We decided not to stand our ground regarding purchasing through our corporation and purchased in our personal names.

We have owned these properties for almost ten years, and the cash flow has been awesome, the mortgage paydown has been dynamite, and the equity appreciation has been excellent. We can see the mortgage payouts not too far off in the distance.

Sometimes it pays to be flexible and take advantage of the opportunities lenders present to you, even if it's a little different from the way you usually do things.

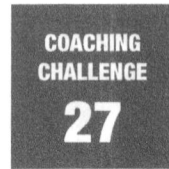 **Test your mortgage financing strength.**

Let's test your mortgage financing strength. Use this coaching challenge to determine what the down payment amount of your mortgage should be and what you feel most comfortable with. Remember, this is an exercise, and you can always change your mind as you make your way to purchasing and renting your first investment property.

- What percentage of the purchase price do you plan to make as a down payment? Remember, even though I have given you a range of 5 to 35 percent, the lenders—depending on your ability to service the debt—will allow you to use a percentage that's not fixed to 5, 20, or 35. For example, you might find that, for your circumstances, your down payment is 17 percent or some other variation. Don't forget that mortgage insurance also impacts what you might use as a down payment percentage.
- What are the elements of your mortgage, and why have you chosen these elements in your mortgage?

How should you set up your mortgage?

Digging a little deeper to discover how you should set up your mortgage requires you to consider how to use all your mortgage's elements. As you pay down your mortgage principal, most lenders are happy to lend you funds against your principal paydown. Remember, lenders are in the business of making money through interest charged on borrowed funds, so it's in their best interest to lend to you.

As an investor, you should be thinking about using your investment property to become self-sufficient. Through principal mortgage paydown, there is a couple of methods you can use. We introduced you to these methods earlier in the chapter, and now it is time to do an exercise to understand what might work best for you. Write your answers in your notebook, the workbook and planning guide, or in the table below.

⇧ What are the pros and cons of a mortgage cash account and a mortgage vacation process for your situation? Which method will work better for you, and why?

Mortgage Cash Account Pros	Mortgage Vacation Pros	Mortgage Cash Account Cons	Mortgage Vacation Cons

Which method works best for you, and why?

Day 13 Key Recap

Record your key learnings and actionable items in your notebook or the workbook and planning guide. (Optional)

- ⇧ Review your funds available and calculate your down payment percentage. Start with a fixed amount of funds you might have easy access to and then calculate your down payment percentage based on that.
- ⇧ Identify if you have any renovation and repair skills you can trade for sweat equity. Could you take a couple of free skill lessons at your local Home Depot or Lowe's?
- ⇧ It is better to look at projected dollar savings and, over time, decide if you should strategically use a mortgage cash account or a mortgage vacation program.

 DAY 14 FINANCING: WHAT CAN YOU AFFORD?

Use this day to identify your resources and the minimum down payment you must make for your lender to approve you for your first investment real estate property. At the end of the chapter, complete the coaching challenges to determine which type of mortgage will work for you. Will you go with high-ratio or conventional mortgage financing?

Each day, we take a step closer to your goal of purchasing and renting your first investment real estate property. But how much can you afford to spend? Many factors influence what you can afford to buy, and we'll go through these today.

Establishing a purchase price range brings the reality of ownership within your grasp. Having a price range to work with gives you a better feel for the real estate marketplace, the neighborhoods, the type of properties, the zoning for rental properties, and the kind of revenue you can expect to earn.

Today, we'll deconstruct the different elements of mortgages: time, financing, costs, income, expenses, options, and how to Uberize your investment.

Time

With any mortgage, time is a critical element, and the term and amortization can have a significant impact on how you manage your portfolio. I can promise you time is a resource that depletes far too quickly.

In investment real estate, you can manage time to be on your side through term and amortization. As an entrepreneur and small business owner, how you manage your resources helps to define your success.

Let's first review the definitions of *term* and *amortization*. Then, we will develop a strategy on how to use both in your investment real estate business.

Term and Amortization Defined

The ideas behind term and amortization are central to your mortgage. This terminology is handled a little differently in the United States than in Canada, so I'll note the important distinctions.

Term: A temporal component of the mortgage describing the length of time the interest rate is in place.

For example, a **short-term component of a mortgage** is often one year in length. An **intermediate-term loan** generally runs more than one year but less than three years. A **long-term loan** generally runs more than three years and to a maximum of five years.

From a lending standpoint, the interest rates drive the term's length. From a borrower's standpoint, other important factors as you build your business include time, payment size, and sometimes payment frequency.

In the United States, term periods tend to be longer; you'll often see fifteen or thirty-year terms. The standard term rate in Canada tends to be five years, but there are other variations—one, three, and four years.

Amortization: The process of allocating the cost of a mortgage asset over a period of time. It also refers to the repayment of real estate principal over time.

In the United States and Canada, we have what is called the amortization period—the length of time required to pay off the entire mortgage amount.

In the United States, the amortization period tends to be tied to the length of the term. In Canada, amortization periods are generally twenty or twenty-five years, and the term in a Canadian mortgage is renewed more often throughout that period.

Any folks purchasing their first residential real estate property try and take their amortization period over a length of twenty-five to thirty years.

Does This Impact You Positively or Negatively?

In some cases, when directed by the government, amortization periods can fluctuate if the real estate market is too hot or too cold and the government either wants to slow the pace of real estate values or activity or increase it.

The reason the government fluctuates the amortization terms is to control the size of your payments. When consumers are flush with cash, the governments tend to reduce the number of years you have to pay off the mortgage because they believe you can handle higher, fewer payments.

When the economy is in rough shape, the governments will allow you a longer period of time to pay off your mortgage, which lowers your payments over a more extended time frame.

Remember, this is a federal government strategy, and not all parts of the country are created equal. Understanding the economics of your city, town, state, or province impacts your decisions.

Controlling Your Costs as a Small Business

When you first start as an investment real estate investor, controlling your costs is extremely important, especially if you are new to investing.

Back on Day 4, in Coaching Challenge 8, we reviewed the fact that owning investment real estate is no different from being a small business owner, and to succeed, you need to develop a small business owner's mindset.

One important statistic I used is worth reviewing again now:

According to a Forbes article, seven out of ten new employer firms survive at least two years, half at least five years, a third at least ten years, and a quarter stay in business fifteen years or more. Fifty-two percent of all small businesses are home-based.

Being a small business owner has its challenges, and the learning curve is steep in the beginning.

Your first five years are critical to your success. And as stated above, just half of small businesses survive at least five years. This article from the U.S. Small Business Administration gives you more insight into surviving as a small business for five years.

Small Businesses

Small businesses are the heart and soul of the American and Canadian economic engine. It is hard to watch as the coronavirus devastates small businesses worldwide; it might take decades for many of these small businesses to bounce back.

You will see our family story below about operating a small coffee shop business, describing some of the nuisances of operating a small brick-and-mortar business compared to owning brick and mortar.

I want you to think about how you are going to invest your hard-earned cash and the cost of operating various types of small businesses. Why, and what does this have to do with mortgages and affordability?

Starting and creating a small business requires more than money. Small business owners are often prepared to give their time away freely. As a small business owner, if you give up your time freely, you disguise many expenses, including underestimating wage costs. Your intention as a small business owner may be good, and you may plan to repay yourself through the net profits of your business. However, according to the Bureau of Labor Statistics, about 20 precent of small businesses fail in their first year and about 50 percent in their fifth year.

I am not trying to kill your small business dreams; I want to show you how investing your hard-earned savings in real estate might be a better investment and a much better return on your time into the business if you apply this time to mortgage and affordability.

Below, I discuss our experience of buying a small coffee shop. I gave my hours freely to the business, doing the bookkeeping, some of the offsite purchasing, and some of the cleaning and maintenance labor. My hours were about ten hours weekly, or approximately forty hours a month. Using an hourly wage rate of ten dollars, I was contributing an unaccounted labor amount of over five thousand dollars a year.

I would like you to think about this as you do your mortgage and affordability exercise: What if we had taken our initial down payment for our coffee shop of $70,000, used this amount as a down payment on an investment real estate property, and then I went to work part-time for someone who actually paid me for my time and took the salary of $5,200 and applied it to the mortgage amount or showed this salary to the lender? The lender would add this amount to my salary, and it would impact the affordability equation of purchasing the property. Interesting, right? You'll find more thought-provoking ideas like this in the introduction to Uberizing your investment later in this chapter.

Let's not stop at unpaid labor; let's review one other important expense line.

Monitoring and Optimizing Your Income

As we discussed on Day 3, understanding and putting together your personal net income and net worth statement is essential.

From a financial perspective, monitoring the success of operating a small investment real estate business is easy when you pay attention to your financial statements. This is worth repeating: you will benefit from the ease of running a monthly and year-to-date income statement.

One of the most complicated financial lines for many small businesses is the cost of goods sold (COGS) line.

A Case Study: Our Coffee Shop

My wife and I owned a coffee franchise business, and I managed the financial side of it. The cost of goods sold was the trickiest part of the business. I would run a financial statement each month, and I would have to look at the value of goods sold during a particular month.

In many small businesses, there are costs associated with particular goods. To calculate these, you use one of several formulas. For example, in any coffee shop, the goods sold generally are brewed coffee, specialty coffees, cold specialty drinks, bottled drinks, packaged coffee beans, baked goods, and food items.

The costs of these items include all costs of purchase, the costs of making (e.g., baking), and other costs incurred in bringing the inventory to our coffee shop and getting the items to a saleable condition.

The cost of goods includes material, labor, and allocated overhead. The cost of those goods that are not yet sold are deferred as inventory costs until the inventory is sold or written down in value.

While we owned and operated the coffee shop, the amount of time we spent acquiring goods to sell to operate our business was mind-boggling.

The reason I tell this story is to have you put yourself in the shoes of a small business operator and think about the cost of goods. Imagine how complex it can be to stock and operate a coffee shop, restaurant, or retail business. Am I trying to dissuade you from operating these types of small businesses? No. I simply want you to compare the complexity of the cost of goods in relation to running an investment real estate portfolio and think outside the retail box when it comes to investing your money.

When you acquire a piece of investment real estate, ensure it is in rental-ready condition. Then there is no other cost of goods. You receive the rent (income line), and each month, you have a few items to track: bank charges, property taxes, condo fees (if applicable), insurance, property management fees, bookkeeping/accounting, repairs, maintenance, supplies, renovation charges (if necessary), and taxes. Those go on the expense line, not including principal and interest payments, and then you have the net income line. As part of the appendix, I have included a template for the monthly and year-to-date income statement that you can use to keep track of your income. I developed this simple income statement over twenty years ago and have had to make very few changes to keep it current.

I recommend you keep a separate bank account for your investment real estate property. You must keep your business expenses separate from your personal expenses. You don't want to run into issues with the IRS or CRA.

From twenty years of doing a monthly income and expense statement for each of our properties, my experience is that it's quick. Each property takes less than fifteen minutes to complete.

Keeping a separate bank account for your investment real estate property and setting up your rent to automatically be deposited to this bank account, plus all of your expenses to be withdrawn from the same bank account, keeps everything transparent. Moreover, with all the info in one place and separated from your personal affairs, it'll take you a matter of minutes to transfer the information to the income and expenses statement.

Making the income and expenses statement part of a spreadsheet workbook and linking each month together to create a running year-to-date statement means you are not only on top of your monthly investment real estate net operating return, but with each month linked to the year-end sheet, you automatically have a year-to-date net operating statement.

Our accountant uses our income statement, year-to-date, for income tax work in submitting our yearly income tax returns.

At the end of each fiscal year, I only have to wait for the lender's mortgage statement to arrive, showing the actual amount paid for the principal and for the interest. (You cannot claim the principal repayment amount for income tax purposes.)

Talk to your accountant—part of your Team REAL—or do a little research on income and expense statements, and you will soon learn the simplicity of running an investment real estate business.

Tips for Paying Expenses

Here are a couple of tricks I suggest you take advantage of when paying your expenses.

First, set your mortgage payments up on the second of every month. Why? It gives you a little insurance that the rent check has been deposited.

Second, I would also set up your mortgage payments to be withdrawn by the lender twice a month, minimum, and ensure your extra payment each month helps pay down the principal on the mortgage sooner.

I know from experience that paying your mortgage twice a month is a good idea. This means you can save on interest, and you will be free of your mortgage payments early. You must check with your lender and ensure they allow this, and that the extra payment will pay down your mortgage sooner. Make sure there are no additional fees for processing extra payments or prepayments.

In some cases, banks or lenders will collect the property taxes as part of your payments; however, if you have a conventional mortgage, you can pay the property taxes yourself. Most towns or cities have a monthly payment system you can join and pay your property taxes monthly.

Other expenses should be paid monthly, as in most cases, you'll collect the rent from your tenant on the first of every month.

Types of Mortgages

With a variety of mortgage types available, the door is open to almost anyone who would like to be an investment real estate investor. That's the first reason to review the types of mortgages out there.

The second reason is that, if you follow my advice, trade your spare time for a part-time salary, and have a mortgage that allows you to make extra payments to your principal amount, think of the impact it would make. Go ahead—calculate what making extra payments every two weeks, semi-monthly, monthly, etc. would do for your mortgage balance and amortization length. Use the mortgage calculators I have provided via my website, the ones available on your banking website, or through software such as Excel. These calculators are all free to use, so take advantage of the little time it takes to see the impact.

High-Ratio Mortgage: We talked a little about this on Day 13. In North America, a high-ratio mortgage means the loan value exceeds 80 percent of the property's value. The calculation to determine if a mortgage is high-ratio is called a loan-to-value (LTV) ratio.

The lenders take on more risk when lending funds for these mortgages, and having a high-ratio mortgage comes with additional costs. The most-used technique lenders use to mitigate this risk is private mortgage insurance. In many cases, in the United States, there are high-ratio mortgage loans given out by the Federal Housing Administration (FHA), and in Canada, the Canadian Mortgage and Housing Corporation (CMHC); these government agencies will offer programs lending up to 96.5 percent (FHA) or 95 percent (CMHC), requiring you to have 3.5 percent (FHA) or 5 percent (CMHC) down payment. In both countries, your credit score comes into play and can affect your down payment percentage required. This could mean a lower credit score might require you to have a down payment as high as 10 percent.

There is some good news if you are able to have a larger down payment percentage: the cost of your insurance premiums will decrease.

You will need to do your homework because purchasing a real estate property for investment purposes may not qualify for a high-ratio mortgage. This is another reason to have a mortgage broker as part of your Team REAL: they can advise you in advance of the route and lenders available to you if you decide to go the high-ratio mortgage route.

Remember, you are running a business, and you need to show positive cash flow. A high-ratio mortgage may make all the difference in the world, and if the rental rates in your chosen area have had consistent stability or even seen moderate increases, this might be the best way to go.

I would never recommend a high-ratio mortgage if you are in an area of rental volatility. Having a high-ratio mortgage already puts pressure on your ability to keep your cash flow positive as it means your monthly payments will be higher. You don't want to find yourself in a position where you have to access your own personal funds to subsidize your investment real estate property. Running a successful small business should give you a positive return at the end of every year.

If you are fortunate, you decide the numbers work (positive cash flow), and you can use a high-ratio mortgage, this is great.

The good news is that with a high-ratio mortgage, the good times are rolling. This allows you to have a smaller amount invested, you see a quicker return on your original investment, and you're left with more working capital for your next investment real estate property.

Conventional Mortgage: In North America, a conventional mortgage is any type of home buyer's loan that is not offered or secured by a government agency or department. Generally, conventional mortgages are available through private lenders, such as banks, credit unions, and mortgage companies.

These conventional mortgages require you to have a minimum down payment of 20 percent. A conventional mortgage means the loan value cannot exceed 80 percent of the property's value. Like in a high-ratio mortgage, the calculation to determine if a mortgage is deemed a conventional mortgage is called a loan-to-value (LTV) ratio.

Fannie Mae and Freddie Mac (USA) or CMHC (Canada) are agencies that charge a premium to qualify for mortgages with less than a 20 percent down payment. These agencies will insure conventional mortgages, but I would suggest you do your homework to get the true costs on insurance premiums before using their services. You also need to find out if you can qualify for these services in the first place.

Conventional mortgages have several advantages over high-ratio mortgages, such as the following:

- ⇧ Lower fees to borrow mortgage funds
- ⇧ Lower insurance premiums
- ⇧ Less time for loans to close
- ⇧ Less paperwork
- ⇧ Lower mortgage payments
- ⇧ Paying down or paying off mortgage principal sooner
- ⇧ More flexibility due to lower costs (e.g., should you have to lower your rental rates, lower costs can keep your property in a positive cash flow position in bad economic times)
- ⇧ Can change payment terms easier

What the bank or lending institutions require in terms of time and information from you can vary. A mortgage broker can help you know what to expect and what is required of you.

In general, you can expect a processing time of anywhere from five to forty-five days. On your application, you will need to provide your income, assets/liabilities, other real estate you own, type of property you are buying, proof of two years of employment, and, in some cases, country of residence.

You will also be asked for a purchase and sale agreement, confirmation of down payment, and closing costs, typically around 2.5 percent of the purchase price.

If you have completed the coaching challenges to this point in the book, you should have much of this information at your fingertips.

Which Option Is Right for You?

Choosing whether to use a high-ratio or conventional mortgage may come down to a few simple things: your eagerness to get started; the amount of working capital you have; your down payment amount and closing cost funds; your comfort level with taking on higher financial risk versus lower financial risk; taking advantage of first-time homeowner government programs, including restrictions these programs might have; government programs you can access to create a secondary suite in your first property; and more. The options you have to develop a strategy are endless, and this is why I have weighted this book around the Ready phase.

The trick is to get started and take action.

Taking Advantage of Your First Investment Real Estate Property

The main purpose of this book is clearly stated in the title: *31 Days to Purchasing and Renting Your First Investment Real Estate Property*.

Taking advantage of your first investment real estate property helps you create a strong financial foundation that will impact you and your family for the rest of your lives.

Strengthen your foundation right up front when your interest, passion, and energy are at their highest levels on your investment real estate journey.

Uberize Your Investment

Don't manage your investment real estate portfolio like most governments manage their funds in good times. Most governments will spend every dime and more of the taxpayers' money during good times, never thinking there will be a downturn in the economy.

The governments continue to run huge deficits. Remember, as an individual or a small business, you are not allowed to use this method and will find yourself out of business if you run a deficit for too long.

My recommendation is to get a jump on the good times and **Uberize** your investment. Look for a part-time job for a couple of years and use your paycheck to pay down the principal on your investment property.

You can always access these funds if you need to, based on the type of mortgage and term length you decided upon.

You might have a shorter-term mortgage and can remortgage the property in two or three years. This would give you access to your Uberizing funds, and if the property has gone up in value, you can borrow a larger amount to invest as the down payment of your next investment property.

You can also look at the mortgage payment vacation technique or your mortgage cash account (MCA), which we discussed in detail on Day 13.

The neat thing about accessing the mortgage cash account is your payments don't change. If you have a five-year term, your payments remain the same. If you have paid down substantial funds, you can use your MCA and gain access to some or all of a down payment for another investment property.

That means your tenant in your first property is paying rent and covering the cost of your original investment property mortgage as well as the cost of your down payment on your second investment real estate property. Sweet!

Time can really work to your advantage if you set a sense of urgency. With the learnings from this book, you'll be able to make good and speedy decisions about investment real estate.

 **Think about your mortgage choices.**

As you learned today, the type of mortgage you choose can have big implications for your investment real estate future. In this coaching challenge, you're going to spend some time considering your options.

⇑ Review your choice of mortgage for your investment real estate property (high-ratio, conventional, other) and explain why you decided to go with the option you chose. (Remember, your answer is not etched in stone; it's simply time to start thinking about what might work for you and why.)

1. Would you prefer a high-ratio mortgage, conventional mortgage, or other?
2. Why did you choose this option?

In your notebook, the workbook and planning guide, or in the blank spaces below, write out the scenario of what your potential mortgage might look like:

Price Range: $_____

Down Payment: $_____

Mortgage Amount: $_____

 **Familiarize yourself with a mortgage account activity sheet.**

The goal of this book is to have you purchase and rent your first investment real estate property. I also like to give you a few options to look ahead at the potential future impact of your decision.

For example, I have given you a couple of options surrounding your mortgage's principal amount in the "Uberize Your Investment" section. You could pay the property off sooner, or build a cash reserve through an MCA to use as a down payment for another investment property.

You can get informed about these options through your mortgage account activity sheet. In this coaching challenge, we'll review an example sheet and understand what it means.

Right now, let's focus on paying down the mortgage principal on your first investment real estate property.

One of our properties currently has an approximate mortgage balance of $125,000 with seven years and eight weeks on the amortization period. Paying this property off is within our grasp. Can we get it done sooner?

With today's technology, our mortgage lender posts this information online, and the details of the mortgage are very transparent.

The mortgage detail sheet, referred to as the account activity sheet, is broken down into the right and left side of the form with the following main headings and details:

Right-hand side: mortgage number, mortgage statements, mortgage account details, payment details, and prepayment details

Left-hand side: options for your mortgage

(See the sample Online Mortgage Account Activity form below.)

The **options for your mortgage details** are important because the lender outlines the impact of increasing your mortgage payment by a certain amount, the impact on your savings in interest, and how much sooner you will pay off your mortgage.

There are also details regarding lump-sum payment, including the impact on interest amount saved and the time taken off your mortgage.

The **prepayment details** area is also important because most lenders limit the amount of money you can pay down on your mortgage balance each year. The lender is in business to make money off the interest you pay, and if you pay down sooner, they make less profit.

One of my lenders, for example, allows a maximum of 20 percent each year of the original amount of the mortgage. (Make sure you check with your mortgage broker about each lender's prepayment rules.)

You'll find a blank copy of this form in the appendix, or https://www.vaulttoinvestmentrealestatesuccess.com/resources/.

Online Mortgage Account Activity sample form

Mortgage	Mortgage #	Mortgage Balance	Options for Your Mortgage
Mortgage Statements			
View Your Mortgage Statement			Increase Your Payment by $
Balance of Last Payment	$		Details: You will save $ in interest and pay off your mortgage __weeks sooner.
Accrued Interest	$		
Current Interest Rate	%		Make a Lump Sum Payment
Maturity Date			
Term Start Date			Details: You will save $____ in interest and pay off your mortgage __weeks sooner.
Term	Months		

Remaining Amortization Period	Years, Months		
Original Amortization Period	Years		
Original Mortgage Amount	$		
Payment Details	View Payment Options		
Amount Payable	$		
Payment Due Date			
Payment Frequency	Weekly, Bi-Weekly, Semi-Monthly, Monthly		
Principal + Interest Portion of Payment	$		
Prepayment Details	Make a Payment		
Annual Prepayment Limit	$		
202_ Available Prepayment Amount	$		

For example, if we added fifty dollars to our payment (we pay every two weeks) for the duration of our mortgage, we would save $578.33 and pay our mortgage off twenty-six weeks sooner.

Let's put that in context to Uberizing your investment. Fifty dollars every two weeks as an extra payment works out to $108.33 a month. If I got a part-time job (Uber or other part-time work) and made $12 an hour, I would have to work nine hours part-time for the month to add this additional money to my mortgage principal paydown. Wow, just over two hours a week in part-time work, and I would pay off my mortgage a half a year sooner.

Now it's your turn. Use a mortgage balance of $100,000 to get comfortable and use the above form to develop your own scenario. See how you could impact the amount of time reduced on the mortgage balance and the amount of interest you would save. You can find mortgage calculators on our website (linked below to the Resources tab), your bank's website (look for their mortgage calculator), or software such as Excel (search "mortgage"). These tend to be free resources and are very helpful in understanding the full financial picture.

What if you are more skilled than me at a part-time job and could make $20 an hour? What if you were more ambitious than me and decided to work eight hours a week part-time? What would be the impact of your Uberizing? As you'll see, a little goes a long way.

Have fun—and remember, figures don't lie.

Day 14 Key Recap

Record your key learnings and actionable items in your notebook or the workbook and planning guide. (Optional)

- ⇧ When evaluating affordability, look at term and amortization. Don't overextend yourself; remember, it is much easier to make additional payments if you have the ability than to try to rework financial terms in the early stages of mortgage financing.

- ⇧ It is better to estimate your reasons for owning a small business and how your funds and time will impact your potential return.
- ⇧ When estimating hours diverted to your small business, determine what financial impact you are having and update your net worth statement once a year at the end of current calendar year.

DAY 15 FINANCING: TYING THE ELEMENTS TOGETHER TO MEET DOWN PAYMENT AND REVENUE REQUIREMENTS

Use this day to build your "base" calculations and understand your purchasing power. At the end of the chapter, complete the coaching challenges to lay out your financial information. You'll need to present these traditional components to your lender in order to secure financing.

When it comes to qualifying for a mortgage, there are many pieces to the puzzle. Two important pieces are your personal income and net worth statements, which we created on Day 3; these are components of your financial borrowing base. Lending institutions have different ways of collecting this information. They will often have their own standard forms for this purpose. Don't be offended if they want you to transfer your information onto their forms or into their system. Remember, it is their money you are borrowing.

Passing the Stress Test

When you go for a medical examination, the doctor might send you for a stress test if she suspects your heart might not be functioning properly.

Just like the doctor, the banks and lending institutions have their own stress test for your financial health. You might think you are a financial genius, only to find out you don't even have a passing grade. In a survey of major lenders, as many as 50 percent of borrowers didn't understand what a stress test was. You won't be one of them.

Having income and net worth statements is great, but do they show that you have a healthy, regular financial pulse? The banks and lending institutions will conduct their examination and give you their opinion.

The stress test is part of their examination of your current financial situation. Passing the stress test is how you will qualify for a mortgage loan at a bank or lending institution. You will need to prove you can afford payments at a qualifying interest rate, which is typically higher than the actual rate in your mortgage contract. Credit unions and other lenders that are not federally regulated may choose to use this mortgage stress test.

This is another reason you need to have a great mortgage broker on your Team REAL. Your mortgage broker should be fully aware of the stress test requirements wherever you live and wish to borrow mortgage funds, and should explain them to you.

Part of your stress as an investment real estate investor involves covering the payments on your own in case things go wrong. Can you make the mortgage payments on the investment real estate property if you don't have a tenant for several months? Some lenders will expect you to be able to cover all of the mortgage payments, and some lenders may require you to be able to cover part. Your mortgage broker will know the requirements for each lender.

Lenders reviewing your application will consider whether you can afford a higher interest rate. They take into consideration the higher of the five-year benchmark rate or your approved rate plus two points.

Because of the recent pandemic, we are seeing interest rates at an all-time low, and the U.S. Fed has indicated interest rates will stay low through 2021 and beyond. This is also true for Canada and other nations. But it won't last forever. This pandemic is global, and as vaccines come on the market and the general population gets vaccinated, all governments will need to service the heavy debt from all of the government funds spent on programs to keep their nations operating. At some point, we will see increases in interest rates. Your lender knows this and is keeping one eye on the future.

For example, if you are taking out a mortgage with a 4 percent interest rate, you must be able to afford a 6 percent interest rate. Similarly, someone with a mortgage with a 3 percent interest rate must qualify for a mortgage with a 5 percent interest rate. If the ending rate (in this instance, 4 percent) is lower than the benchmark rate (currently 4.9 percent), you must meet that requirement. If you don't meet at least the benchmark rate, you don't qualify.

Remember, getting the lowest mortgage rate from a lender may not be a good enough reason for you to use them. Instead, you may need a lender who, for example, is more liberal about your ability to cover all or part of a mortgage during a property vacancy. This is an important lesson to learn.

I love the idea of a stress test. Setting your costs higher when budgeting is never a bad thing. The costs to own investment real estate are always fluctuating; after all, few costs ever go down in life. If ten or twenty dollars a month of extra payments on an investment property will put you in a negative cash flow or under financial pressure, don't buy the property.

Remember to work with your mortgage broker and get them to run the scenarios for you based on the current rates in your area. Most lenders have mortgage calculators on their websites, and they are free to use, or you can work with Excel or other software programs. Type in "mortgage," and a free spreadsheet will pop up that you can use to run your scenarios.

Throughout this book, I discuss building a contingency expense into your monthly budget. The more you know about the breakdown of expenses, how an income statement for your investment real estate property works, and how to read the income statement, the better you will be able to present your case to your lender. As Sir Francis Bacon said, "Knowledge is power."

Sweat Equity

Don't underestimate the power of your skills. When purchasing a property, can you look for an underpriced property that has good bones and only needs some TLC to add instant value to the home?

If you are required to get an appraisal done, see if you can pay a little bit more to have the appraiser give you a price for if certain work like painting, replacing the carpet, and landscaping is done to increase the value. This additional value will come in handy down the road.

I will mention the added value of the property during Day 15, when we are discussing the length of term and how financing renovations can produce more value.

A Word About Team REAL

Before we look at how to present your information, here are a few items to think about.

At the end of Day 18, we will move into Stage II of the book. Stage II is all about assembling your Team REAL—your personal real estate advisory league.

Each member of your team can and will make purchasing and renting your first investment real estate property much easier. Your team members are skilled and educated in their respective professions. These folks have spent years in college or university, being supported and trained by their employers and the organizations of their professional designation.

Don't try and circumvent using these professionals on your team. They have the knowledge and skills that will lead you to success. And in most cases, you won't pay them any fees until you have purchased a property.

Fault Lesson

Early in my career, I started my first attempt at entrepreneurship. We built a company of multiple convenience stores, restaurants, and clothing stores. Half of our stores were in great locations, with great revenue and net earnings, and the other half weren't in such good locations, with low revenue, and we were losing money at the bottom line.

When we were setting up our company, our lawyer recommended we keep each store incorporated separately so if any location did not work out, we could close that store without affecting the other stores. It cost money to incorporate each store on its own. We didn't listen and set up a holding company instead.

What took us five years to build came smashing down. The poor-performing stores' financial weight was too much. We tried to liquidate the bad stores and keep the good stores, but it was too late. I had started out as a twenty-one-year-old owner of a thriving retail company, and it abruptly came to an end. And by this time, I had a wife, two children, and a mortgage payment. My entrepreneurial dreams were put on hold for a decade. Had we listened to the advice of the lawyer, things might have turned out differently.

Soliciting the advice of your Team REAL can help you avoid making mistakes that could topple your investment real estate business, or prevent it from even getting off the ground. Part of your presentation to your lender will be about how you are using your Team REAL to purchase and rent out your first investment property. Your lender will see you are mature and smart enough to realize you are not the expert in most areas of investment real estate.

There is a story about someone asking Albert Einstein for his telephone number, and Einstein said, "I don't know my phone number." The person looked at Einstein, dumbfounded. Einstein said, "No worries, I know where you can find my phone number: in the phone book." Pure genius.

Through your Team REAL, you have a chance to create a solid presentation to your lender and look like a pure genius.

Your Financial Information

Your financial information is the biggest determining factor in whether or not you get a mortgage loan. The most important rule for laying out your financial information to present to a lender is don't complicate things—keep it simple.

First, collect your net income and net worth numbers, which we determined on Day 3. In addition to these, there is one other important number you should know.

Your Credit Score

A credit score is a number assigned to an individual to represent their ability to repay a loan. It is considered by lenders when deciding whether or not to lend someone money.

Therefore, it's important to understand your credit score as you put together your presentation.

But before looking at your credit score, it is vital to understand who is creating your credit score and how your score is derived. Your credit score is not like a credit rating. You might have heard about credit ratings on the news when they refer to a country or company's credit rating. This rating is a letter: Triple A, Double A, A, and so forth, down to Triple C. Companies that deal with credit ratings are credit rating agencies.

A personal credit score is generally a three-digit number. In simple terms, your credit score impacts the size of a loan you might qualify for or the interest rate of the loan. Many property management companies will source your credit score before they rent to you, and I have even heard that employers will check your credit score before offering you a job.

Credit bureaus supply your personal credit reliability information. There are three large credit bureaus: Equifax, Experian, and TransUnion. They are all headquartered in the United States, but in many cases, they have a global reach. These bureaus all collect much the same information.

What is the range of credit scores, and what does it mean? While every creditor defines its own range for credit scores, the average FICO score range (a score created by the Fair Isaac Corporation) is often used:

Excellent: 800 to 850

Very Good: 740 to 799

Good: 670 to 739

Fair: 580 to 669

Poor: 300 to 579

You may also find that your credit score varies from bureau to bureau. Why? Not all companies will pull your credit information from all three bureaus. These bureaus charge a fee, and companies may have a stronger relationship with different companies.

There are also free credit score companies like Credit Karma. I signed up for Credit Karma's free service, and when I ran my report, I noticed something interesting. I deal with two primary banks, and I noticed one bank had supplied more information about me than the other bank and other credit card companies.

You should be aware of your credit score and how it affects your borrowing amount and interest rates. Signing up for a free service like Credit Karma is a great place to start. As I have mentioned in the past, you should know as much about yourself as your lenders do. Forearmed is another excellent way to look like a professional investor.

Julia Kagan authored a great article about credit scores on Investopedia. I encourage you to read it for a deeper understanding.

Do your research and make sure you know your credit score before contacting a lender. If there are any discrepancies on your credit score, make sure you reach out to the service and clear it up.

It is also important to remember that the rules are always changing. The federal governments and lenders change their requirements all the time. A recent example was when the Canadian Mortgage and Housing Corporation (CMHC) announced they were changing their credit rules. They had been accepting personal credit scores of 600 or higher, and on July 1, 2020, they revealed they were increasing the personal credit score requirement to 680.

Don't get caught up with the aforementioned date or number. The government and lenders will always be moving the goal line; after all, it is their money they are lending you.

Your credit history is one other element that the lender will uncover. Making payments on time and staying within your credit card limits are critical to your ability to borrow, and they contribute to determining the interest rate you will pay.

Laying Out Your Financial Presentation to Your Lender

A mortgage loan is a significant amount of money. Therefore, it shouldn't come as a surprise that lenders are never going to take your word about your financial situation. They will do their own research and due diligence to verify that you are telling them the truth. This is why there are credit bureaus, appraisal companies, and many other services that will verify your information for lenders.

When I first started on my investment real estate journey, I went to great lengths to put together my financial information. While preparing for my first presentation at my bank to secure a mortgage for my first-ever investment real estate property, I worked for hours on what I thought the lenders would need. I even developed my own personal financial information binder with beautiful tabs, an index, and pictures of my properties. I thought, "Man, have I ever done a great job." But my enthusiasm came to an abrupt end when I presented to a lender and they went through my binder, pulling out the information they said was relevant to them. They didn't care about the pictures. The lender handed me back my binder and said, "Please take this information and bring it back to us on our forms to be transposed to the banking computer system."

All the information the lender wanted was on my net worth statement, a couple of years of our personal net income statements, and my current payroll voucher.

Step 1: Find Out What They Want, and How They Want It

Either through your mortgage broker or lender, find out what information the lender requires for you to secure a mortgage from them. This one simple question can make your chances of success much better.

It is also important to remember that each lender's rules are different, and what you might have to supply for one lender could be different from what another lender wants. As you assemble your personal financial information, know that having more is good, but all the personal information you gather is, in the end, for you.

Remember, as you work with your bank or lenders, only offer the information they request.

Your personal net income and net worth statements contain much of what the bank or lender will need, such as your income, debt-to-income ratio, assets, and liabilities, but other information will be asked of you as well.

On Day 3, we taught you the importance of both these statements and how to assemble the information. You must keep your financial information current because the credit bureaus collect your personal financial information and update their records every month. You should be as current or even more current than the credit services that are collecting your personal financial information.

Step 2: Gather Your Personal Data

A lot of information is required to apply for a mortgage loan. The standard information includes your tax returns for the last two or three years, your bank statements for a minimum of six months, several pay stubs, and a copy of your driver's license. If you are applying with a partner, spouse, family member, or joint venture partner, you will both be required to provide this information.

As previously discussed on Day 3, your net worth statement should reflect your credit cards, personal and student loans, car loans, child support, outstanding balances on your personal income tax, and any other lines of credit or personal loans. Don't be surprised if some banks or lenders even want the file number for each loan.

Be totally honest, and don't try to conceal any financial information. The bank and lenders will follow up to see that you have not omitted anything. Don't put a bad foot forward—the moment you raise suspicion, you hurt yourself.

A mortgage broker can help you get some idea of what amount of a mortgage you can qualify for and the down payment required. It will help the process along if you know a ballpark figure of what you can qualify for.

It is great to work with the bank or lender and get preapproved for a mortgage amount. With the preapproval, you can move the property purchase along more quickly. Sellers can be impatient and unhappy if you need a long time to get your funds in order. Sellers will often take less if they are sure your funds are in order right off the bat.

High-Ratio Mortgage Lenders

Whether you are in the United States or Canada, if your down payment is less than 20 percent of the house's purchase price, you are required to use a high-ratio mortgage lender.

A high-ratio mortgage lender is a government agency or private company that is prepared to lend you funds for a mortgage that is higher than the traditional loan-to-value ratio of 80 percent. Because there is generally a higher risk to loaning these funds, only the government and a limited number of private companies become high-ratio mortgage lenders. Be forewarned that the interest rates for high-ratio mortgages tend to be higher, and you are often required to pay a percentage of the mortgage amount in advance as insurance against your inability to repay the loan.

The insurance rates for high-ratio mortgages can range from 2.4 to 4.5 percent; you need to do your research. Being aware of these additional costs is important as you go through the loan process.

Some of the private high-ratio mortgage lenders may use an underwriter to arrange for insurance. These underwriters will also confirm all of the financial information you have provided.

In Canada, there is also a government agency called the Canadian Mortgage Housing Corporation (CMHC) that will lend you money for a high-ratio mortgage.

Lending institutions will require an appraisal of the property to ensure it is in the general worth of what you are paying, and you, as the borrower, will have to pay for the appraisal service.

You will also be required to pay the legal fees (to a lawyer, another member of your Team REAL) for closing the deal at your end.

If you are starting to think there are costs associated with investment real estate beyond just the property's price, you are correct. On Day 16, we will start to lay out those costs.

Develop your own credit stress test and lead yourself to approved mortgages, loans, and credit cards.

In this coaching challenge, we're going to test your credit position.

First, let's talk about your credit history. Let's review your tendencies with credit over the last twenty-four months. Answer the below questions honestly; remember, this is a self-assessment.

1) How are you paying your accounts? Are you paying more than the minimum amount due? (Circle Yes or No). Credit bureaus tend to reward those who pay more than the minimum.

2) Debt amount trends – Is your debt higher or lower through the last twenty-four months? Circle Higher or Lower.

3) Available credit card debt – Imagine you have multiple credit cards and your credit available to you, combined, is $10,000. What percentage are you using every month? As a general rule, credit bureaus like to see you using no more than 35 percent. Are you lower or higher than 35 percent every month? Circle Higher or Lower.

4) Have you had any bankruptcies, collections, or late payments? Circle Yes or No. Credit bureaus tend to frown upon these items.

Did your self-assessment credit score ready you for mortgage time?

Mortgage stress tests assess your ability to repay a mortgage. In most cases, a mortgage stress test only applies to borrowers who have at least a 20 percent down payment. But I believe that this part of getting ready to purchase and rent investment real estate applies to everyone. You should always be testing yourself to see where you are at financially and ensure you can pass a mortgage stress test with confidence. Why would you go to a lender and not know yourself and your financial situation better than they do? That's why today's coaching challenge is in two parts: your big-picture credit score and your mortgage stress test.

Don't get stressed out—it is fun to know your numbers instead of relying on others to do it all for you.

The bottom line is this exercise is all about calculating your base—your purchasing power. Bring forward the net amount from your current income statement and your net worth statement, determined in Day 3's coaching challenges, including funds identified for a down payment.

COACHING CHALLENGE 32
Lay out your financial information to present it to a lender.

Each lender has different requirements, so you need to understand each lender's unique needs. For my first presentation to a lender, I went all out, crafting a special binder just for them with pictures of my properties and tabs organizing tons of information. After my presentation, the lender's financial agent took my binder, removed what they needed, and handed back the rest—about 70 percent of the binder's content. I don't want this to happen to you.

You'll have to fill out most of the information on a lender's internal form. In today's digital world, the person making the ultimate decision might be thousands of miles away in a different part of the country. If the lender's agent has to transfer your information from your form to theirs, it will cause delays and aggravation.

The first step in today's challenge is to ask your mortgage broker or lender for their specific list of items; don't give them any more information than they need. The lenders have a system and you need to stick to it.

Don't let the digital age stop you from meeting the lender's lending specialist in person. Building a relationship with them is important to your success. If you have an in-person relationship, great; if you don't, talk to the specialist over the phone, and get them to email you the form you will be required to fill out. Make an appointment with the specialist in person, and give yourself some time to fill out the form completely, with accurate information. Don't email the form if you have never met the person.

At the appointment, you will present the information to the lender. Make sure you have completed the information to the best of your ability. Take hard copies of information they have requested through their form.

Now it's your turn. Lay out your financial information to present to a lender.

- Don't present any property information, including pictures, that does not pertain to the property you are purchasing. Bring in a copy of the offer to purchase.
- Fill out the lender's form to the best of your ability. This will include personal information (e.g., a copy of your photo ID, employment information, financial statement, and your assets and liabilities with a net worth line). You will also need to provide any information regarding you providing indirect liability as a guarantor.

- The reason for borrowing the money, such as first mortgage, secondary financing, down payment amount, or purchase price.
- Review the lender's filled-out form with them. If you have a laptop or tablet, it would be neat to review the form with the lender right in their office, and if any changes are made, you can email them the corrections before you even leave their office. By making the lender's agent's job simpler, it shows how organized you are and helps them say yes to your financial request more easily.

Remember to digitize everything that a lender's specialist might want a copy of. If they don't have to scan your information, you have saved them time. Also, make sure you title each attachment with the proper name or description of what it contains. If you are self-employed, you may be asked for additional information; each lender is different.

Day 15 Key Recap

Record your key learnings and actionable items in your notebook or the workbook and planning guide. (Optional)

- ⇧ When creating your personal stress test, you must be totally honest with yourself. (Remember, it is part of the credit bureaus' job to unearth discrepancies you might omit.)

- ⇧ It is better to estimate the value of sweat equity to see how a small investment for improvements can impact the appraised value of the property once the renovation or repair work is done.
- ⇧ Update your understanding of what information lenders require, and assemble these items in advance of your first visit to a lender. Think of how being prepared will offer a great first impression.
- ⇧ Knowing in advance the percentage you will require for the down payment helps. Being self-employed can carry a different set of financial down payment requirements and result in higher scrutiny by lenders.

 DAY 16 THE COSTS TO PURCHASE

Use this day to identify all of the costs involved in purchasing your first investment real estate property. At the end of the chapter, complete the coaching challenges to discover how much you need to save or acquire. There are more upfront costs to purchasing than simply the down payment percentage.

Most high-value purchases, whether it's a home, a vehicle, or a luxury item, have something in common: they tend to involve additional costs.

An excellent example of this is the purchase of a new car. While the car has a sticker price, that figure doesn't reflect everything that you might pay in the end. The additional costs could include safety features, rust-proofing, maintenance package, insurance beyond collision, upgrades, and other such things. Typically, the dealerships or lenders will offer you the chance to add these extra costs to your monthly payment, easing the financial burden.

Just like a new vehicle, investment real estate is a high-value purchase, which means it's no exception to this rule.

Today, I am going to outline the additional costs you may encounter when purchasing an investment property. Have you set aside funds for these expenses, or do you need to think about requesting these expenses get added to your mortgage principal? How much of these costs will your lender allow you to add, and what will you need to save to purchase the house?

Property Appraisal

When you apply for a mortgage, the lender will request that you get a property appraisal done before they agree to the specific amount. Having an appraisal done will give you the peace of mind that you have paid the right amount for the property. In general, an appraisal fee will range from $300 to $500.

Legal Fees

As the buyer, you are responsible for your legal end of the transaction and all the closing costs. This is one of the most important expenses you have.

A lawyer will protect your investment. Real estate is an important asset; in fact, for most people, it's their most valuable asset. People have been known to use their real estate as collateral to secure funds or loans for other items they may want to purchase.

With your legal team's help, you can ensure there are no caveats registered against the property.

Simply put, *caveat* means caution or warning. Think about a pie. It is tasty, but the caveat about the pie is that if you eat too much, you could pack on the pounds.

A caveat is a notice that certain actions may not be taken without informing the person who gave the notice. You don't want to be responsible for other people's debts.

Legal fees can be either a flat fee or a percentage of the mortgage, such as 1 percent. Do your homework—flat-fee rates tend to be less expensive, from $500 to $1,000, and the results are the same.

Property Taxes

Generally, property taxes are your responsibility after the purchase of the property; however, if the current owner has paid the property taxes in full for the year, you will be assessed your portion for the balance of the year. In other words, if you take possession of the home on October 1 and the full year's taxes have been paid, your portion in the sale transaction would be three months.

Property Inspection Indirect Costs

A property inspection can be critical to the purchase of your investment real estate. Always have the property inspected before committing to purchase. You may be happy with the price for the property until the property inspector uncovers certain deficiencies you had not expected. The positive thing about any deficiencies you may not have seen yourself is that, as a buyer, you can always add that the work be done at the owner's expense before you agree to purchase and take possession of the property.

Some common examples of deficiencies include the home's insulation, roofing, or hot water tank venting. Over the years, building regulations change, and people sometimes unknowingly will have something replaced (e.g., a hot water tank) according to the old bylaws.

You will often be able to ask the property owner to address and fix these deficiencies at their cost, or you can ask for them to drop the price of the property, and you will deal with the issues when you take possession.

Remember, the property owner may not agree to all of the deficiencies or to paying to address these issues. There are some items you might have to pay for out of your own pocket. Fees for these types of things may range, on average, from $300 to $500.

Miscellaneous Regional Costs

Each jurisdiction has their own expenses. Remember, you need to work with a lawyer, real estate agent, and mortgage broker to see what may pertain to your area. Such expenses can include things like land surveys, land transfer tax, harmonized sales tax, etc.

Maintenance and Equipment

Sometimes there are costs associated with maintenance or equipment, such as appliances, renovations and repairs, service hook-up fees, condominium fees, gardening expenses, or snow-clearing equipment. Not all these expenses may impact you, but be aware.

Insurance Costs

When it comes to investment real estate, there are different insurance costs involved. These include life insurance, mortgage insurance, owner's insurance on the property, and title insurance.

You need to look closely at life and mortgage insurance. Generally, with mortgage insurance, the rate stays the same for the duration of your amortization period. Another option is term life insurance, which means you take out insurance for the length of time of the term of your mortgage. As you pay the principal amount down, you can reduce the amount you need to cover.

For example, say the original mortgage was $100,000. At the end of the five-year term, the mortgage balance is $85,000. This means you could lower your costs by covering less of the mortgage balance. Most insurance is based on your age. Don't forget, you are aging, and there may not be huge cost savings at the end of five years on a lower amount. To determine what's best for your situation, talk to the insurance agent on your Team REAL.

I hope all of these potential expenses don't scare you off. The fact is, all investments come with costs. You need to determine which costs affect you and which costs are necessary for your circumstances.

Costs That You Can Finance

Sometimes it's possible to finance some of your costs of purchase. For example, you could add other costs to your mortgage, such as mortgage insurance for high-ratio mortgages, and renovation and repair costs.

As an investor, you need to watch the upfront costs of covering all the costs you add to your mortgage; it can be tempting.

But can the rent for your investment real estate property cover the additional mortgage amount and still give you positive cash flow?

According to Mortgage Managers Brokerage Inc., to obtain high-ratio mortgage insurance, your lender will pay the insurance premium. The lender will usually pass this cost on to you. The premium payable is based on a percentage of the home's purchase price that is financed by a mortgage. You can pay the premium in a single lump sum, but most clients finance it in their mortgage and pay for it in their monthly payments.

Make sure you shop around on the cost of high-ratio insurance. Like in all areas of finance, costs for services vary and the difference can be significant on a mortgage of several hundred thousand dollars.

In the United States, there are several private mortgage insurers (PMIs) that work with your mortgage broker to review rates in your area. In Canada, there is CMHC (the Canadian Mortgage and Housing Corporation), which will provide high-ratio insurance that generally runs between 2 and 4 percent of your mortgage amount. There are also PMIs in Canada, but you have less choice.

Adding renovation costs to your mortgage can be a bit more difficult. Generally, lenders like the renovations to be done before closing and are not big fans of adding the renovation costs to the mortgage. Lenders tend to allow renovation and repair costs to the mortgage as long as the property appraisal is higher than the purchase value.

You may have to wait a few years before you can refinance your mortgage to fund renovation costs. You're hedging your bet that the property will appreciate in value over the next number of years, and your mortgage paydown will be substantial enough to add this amount to your mortgage refinancing.

This does not mean a lender will never add the renovation costs into the mortgage amount. Each lender has different lending rules. Some lenders allow you to compile these additional costs and add them to your mortgage amount. Your mortgage broker can help you find a lender who is friendly to this.

Your appraiser might also be prepared to add the costs of renovations and repairs to the property appraisal with the assurance you will have the work completed upon possession of the house.

It is also important that you use your real estate agent to negotiate any renovation or repair costs into the price on your behalf and leave you some wiggle room. Many times, the seller will pay to have repairs and maintenance done and purchase new appliances. Don't be afraid to ask. Some sellers may not want to handle the work but will take the cost of repairs, maintenance, and appliances off the property's price.

Always try and make the purchase a win-win for both the buyer and seller. Don't miss out on purchasing a great property over the cost of a dishwasher or a small incidental.

Saving Money on Renovations and Repairs

The best way to save money on renovations and repairs is to do it yourself. In the beginning of becoming an investment real estate investor, you should take inventory of your trade skills or those of your spouse, partner, or joint venture partner.

There are also plenty of trade schools where you can take night or weekend courses on certain skills. Painting tends to be a skill many folks can acquire, along with framing and drywalling. If you are not up for the trade-skills learning, or can't see yourself being any good at it, don't do it. Tenants and potential buyers can spot a hack job a mile away.

If you are up for the challenge, though, you can save yourself hundreds to thousands of dollars in renovation costs and add real value to your home. You get paid on the back end when you go to sell the property, or receive upfront and immediate payback when tenants are willing to pay a higher amount of rent.

Conclusion

When you are making an investment of this size in your financial future, you need to be aware of all the costs associated with the purchase. Unlike most purchases, many factors affect this acquisition. For instance, not many purchases require you to assemble an experienced team to carry them out! Remember to keep all your receipts and records of expenses. You are running a small business, and as an entrepreneur, good record-keeping goes a long way to ensuring you have captured all your expenses. Most of these expenses will be tax-deductible.

 **Identify the costs to purchase.**

We learned today about the many additional costs associated with purchasing your first investment real estate property. In this coaching challenge, we're going to put together a list of the additional costs to purchase, so you understand how much money you truly need to make this happen, and how you might manage these costs.

Use the table below to determine your costs to purchase. Once you have a number identified, you need to review and decide how you might address these additional costs. In Coaching Challenge 34, we will set out a task to assign the amounts.

We will decide what costs you can get the seller to cover by either lowering the price of the property or negotiating with the seller to have the work done at their expense before you take possession of the property, or decide what funds you can set aside.

List of Additional Costs to Purchase

Type of Expense	Cost ($)	Who Covers the Cost and How
Property Appraisal		
Legal Fees		
Property Taxes		
Property Inspection		

Miscellaneous Regional		
Maintenance		
Appliance Replacement		
Insurance		
Reno Repairs		

Members of your Team REAL should be able to recommend several companies for each of the expenses outlined above. Ensure you get a minimum of two quotes per service, product, or professional. Don't forget, there is also a personality fit to consider. Saving a few dollars is not worth the hassle if you don't get along with someone. Ask for references for these professionals, and ensure you follow up.

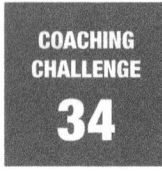

COACHING CHALLENGE 34 — Identify the costs you might be able to finance and why.

In the purchase of investment real estate, there are often extra costs involved. Some of these costs can be negotiated with the seller; either they can lower the purchase price or they can take care of the issue before the possession date. In other cases, the costs will be your responsibility. Sometimes these can be included in the mortgage balance.

In your notebook or the workbook and planning guide, determine the costs you might be able to finance in each of these categories and state why.

Option 1) Total Costs and Lower Purchase Price:

Option 2) Total Costs and Pay by Seller before Possession Date:

Option 3) Costs to be Covered by Buyer upon Possession:

Before making a decision to add any amount to your mortgage balance, consider how it will impact your monthly costs of operation for your investment property. Keep this additional charge in mind as we move forward in reviewing your monthly cash flow. Is it remaining positive and healthy?

Day 16 Key Recap

Record your key learnings and actionable items in your notebook or the workbook and planning guide. (Optional)

- ⇧ When identifying additional costs to purchase the investment real estate property, you must decide the best option to fund these: having the seller lower the price, having the seller take care of the issue before the possession date, or paying the cost yourself (either out of pocket or on your mortgage).
- ⇧ Before locking in the final price with the seller, it's better if you can negotiate for the seller to lower the selling price to offset the additional expense items.
- ⇧ Keeping a positive monthly cash flow is critical to the value of the income property.

DAY 17 FUNDING: YOUR SOURCE OF FUNDS DETERMINES YOUR FINANCING NEEDS, AND HOW TO PRESENT YOUR CASE

Use this day to dive into the funding of investment real estate. At the end of the chapter, complete the coaching challenges to discover what your funding success will look like, set your funding goals, and take your next step toward readying your presentation.

Funding is the act of providing financial resources, usually in the form of money or other values such as effort or time, to finance a need, program, or project.

Sources of funding include banks, credit unions, financial institutions, joint venture capital, gifts, grants, savings, subsidies, family, lending clubs, and more. Funds can be allocated for either short-term or long-term purposes.

Short-term funding purposes are one-offs and range from several hundreds of dollars to a couple of thousand dollars. Some examples are purchasing professional services, home appraisals, home inspections, legal work beyond the property purchase (e.g., joint venture agreement), appliance or heating and cooling system maintenance, light landscaping work, and touch-up work around the interior and exterior of the house. If you make a list of these short-term costs, you can develop a plan to pay for them.

Long-term funding purposes include mortgage financing, possibly mortgage insurance, liability and work-interruption insurance, other forms of insurance coverage, property taxes, and condo fees.

Remember, your tenant should be responsible for tenant contents insurance and utilities.

All About Lenders

There are so many types of lenders and lending practices in today's world.

The good news is that means there is a lending solution out there for you and your circumstances. Taking the time to research this area of financing is so important. Long gone are the days of thinking your bank is your only mortgage solution.

So what are these other options? Easy: they're mortgage lenders, which differ from mortgage brokers. The broker is your representative between you and the lender. The lender pays the broker's fees. Mortgage lenders come in several categories, which we'll get into in a minute.

Every location is different, so it is important to research mortgage lenders and mortgage brokers in the jurisdiction in which you'll be making your investment real estate purchase.

When you are looking at lenders and brokers in your area, dig a little deeper. Most lenders' websites have their interest rates posted, along with the length of time for those rates. All you have to do is visit these sites to learn more about their services.

As a borrower, you need to look at the fine print and know your credit rating. Many times, the posted or advertised rates are for clients with the best credit scores, and when you get in front of the lender, you'll often find you are not offered these rates.

On the other hand, if you have an excellent credit score and history, you might be able to negotiate a better rate. If you don't ask, you will never receive. Remember, the lenders make more profit from your transaction if they can get you to accept a higher interest rate.

Listed below are the different types of lenders. Often, each lender is sourcing the money they are lending to you. If they are borrowing money to lend to you, they are paying someone for these funds, and as a result, you will pay more.

If you need to build a credit history and a better credit score, you might pay more for the privilege to borrow money. You may borrow money at higher costs, having a plan in mind to refinance these funds with a different borrower at a lower interest rate down the road.

If the numbers work and you can purchase a property at a higher interest rate and still maintain a positive cash flow each month, the cost to borrow may not be an issue. In the short term, you are looking to acquire your first investment real estate property.

Review the list of lenders and their processes below, and shop around for a mortgage broker who gives you access to multiple categories of lenders.

When reviewing mortgage brokers, ask each mortgage broker what type of access they have to lenders. All mortgage brokers are paid fees to bring your mortgage to the lender and are compensated accordingly. Some mortgage brokers try to influence you to use a particular lender; a broker should do their analysis on you and the financial conditions required to buy the property you are interested in. Don't forget—the lowest interest rate may not be your primary need.

Types of Lenders and Their Process:

1) **Bankers** may lend you the funds and then sell your mortgage into a secondary market. For example, in the United States, this might be Fannie Mae or Freddie Mac.
2) **Retail lenders** have physical branches or outlets offering checking and savings accounts and other financial products.
3) **Direct lenders** have limited branches, mostly online. You'll rarely deal with them face-to-face.
4) **Portfolio lenders** use their own money, and their lending guidelines are different from other lenders.
5) **Wholesale lenders** use third-party funds.
6) **Warehouse lenders** tend to offer short-term money (loans for a year or two), and these funds are sold to a secondary market.
7) **Hard money lenders** should be used as a last resort. The loans are shorter term, with higher interest rates. These lenders tend to attract house-

flippers. House-flippers like to purchase, renovate, and turn around and sell the house quickly.

Alternative Funding Options: Thinking Outside of the Inheritance Box

A friend of mine who is an investment real estate investor approached me with a dilemma. We'll call her Rachel. She and her husband had run out of sources of down payment funds. I wrote an article on this subject for a major investment real estate magazine and have posted the full article, "The Gift That Keeps On Giving," under the media tab on my website, vaulttoinvestmentrealestatesuccess.com.

Rachel's mother told Rachel she was going to leave her $70,000 as part of her inheritance. The only stipulation was that Rachel would receive the funds when her mother passed away. Rachel's mother's health was great, so Rachel wouldn't see these funds until sometime in the distant future.

In this book, I've been discussing the idea that investment real estate will help you build a strong financial foundation, unlock sustainable wealth, and create a living legacy. Can you guess how this idea applies to Rachel's situation?

My advice to Rachel was to demonstrate to her mom how the inheritance could help Rachel's family now, when Rachel's kids were in contact with their grandma every week, and the kids were a big part of their grandma's life.

The idea I shared with Rachel was to approach her mom with a radical idea: "You don't have to die to enjoy your inheritance gift." Instead, Rachel's mom's inheritance gift would be part of her living legacy.

Hand-Up

I personally don't believe in the "feet first" method of distributing your wealth to your family—meaning it only happens when you die—but this is how most people go into death. They leave their estate behind to be distributed to family members. The family members generally take these funds and put them into lifestyle spending. It does not take long to forget where the funds came from; there's no evidence of any legacy to be had. I really believe this story about Rachel's mom demonstrates my point.

I have had the great fortune to work with many younger clients throughout my career, and their energy and generosity have always been appreciated.

Rachel is a Gen Xer, a past business associate who is now a friend. She and her husband have been investing for a few years now, but as I mentioned earlier, they have been roadblocked by the lack of investment funds to purchase more investment real estate.

Rachel's mother and father retired several years ago to a warmer climate and started to live the dream; a few years into the parents' dream, Rachel's father passed away. Her mother, who had made friends in her new hometown, realized as she aged that these friends her age were not in any position to take care of her in her old age, as they were all facing the same issues.

Rachel's mother had been toying with moving back to the colder climate to embrace her family's support and love. And with Rachel's mother being in excellent health, the family support could be a two-way street.

Rachel's mom did not want to give Rachel's inheritance to her early because of Rachel's sister. The mother was planning to split her wealth between her two daughters. Both daughters were close in age, but one was very much about lifestyle and frivolously spent everything she and her husband earned. Rachel's mother was worried that this daughter would just blow the money, and it would all be gone before the mother even left this world. Rachel's mom knew giving this daughter the funds would bother her all the way to the grave, and she'd have to watch her legacy go down the proverbial drain.

A Hand-Up

The "hand-up" philosophy I propose is to hand out your inheritance before you leave this world so you can see how the people you are leaving your estate to are building a better life for their family.

Rachel had her kids involved in helping to clean the houses they rented when the houses became vacant. I suggested to Rachel that, with the love and attention her mom was giving her girls, why not invite her mom to the next rental house they cleaned and let her see how engaged the girls were in the family rental housing business?

Taking my advice, the family headed to the next rental house cleaning together. Rachel's mom was impressed at how her granddaughters jumped into action and helped clean the home, and how much they understood about the business. She also knew the goal for Rachel and her husband was to earn enough positive cash flow by the time the girls went to college or university to fund part or all of their schooling.

A few days after working with the girls on the rental property, Rachel's mom surprised Rachel by telling her she would give her the inheritance now to help the family purchase more properties. The excitement Rachel and her family showed to Rachel's mother was incredible; they knew this hand-up would help them achieve more positive cash flow to enrich all of their lives.

Showing your folks or someone who is going to leave you an inheritance the advantages of leaving a living legacy is a great way to secure the funds you need for a down payment on an investment real estate property. Remember, you need to have a clear paper trail with your banker and accountant. These funds will be viewed as a gift, and each lender has a form you must have filled out by the person giving you the gift of funds for the down payment. You must handle this properly so you don't get in trouble with the taxation department. To help ensure you are approaching it correctly, talk to the members of your Team REAL. Speak to your accountant first; they should have experience with gifting and how the funds should be handled on your tax return. Many lenders have their own forms for money given as a gift—talk to the lender, get the form, and review the form with your accountant and the person gifting you the money.

Take time to review your investment real estate strategy and choose a lender whose process best fits you. And don't be afraid to be a little flexible. As you start your investment real estate business, you might adopt a different business model down the road.

This is where I appeal to all boomers to use this book as a blueprint to avoid distributing your wealth feet-first and instead look at leaving this world and your inheritance as a hand-up. Now is the time to open your vault to smart investing that creates returns for generations to come while giving you a first-class life.

It's Someone Else's Sandbox, So Learn to Play Nice

In today's world, there is more pressure than ever for proof of a down payment. It was tough enough for you to earn and save the funds, and now how you put these funds together will be questioned.

As I have mentioned before, you are the one borrowing someone else's money and playing in their sandbox. If you want access to the mortgage funds, you need to adhere to the lender's rules.

In Canada, for example, due to the [Proceeds of Crime (Money Laundering) and Terrorist Financing Act,](#) you are mandated to provide a full ninety-day history of the account or accounts (checking, savings, RRSP, mutual funds, etc.) where your down payment is. You are required to provide proof of the source of deposits over $1,000, excluding payroll.

Remember, the people asking the questions are only doing their job and complying with the law. You need to keep your cool and be forthcoming with the information regarding your down payment.

The down payment can come from a combination of sources. These sources can be, for example, a secured or unsecured line of credit, the sale of a property, the sale of an asset (like an RV, boat, etc.), a gift from a family member, an RRSP, stocks, mutual funds, or multiple bank accounts, savings or checking.

There is also a popular savings account vehicle in the United States and Canada called a Tax-Free Savings Account (TFSA). Make sure you understand the rules behind your TFSA in your country.

You will need to provide proof in the form of bank statements, a gift letter, proof of sale, statement of accounts, sales contracts, and/or any other documentation that will support your ability to have proof of the down payment.

If you have to liquidate these assets for cash, make sure you leave yourself ample time before closing.

If you are sourcing your down payment from multiple sources, double-check your math and make sure all these sources add up to the total down payment required. You don't want to create problems at closing because you have come up short on your down payment.

This is why having great members of your Team REAL is critical to keep you on course. They're your checks-and-balances team.

Preparing Your Presentation to Obtain Funding

When preparing your presentation to obtain funding, your mortgage broker can be invaluable. Why? Because they will go through everything the primary lender will need for you to secure the mortgage funding.

Working with a mortgage broker, you will not be embarrassed or unprepared for your presentation. Your mortgage broker will ensure you get your documentation in order.

The broker will give you a guide to what is required. Remember, each lender has its own rules and regulations, and the mortgage broker will sift through your information. The mortgage broker may collect more information than required. It is this preplanning that gets you to "yes" more quickly.

By following the information I provide and having it available at your fingertips, you will be your mortgage broker's new best friend. If you set a good impression from the start, when you go to put your next investment real estate purchase together, your mortgage broker will be more engaged and happier to help.

Steps on how to present are included in Coaching Challenge 36.

Two Words: Over-Deliver

When putting together your investment real estate presentation for financing, the most important thing is to over-deliver. If you are not familiar with the term *over-deliver*, I encourage you to adopt these two words into your investment real estate life.

Most folks like to do just what is expected of them and no more. When you go above and beyond, it's reflected in the results.

Success comes from you adding value to everything you do. I can tell you from experience that adding just one thing someone never expected from you comes as a pleasant surprise to most folks, and this is how people remember you.

Ask questions, find out what is expected of you, and then add one more item or action.

Documents Required for Your Lending Presentation

Below is a list of the documents commonly required when making a presentation to a broker for your investment real estate. There may be other documents; check with your mortgage broker about the detailed requirements for your targeted lenders or situation.

Proof of Income from Employment: This can be an employment letter, recent pay stub, or any bonus, overtime, or shift differential. If you are on maternity leave, you will need an employment letter confirming the date you return to work and your income.

For Self-Employed Individuals: You'll need personal T1s, two years of tax returns, and your company's financials for the most recent year.

For Commission Sales Employment: You'll need a document confirming your length of employment, base salary (if one is provided), and commissions earned year-to-date. Like self-employed individuals, you will need proof of commissions on your T4As, year-to-date payroll stub, or your Notice of Assessment.

On the Homefront: This can include child support and/or alimony and child tax credit information.

Income from Rental Property: As this course is about purchasing your first investment real estate property, you are probably not in a position to worry about this information, but it's important to remember down the road when you go to purchase your next investment real estate property.

Preparation Is Key

Searching for a lender can be intimidating when you've never done it before. But now that you're forearmed with knowledge about the different types of lenders and the information that will be required of you, you'll be in a stronger position to secure a mortgage and present your case with confidence.

> **COACHING CHALLENGE 35** Identify your ideal lender and lending method.

When you are identifying your ideal lender, you must always look at your needs first. Even though you are playing in the lender's sandbox and have to play by their rules, don't get in the wrong sandbox. The world is full of sandboxes, all of different shapes and sizes. Each lender has different lending rules regarding investment real estate; just because your lender is happy to lend you funds for your primary residence doesn't guarantee they will be willing to lend you funds for investment real estate.

Let's look at your conditions. Big-picture answers will work here; each day, we get into more detail. What do you need to address when purchasing your first investment real estate property? Write your answers in your notebook or the workbook and planning guide.

- If you own your own property with a mortgage, would your lender be interested in lending you additional funds for an investment property?
- Is your primary home lender the correct lender for investment real estate mortgages?
- Is there a restriction on what type of property your lender would lend you funds for?
- Will your lender allow you to add the rental income to your income?
- Not to get you off-track, but if you own a bungalow with a separate entrance, for example, your first investment real estate property might be under your feet. Does your zoning allow for secondary suites? Are there grants by your municipality that would enable you to add a secondary suite? Is this a strategy you would consider? If you can convert your basement into a rental suite, the funds to convert may be as simple as seeing if you could remortgage your home to pay for the renovations.
- There might also be a chance that by lengthening your amortization term, you could keep your mortgage payments the same, generating additional revenue while your costs remain static.

COACHING CHALLENGE 36 — Determine your financial resources.

Accessing your financial resources for your investment real estate down payment may be as simple as using your own funds you have saved in a savings account. It could be approaching a family member about an investment opportunity or early inheritance, or it could be using funds you had set aside for another type of large purchase, such as a recreational vehicle.

Take a blank piece of paper and write the heading "Accessing Financial Resources." Start to write down areas in your life through which you may be able to access funds. This is a brainstorming method; no idea or source of funds is unreasonable. Jot down all of your ideas. If you get stumped, walk away from the list for a couple of days, and come back when you are more refreshed. Don't be afraid to ask others for ideas.

 **Prepare a presentation to obtain funding.**

On Day 15, in Coaching Challenge 32, I had you lay out your financial information and get it ready to present to the lender.

In this challenge, we're going to build on that. It is crucial to understand you are not applying for a residential mortgage for a home you are going to live in. This is an investment property that will generate revenue, and you will have tenants.

As we discussed on Day 4, you are going to enter the world of entrepreneurship and small business.

Your presentation is your opportunity to put your best foot forward in hopes of securing a mortgage to purchase an investment real estate property. Learn your lender's needs and give them exactly what they request.

Here are the steps of presenting your business loan proposal. Write down the details to each step in your notebook or workbook and planning guide).

1. Make an appointment. You cannot simply walk in off the street; instead, you need to call ahead and make an appointment for a specific time. You need to have a plan, so gather the information from Day 15 and the business plan

you prepared. It should be as perfect as possible, accurate, and complete. (Time and Date of Appointment: _____)

2. Overdress. In today's world, we all tend to dress casually. Dress to impress, looking sharp and like you are serious. Remember, the amount you want to borrow is a serious amount of money. (What are you going to wear? _____)

3. Be thorough. From Day 15, you already know what the lender is looking for, so have all of this financial information ready. The lender should be pleasantly surprised by the information you present.

4. Have the other information the lender might need with you. Refer to the list above, with items such as letter of employment, the last two years of tax returns, etc. Know your lender! (List of information you will need: _____)

5. Be brief and know what you are going to say. People are busier than ever, so don't waste their time. Do a mock presentation in front of your spouse or partner and time how long it takes. (Did you set a time to present to your spouse or partner? When and where? _____)

6. Thank the lender for their time.

Lastly, don't put all your eggs in one basket. Have a backup plan and consider alternatives.

Details to Support the Steps Above

If you are using a mortgage broker, they will have access to the requirements of all the lenders they might recommend and how they want your financial information presented.

We talked about playing in your lender's sandbox, and how each lender has different borrowing rules.

Talk to the lender or your broker. Find out what they need to see in an ideal presentation for when you ask them for funding; ask them to describe the perfect presentation and the elements they require (e.g., net worth statement, net income statement, payroll stubs, income tax returns, etc.).

When I first started to present to lenders, I would over-deliver the information they requested. Even though this is a great idea, most lenders are particular in their needs, and too much information is unnecessary documentation. Much of the time, they will hand you back the extra information.

Remember to give them what they have requested from you. It will move the process along in a timelier manner.

In today's digital world, your lender or broker will send you a link where you can fill in their requirements; make sure you are aware of when they want this information completed.

Day 17 Key Recap

Record your key learnings and actionable items in your notebook or the workbook and planning guide. (Optional)

- ⇧ Update your short- and long-term funding needs.
- ⇧ When creating your source of funding, ensure you think about alternatives. Traditional financing sources may be fine, but review all that are available.
- ⇧ It's best to practice your presentation before your actual meeting with the lender.

DAY 18 SMART (SPECIFIC, MEASURABLE, ACCEPTABLE, REALISTIC, TIME-BOUND)

Use this day to review your decision using the SMART goal-setting framework and ensure your foundation is in place. At the end of the chapter, complete the coaching challenges to set your own SMART goal. With a strong foundation, your investment real estate purchase is sure to be a success.

There is a theme in my book that I don't want to conceal. This theme was first attributed to Aristotle, the Greek philosopher, and I first came in contact with this theme, or learning technique, at Toastmasters. Toastmasters is a worldwide organization dedicated to helping individuals improve their public speaking skills.

To write a great speech that the audience will remember, Toastmasters recommends you structure your speech in the following manner:

"Tell them what you are going to tell them, tell them, and then tell them again."

On Day 2, we talked about the concept of goal-setting and its importance; today, we are looking at goal-setting and its application using the SMART method.

You've probably heard of the SMART goal-setting framework before. This acronym has been around for years, it's used in many different fields, and everyone has their own spin on it. Here's my take.

Let's Get Started and Get Smart

Remember Don Adams, aka Maxwell Smart, Agent 86, who starred in the 1960s TV show *Get Smart*? (Yes, all five seasons are available on iTunes.) Or what about the more recent film version with Steve Carell and Anne Hathaway?

Maxwell Smart always tried to complicate every situation, it always got him into hot water, and we all had a good chuckle.

I am not asking you to be a secret agent and complicate the investment real estate world.

You can, however, be knowledgeable, be well trained, and have the tools and tactics you need to complete a successful mission.

Your mission? To purchase and rent your first investment real estate property in thirty-one days.

What Is SMART? The Framework and the Application

Albert Einstein once said, "If you want to live a happy life, tie it to a goal, not people or objects." Well, SMART is all about determining that goal.

SMART is an acronym that stands for Specific, Measurable, Acceptable, Realistic, and Time-Bound. It will give you the knowledge, the tools, and the tactics you need to succeed.

Remember when we discussed the idea of focus and the acronym FOCUS—Follow One Commitment Until Success, back on Day 12? Just like with FOCUS, I'm going to take you through an example of using the SMART tactic. My aim in this book is to get you FOCUSed and SMART, all at the same time.

So let's GET SMART.

SMART Time: Evaluating Your Goals Is the First Piece of the Puzzle

First, you need to evaluate your goals. Take the time to review the following:

1. What am I trying to accomplish?
2. How am I trying to accomplish it?
3. Could there be a better method?

Breaking Down the SMART Acronym

The SMART acronym tells you everything you need to know about goal-setting.

Specific – It should clearly state what you—the who in this equation—want to accomplish, what needs to happen, why it is an important goal, where this goal will take place, when it will take place, why this is happening, and how you intend to accomplish the goal.

When it comes to setting a SMART goal, Specific looks like this:

Goal: To purchase and rent my first investment real estate property in thirty-one days.

Who is setting this goal? *Me and perhaps my spouse or significant other (if applicable), a family member, or a joint venture partner.*

What's the importance of the goal? *It will help me to build a strong financial foundation or portfolio.*

Where will the goal take place? *An area with a high rental demand for the type of property I am are purchasing.*

When will it take place? *In the next thirty-one days.*

Why is this happening? *I'm dissatisfied with my current financial situation and want to control one part of my financial portfolio.*

How do you intend to accomplish the goal? *I'm going to follow the thirty-one days and sixty-one coaching challenges in the book 31 Days to Purchasing and Renting Your First Investment Real Estate Property.*

Measurable – It should include a plan with targets and milestones that you can use to make sure you're moving in the right direction.

In this case, this book provides those targets and milestones over thirty-one days.

Acceptable – It should be a goal that you are willing to put your energy and effort into, and it should include a plan that breaks your overall goal down into smaller, manageable action steps that use the time and resources available to you within the timeline you've set for yourself.

Thirty-one days is a reasonable timeframe; however, you don't necessarily need to execute the days consecutively. For example, you might plan to complete the days and coaching challenges over three months, giving yourself a chance to reflect on and review the work you have completed each day.

Realistic – It should make sense to you when measured against your investment real estate plan, your investment real estate marketplace, your joint venture partner base, or the investment real estate industry.

You should feel comfortable and confident that you can purchase and rent an investment real estate property after following the days and coaching challenges as laid out in the book.

Time-Bound – It is limited by a defined period and includes a specific timeline for each step of the plan. The word *bound* gives the connotation of being compelled, taking a leap of faith, or vaulting to.

In the end, you should have the confidence that, if you follow the work and coaching challenges as laid out in this book, you can meet the target time frame of thirty-one days from start to finish.

I believe that the principles in this book will give you a sense of faith and you'll be able to follow the words of American author John Burroughs: "Leap and the net will appear."

Asking SMART Questions

Part of SMART self-coaching is to ask yourself questions:

- Do you know your investment real estate outcome? (Specific)
- What actions have you taken to make the purchase of investment real estate possible? (Measurable, Acceptable, and Realistic)
- Have you established a date or timeline to purchase your first investment real estate property? (Time-Bound)
- Are you getting closer to or moving away from your investment real estate goal? (Time-Bound)

The best way to achieve your investment real estate dream is to use the SMART formula of goal-setting. Remember, your goal is the final result or outcome of this endeavor—purchasing and renting your first investment real estate property in thirty-one days—and your objective is the specific result that helps you achieve this final goal. Completing the sixty-one coaching challenges is a specific step you can take to help you achieve the purchase and rental of your first investment real estate property.

Applying SMART

The goal "to purchase and rent my first investment real estate property in thirty-one days" is very **Specific**—you want to purchase and rent your first investment real estate property.

It's **Measurable** because each day comes with coaching challenges for you to complete.

Is purchasing and renting your first investment real estate property **Acceptable** to you?

Acceptable is the most difficult of the five steps in the SMART method of goal-setting because this question is solely based on your comfort level.

And is it **Realistic?** By the end of thirty-one days and sixty-one coaching challenges, you will have a plan and feel confident that you can purchase and rent your first investment real estate property.

Finally, is your goal **Time-Bound?** This book comes with a couple of stipulations. The first stipulation is that the process in this book focuses on residential investment real estate. That is not to say you can't buy commercial or multi-family properties in thirty-one days. However, the process would be somewhat different from the one explained here.

It will be up to you to decide if owning multiple investment real estate properties is a path you want to take. Every investment real estate investor has his or her own set of goals, and no one can dictate your goals but you. What I can do, as your coach, is help you realize your goal of owning your first investment real estate property. Whether you're happy to stop at one or you want to go on to purchase more is up to you.

Your First Combined FOCUS and SMART Goal Sample

The Focus: Purchase and Rent My First Investment Real Estate Property

Specific: Myself and My Spouse/Partner (Who)

Measurable: Neighborhood/City/Town (Where)

Acceptable: Start the Investment Real Estate Part of My Financial Portfolio (Why)

Realistic: Do My Income Statement, Net Worth Statement, and Entrepreneurial Profile Set the Financial Base for Purchasing My First Investment Property?

Time-Bound: Specific Date (When)

By setting your investment real estate focus from Day 12 and laying out your SMART goal, you are creating a strong financial base that will lead to lifelong success and economic sustainability for you and your future generations.

Thirty-One Days to Purchasing and Renting Your First Investment Real Estate Property can break down barriers to a road of financial freedom. Are you ready?

Or

Do you find yourself roadblocked because you don't know what success looks like?

Are you unsure how to clarify what you want through investment real estate success?

What will be your catalyst to achieving success?

Is your financial success catalyst tied into time?

Dr. Edward Banfield, a political scientist, did a lot of work on understanding people's financial success and how this success was built up over years and generations. He referred to this attitude as a "long-time perspective." He said that people who were the most successful in life and the most likely to move up economically were those who considered the future with every decision they made in the present.

COACHING CHALLENGE 38

Set a SMART goal.

Wow! The decision to make investment real estate part of your financial foundation sets you on the path Banfield referred to as "long-time perspective."

You are entering a SMART stage in your life that will have a lasting financial impact, create sustainable wealth, and affect generations of your family now and long into the future.

Homes are where many incredible fun and exciting life memories are made. Not only are you creating generational wealth, but you are also building a home for tenants who will make many memories in the housing you provide.

In today's coaching challenge, we're going to apply the SMART framework to your goal, and get some concrete answers.

SMART Goal – "Let's Get SMART"

It's go-time!

We are now more than halfway through the book.

Today is the last day of the Ready stage; tomorrow, you'll start assembling your Team REAL. That means you're well on your way to finding a lender, putting the funds in place, making the offer, and closing the purchase.

Let's try an exercise used by many top athletes. Close your eyes and visualize that you are moments away from getting set in the blocks to start a race. Your blood is flowing as you anticipate the starter firing the pistol.

All of your training has led up to this moment.

- In your notebook, using the workbook and planning guide, or writing in the blanks below, identify "Specific," "Measurable," "Acceptable," "Realistic," and "Time-Bound" in relation to your goal of purchasing your first investment real estate property.

Let's use the general description above and apply it specifically to you:

"S"(WHO?)_____

"M"(WHERE?)_____

"A"(WHY?)_____

"R"(HOW/WHO?)_____

"T"(WHEN?)_____

The purchase and rental of your first investment real estate property is starting to take on a life of its own. Close your eyes, and breathe in and out as your dream becomes a reality.

Day 18 Key Recap

Record your key learnings and actionable items in your notebook or the workbook and planning guide. (Optional)

- ⇧ Use the SMART goal-setting method to lay out the blueprint for a strong investment real estate foundation.
- ⇧ A goal-setting framework can help narrow down your vision of the right investment real estate property.
- ⇧ SMART questions can help you dive deeper into what a successful investment property will look like for you.

Stage II:
Set

Days 19 to 24

STAGE II: SET

SEARCH FOR YOUR INVESTMENT REAL ESTATE TEAM

It takes a village to raise a child. — African proverb

Just like the common saying, "It takes a village to raise a child," it takes a village of people to help you build a successful investment real estate portfolio. That's what Stage II is all about.

Your first investment real estate property and rental is a little like having a child. A child needs plenty of nurturing, care, and attention to grow up and become a fruitful member of society.

When raising children, it is not only Mom and Dad, but also grandmothers and grandfathers, uncles and aunts, sisters and brothers, extended family and friends, teachers and coaches, and a never-ending list of others who contribute to their development.

Similarly, adding a major investment like real estate to your financial portfolio requires a village or a team.

In the next few days, you'll determine who the members of your team should be, what their roles are, where you might find them, at which stage you need them, why they all have a role, and how to assemble the best team for you.

Many folks try and go it alone. If you have ever belonged to a sport, academic, or activities team, you know there is no "I" in team.

There is a common misconception that assembling an expert investment real estate team comes with huge costs. The reality is it's not as expensive as people think. Often, all you have to do is watch someone's YouTube channel to get coached for free.

We will go into depth on creating your own team of experts—your Team REAL (Real Estate Advisory League). In most cases, the cost of assembling a great team is only paid when you use their services.

The golden rule of building a great team is not only to have folks who are like-minded but who have themselves taken the actions you wish to take. Find team members who purchase and rent investment real estate, and you'll position yourself to win.

DAY 19 IDENTIFYING, ASSEMBLING, AND MEETING YOUR TEAM REAL

Use this day to learn to identify, assemble, and work with a personal investment real estate team and other real estate industry intermediaries. At the end of the chapter, complete the coaching challenges to build your own Team REAL. These professionals will help you on your journey.

There is a saying that has its roots in Africa: "It takes a village to raise a child." Purchasing investment real estate is much the same—you need an investment real estate village of folks to help you develop your vault to investment real estate success. This is your Team REAL (Real Estate Advisory League), and having one will make your investment real estate journey a win.

When I first started my investment real estate journey, I found myself in the trap that many of us fall into when assembling an investment real estate team: I did it haphazardly. For example, we found a real estate agent through friends or family when we purchased our primary residential property.

The bank we used for our mortgage was the bank where we had our personal account. This, for many of us, is the bank that is tied into the direct deposit of our paycheck—the bank that our employer was using.

We used a lawyer recommended to us by the bank.

As for our accounting needs, we saw an ad for a national personal income tax company like H&R Block, and away we went. Whether it was the real estate agent, bank mortgage advisor, lawyer, or accountant, none of these people had investment real estate as part of their investment portfolio.

Earlier, I talked about Peter Kinch, a well-known mortgage broker. He revealed that roughly 4 percent of Canadians purchase investment real estate, and in the United States and Australia, the number is about 8 percent. And of those individuals, half never buy more than two or three properties.

We did not have a formal method or guidance for assembling our team—and why would we? With so few people purchasing more than a few revenue homes, the idea of putting together a great team you can work with again and again is never given much thought.

But I want better for you. I want you, as a new investment real estate investor, to do it right the first time.

Our Early Investment Real Estate Experiences: Pre-Team REAL

Our first investment real estate acquisition was an apartment-style condo.

We didn't use a real estate agent who specialized in apartment condos. The one we used knew we were purchasing the condo to rent. If we had used an agent who understood the condo rental market, we could have gotten higher rents from the start. Also, we didn't pay enough attention to the reserve fund for the building, nor did we review the reserve fund study until we had purchased the property. The reserve fund is a long-term maintenance fund for the building, and a reserve fund study is a multi-year projection of work that would need to be done over each year for up to thirty years.

If we had gone with a real estate agent who understood these types of buildings, reserve funds, and the reserve fund study, we would have known before purchasing that the reserve fund didn't have enough cash to handle the work outlined in the reserve fund study. Within a year of our purchase, the condominium board made a cash call for over a million dollars. We only owned one unit in this building, and our share was an extra hundred dollars a month for five years.

We were lucky that not getting a proper Team REAL member on our team didn't cost us our initial investment. We were able to cover the extra amount because we increased the rent. Unfortunately, this extra hundred dollars that would have been positive cash flow was now part of our monthly operating costs.

We had purchased this property with a long-term buy-and-hold strategy, but after five years, we found out another million-dollar cash call was coming, and it would be years before we saw a good positive cash-flowing property.

Because of that, we sold the property for a profit, including the return of our original investment, but we had to start over again with these funds to find the right investment real estate property.

There may have been some luck in this purchase—both property values and rents were going up.

The lessons we learned along the way were incredible.

At the time, we were not assembling any investment real estate team, just an assorted group of non-investment real estate folks. I am not trying to be critical of these folks—if such a small percentage of us is buying investment real estate, what do you think the chances are that these people we hired for the different transactions would have any type of expertise in investment real estate?

We certainly did not get any advice from our banker; he was just happy to have another mortgage. I don't even think we had an accountant; we used H&R Block. We'd never even heard of a bookkeeper; we thought accountants and bookkeepers were one and the same.

None of the professionals involved in our first purchase—not the real estate agent, the lender, nor the person we dealt with at H&R Block—had investment real estate experience.

After that first purchase, we changed our real estate agent, lender, and accountant to professionals who understood and owned investment real estate. Our lawyer not only owned residential real estate but also owned part of the building he ran his legal offices from.

Over the years, I've spent working with rental investment real estate clients, I developed a Team REAL list so that I can connect my coaching clients with the right professionals for their own Team REAL. The list is incredibly valuable. In fact, I'd say that the lessons you are learning about assembling your own Team REAL alone are worth the cost of this book and much more.

As I share more of our stories and those of our joint venture partners, you will see that the sooner you start developing your team, the better.

Doing It Right the First Time

It has taken me a long time to get the right team supporting me, but now I have few worries because I've assembled a group of experts in the field of investment real estate I can rely on for all my investment real estate needs.

I know that putting together a team sounds like a hassle, but trust me on this. Do you remember a time when your folks gave you great advice, but you chose to ignore them, only to say to yourself, years later, "Geez, I wish I had listened to Mom and Dad."

Well, this is the time to take the advice and build the best team—your own Team REAL.

Why Start with the Best Team?

Whether you never purchase more than one investment real estate property or you go on to buy many, the purchase of investment real estate is a big deal, and you should have the best team possible to ensure everything goes smoothly.

Often, working with a team of advisors who aren't knowledgeable about investment real estate investors means you don't get the proper guidance, and you will find yourself going no further.

Your team should have qualities that inspire you to grow your investment portfolio over time.

Chances are, once you get the investment real estate purchasing bug, you will go on to purchase more than one property.

The Importance of Team REAL

Throughout this book, I've been reminding you of the importance of your Team REAL and how their support can make all the difference in your success. The beautiful thing about Team REAL is that you generally never pay them until you have actually purchased your first investment real estate property. The wealth of information they provide would cost you a small fortune if you were paying a school for the same information.

Buy yourself a personal journal and take notes of every meeting you have with members of your Team REAL. Let them know you are taking notes; people tend to be flattered by this. With today's technology, you could also record the conversations on your smartphone, but make sure you ask before you record anyone.

As I've mentioned, I recommend that, when assembling a team, you find members who are investment real estate investors themselves. Why? These professionals will understand what you are trying to do and will thus provide a tailored service.

They will ask questions, request information, and make notes pertaining specifically to investment real estate. Ensure the conversation is a two-way street and ask them how they access knowledge and resources regarding financing and investment real estate.

For example, our lawyer owns investment real estate, and the questions he asks us are different from those asked by a lawyer who only owns his own residential home.

The Members of Team REAL

The right Team REAL helps you on your journey. You can draw from this team's experiences and know you are growing in a safe environment.

Your Team REAL should have, at the bare minimum, a mortgage broker or bank's mortgage specialist, a real estate agent, a lawyer, and an accountant.

The first criteria in hiring any member for your investment team is to find out if they own investment real estate. The answer should be yes. If the answer is no, move on to a different team member—don't wait until later in your investment real estate career.

While I firmly believe investment real estate "takes a village," through my own experience, it is the quality of the folks who live in the village that lead to the real benefit.

This African proverb is the foundation of Team REAL. It takes a team to develop you as an investment real estate investor, and ensuring a high quality of those team members will help you be the best investment real estate investor you can be.

To be the best investor ever, you must understand how to prospect for the best folks. Think about prospecting for gold—some people get rich, some people get a little wealth, and others end up with nothing. How these folks prospect for gold is what creates the return on their investment of time and resources.

What is prospecting? How do you prospect for the right people?

Prospecting means searching for something valuable. In this case, it's the members of your Team REAL that are your valuable resources. You need to treat the people you work with as resources, right from the get-go of your investment real estate journey. Many of these folks need to be with you right from the start and will stay with you right until the end. You need to minimize as many false starts as possible, and this is what great prospecting does.

Prospect Point Number 1

As I mentioned earlier in the book, all of your team members, especially the core members who will be with you over the long haul of your investment real estate acquisition, **need to be investment real estate investors themselves.**

Prospect Point Number 2

Your team members must have incorporated investment real estate as part of their practice. An example would be an accountant. What percentage of their clients is made up of investment real estate investors? You could easily ask your lawyer, real estate agent, or even a trades professional like an electrician or plumber this question. The more experience your team members have with investment real estate, the more chances you have to acquire new knowledge.

Prospect Point 3

Find out what investment techniques your Team REAL members are using for other clients that are working successfully.

Prospect Point 4

Are your professionals spending any time on investment real estate training during the year, and can they recommend any of this training to you? Can you take advantage of any price reduction with them through their company or trade organization?

Prospect Point 5

Knowledge comes through books, blogs, vlogs, podcasts, YouTube, certification programs, organizations, online courses, and so much more. These sources of knowledge can help you develop an investment real estate base and enable you to use your team to move you to better and best.

Part of developing a team and getting the real benefit from the members is through knowledge acquisition and creating action from this knowledge. Interview potential team members using the prospect points above, and you'll be closer to owning your first investment real estate property. The prospect points will help you to take action and move you toward your goal. It will not take you long to figure out what is working for you and how it is getting you closer to or moving you further away from your goal.

Prospecting allows you to minimize false starts by getting to know your prospects before making your final decision.

It is also important to change your approach if team members are not working out.

Whatever your Team REAL looks like, one thing is certain: you need a motivated team of people who live and love investment real estate.

Minimum Viable Team Members

When you first start to develop your team, you need to think about your minimum viable team members. Buying your first investment real estate property may not require an army of professionals, but you should have a solid base of a few key members.

Your investment real estate team should include a coach, educational organization, or system; an investment real estate mortgage broker; a banking team that may not be your lender; a real estate agent; a legal team; and an accounting team.

Establishing a core team that you trust pays dividends. They can help you assemble the rest of the team members you need. In the beginning, you will find that team members will come and go in the purchasing and rental process. I will go into more detail on Day 20 regarding the folks you need on your team before you purchase your first investment real estate property, the folks you need when you make the actual purchase, and the folks you need after you have made the purchase and are getting ready to rent.

Below, you'll find information about each core member of your Team REAL: the who, what, and why of your team.

Core Member #1: The Mortgage Broker or Bank's Mortgage Specialist

The first member of your Team REAL should be a mortgage broker or bank's mortgage specialist.

A mortgage broker is an intermediary who arranges mortgage loans on behalf of individuals or businesses. And they're crucial for people who are investing in investment real estate.

Many people go to their local bank when they first look for financing. Why? The bank is where many people have their checking and savings accounts and do their daily banking. Also, most people don't own investment real estate; rather, the real estate they are purchasing is their residential home. They're happy to get a mortgage at all and are not thinking about buying multiple properties.

A mortgage broker can give you more lending options beyond your primary bank, and having lending options is critical to your investment real estate success. A mortgage broker finds mortgage loans for individuals or businesses. Remember, banks and other lending organizations tend to direct you to their own products, while a mortgage broker is independent and works with numerous lending providers. The financial world has changed in recent years. Options have opened up, and there is much more choice and competition today. This choice and competition has opened the door for mortgage brokers, who work for you and shop your mortgage around to get you the best terms and rates. The mortgage broker is now a dominant figure in the mortgage lending process.

A mortgage broker can help you assemble your financial information in the format most suitable for lenders. Potential lenders will be judging you based on this material, and mortgage brokers give you the insight you need to do the work and present your financial information in a way that paints you in the best possible light.

Why You Need a Mortgage Broker

As you research how much you will need for a down payment on your first investment real estate property, many different factors will come into play. A good rule of thumb is to budget for 5–20 percent if you are employed by someone else, and as high as 35 percent if self-employed, of the total price you pay for the property. This is one reason you will need to assemble a team—your Team REAL—starting with a mortgage broker.

When you purchase multiple properties over a lifetime, the financing rules are different, and a good mortgage broker is more than someone who helps you secure financing and low rates. A mortgage broker understands the different rules as outlined by each lender. You will find that some lenders don't like investment real estate, some are happy to support your purchases but might try and squeeze higher rates, and some will be willing to finance different numbers of properties.

In addition to helping you find the right mortgage, a mortgage broker adds educational expertise to your team. They understand real estate and are very in tune with each real estate market; in many cases, they even understand the real estate market on a micro-level, by subdivision or neighborhood in a town or city.

A mortgage broker is also connected with other professionals, such as lawyers or home inspectors, to help you in your purchase. They should be one of the first folks you add to your Team REAL.

Core Member #2: The Real Estate Agent

To be totally transparent, after my father retired from the Armed Forces, he found success as a real estate agent. In fact, he was so successful, his firm asked him to open a real estate branch in a different city. My dad went on to have a long second career in real estate. His success inspired my daughter, and she became a real estate agent, too. The reason I'm telling you this is that I have seen the good, the bad, and the ugly of being a real estate agent.

Real estate agents work different hours than most professions, are on straight commission, and have to wait until the new owners take possession of their new home before they get paid.

The industry is changing quickly, and technology is impacting the real estate industry.

Licensed real estate agents must meet certain professional standards and need to study and pass certification programs to become a real estate agent. The real estate agents have yearly fees to pay and these fees are not inexpensive. This is my opinion only, but the annual fees serve as a measure to keep good real estate agents engaged in their profession, and those who don't cut the mustard are weeded out when the annual fees are due. Does this mean all real estate agents are great at what they do? No. When hiring one, like when hiring someone from any profession, you need to do your homework and find a real estate agent that you can work with and who understands your needs.

We have used a real estate agent to sell several properties and to purchase several properties.

Why do you need one? If you are selling, you can expect them to not only know the city you live in and what the selling price of the market should be, but they know the areas. They have access to what is called comparables (information that compares like properties to like properties) and can therefore let you know selling prices and list prices in your area.

The real estate agent should be able to give you a great idea of what you can sell your property for. They can give you information on how long properties are taking to sell in your marketplace, and they can market through a Multiple Listing Service (MLS) system. Most real estate agents have national contacts and have access to folks who are moving into your town or city and may be seeking a property.

Real estate agents are experts at marketing your property, and how they market is no different than how you would market your investment real estate rental. On Day 25, I show you how to market your rental property. There is a list of items you can review; your real estate agent should be doing all of these same types of practices to market your property for sale.

Real estate agents generally have access to great photographers, website experts, social media platforms, home staging, tradespeople, and many other professionals. The long list of professionals they have access to can make your job of selling much easier.

Reaching out to a real estate agent can be a little tricky. There's a reason this is second on the list: in my opinion, you should have contacted your mortgage broker and at least have a range of home prices in mind before contacting a real estate agent.

Too many times, I have seen my dad or daughter work with someone who had either overstated or understated the amount they could spend on the purchase of a home. This is a critical piece of information, and if you don't know your affordability position, it wastes everyone's time.

A real estate agent generally does not cost you a dime until you have sold or bought your home and the new owners take possession or you take possession.

There are also real estate services that say they don't charge you commission for selling your home. Most of these services have a one-time flat fee that you must pay upfront for them to market your home. If you don't sell your home, you have made the investment and gotten no return.

Decide what your time is worth. Do you have the skills and resources to be your own agent? Be honest with yourself. While some might be able to pull this off, the majority of us will need a real estate agent.

Core Member #3: The Lawyer

A lawyer is an important part of the selling and purchasing process. Selling and buying real estate is a vital part of many legal practices.

The role of the lawyer is important because of the legal description of the property, the caveats (warnings that there might be conditions) that could be registered against the property, contact with the seller or buyer's lawyer, the disbursements of the funds, and other legal matters.

Get a lawyer involved when you are making an offer. Make sure you are not making an offer that does not allow you to back out of the deal based on certain conditions. Your lawyer should be able to advise you of these conditions.

Lawyers used to charge a percentage of the purchase or mortgage amount, but this practice has stopped as the real estate part of a legal practice has gotten more competitive. Lawyers generally have a flat rate for this service; ask around and get a few quotes. Also, you generally don't pay for your legal fees until the lawyer has handled the closing of the sale and the funds have been distributed to all parties, including yourself.

Most lawyers will take their payment from the funds being distributed from the sale if you are the seller.

Core Member #4: The Accountant

An accountant is not a bookkeeper. If you follow the methods in this book, you can handle the bookkeeping side of your investment real estate business in less than an hour a month. If you don't want to handle the bookkeeping, an accountant will recommend a bookkeeper and this bookkeeper might be part of their services.

The accountant's role on your Team REAL is crucial because when you add investment real estate to your financial portfolio, you start to complicate your tax return.

If your goal is to have investment real estate as part of your financial portfolio and you intend to use this as a supplement investment without ever turning to investment real estate as a full-time career, having an accountant on your team is more important than ever.

Accountants will advise you of how to handle any positive or negative cash flow to your income, how you can handle appreciation and depreciation of the property, how you can handle your expenses, and what you can legally expense.

If the accountant knows you are a long-term client, they will give you advice without racking up an invoice for their services. My accountant makes himself available to me throughout the year, and this advice is part of his annual tax preparation bill. If you only have one investment property, you are more than likely only looking at a couple hundred dollars as a personal tax bill. You should shop around and get several quotes before locking into a service.

As I have mentioned before, it is not about the accounting firm; it is all about the individual accountant and if they own any investment real estate. If they don't, they should not be your accountant. One of my favorite accountants in my life retired early in her career because of investment real estate; she walked her talk.

Core Member #5: The Coach/Educational Institution/Organization

As a paid coach and consultant, I can give you some insight into hiring a coach. But before getting into the details of coaching, I would like to advise you that there are plenty of great investment real estate education services that won't break the bank.

Many of you will be familiar with a meeting service called Meetup.com. This service is used by folks to set up meetings in their field, whether the meeting is in-person or virtual. Many real estate agents who excel in investment real estate hold these types of meetings, and I have attended a few myself. These meetings tend to be educational and the hosts are hoping to provide you with information to interest you in investment real estate and use their services. I love these meetings as they will bring in guest speakers from different facets of the investment real estate business for you to grow your knowledge. These guests include bookkeepers, repair service folks, other investors, etc.

The cost of most Meetup events is low. I normally pay twenty dollars for a three-hour meeting; this cost covers the meeting room and the AV equipment.

You can also find community colleges that offer courses to teach folks about investment real estate. These classes tend to be through the continuing education segment, consisting of weekend or night classes, and are outside of the normal college curriculum. They tend to be taught by someone in the investment real estate field and cost anywhere from one hundred to a few hundred dollars; the length can vary from a one-off session to a twelve-week course.

You can also find independent for-profit investment real estate organizations that focus on investment real estate education. I belonged to a national organization, the Real Estate Investment Network (REIN). I paid a monthly fee and was committed to joining for seventeen months. I loved the education and was a member for over ten years. (Remember, joining an organization like this can add up to several thousands of dollars in expenses, so make sure you can afford this and are committed to getting the most out of it.)

Last but not least, individual coaching can be a great way to go. Every coach has their own approach, but I'll walk you through mine so you have a general idea of what to expect.

I generally hire my services out over a three-, six- or twelve-month period and charge a monthly fee based on the duration of our contract. My fee tends to run into low to mid thousands of dollars.

The objective behind my services is clear: it is to help you purchase a property and rent this property over the duration of our contract time together. If you have a spouse or partner, you both must agree to meet with me at our first meeting. If I feel you are not both on the same page about purchasing and renting an investment property, I thank you for the opportunity but will not take you on as a client.

Once we are clear on the objective, I will give you a contract to review. This contract will include the following areas: The Objective, The Opportunity, The Project Work and Outline for both parties, The Rationale, Execution Strategy, Project Approach, Project Deliverables, Timeline for Execution, Supplied Materials, and Expected Results Including Financial Results and Other Benefits.

We review pricing, including upfront costs and monthly costs to completion. I will review my qualifications, references, and conclusion. I also provide a list of my Team REAL members as a resource should you choose to use these folks.

Optional Members of Team REAL

In addition to your Team REAL's core members, there are numerous other potential members you can add to your team. I've outlined some of them below.

Partner or Partners – you may choose to have co-investors on your investment real estate journey, such as a spouse, significant other, joint venture partner, family member, etc.

Governments – this can include people at the municipal, state, provincial, and federal levels of government whom you can draw on for information.

Property Taxation Department – there are different taxation rules depending on use; for example, you may pay higher tax as an owner that rents than an owner that resides in the property.

Housewares (see recommended checklist)

Electronics (see recommended checklist)

Home Furnishings

Home Design – know the current trends and themes.

Trades – general contractor, plumber, electrician, fireplace servicing, locksmith, flooring, painter, cabinets, countertops, etc.

Cleaning and Restoration

Utilities – cable, electricity, gas, telephone, internet, etc.

Property Manager

Condominium Board

Not all of these members will be necessary for every investor's Team REAL; you can pick and choose the ones that apply to your situation.

Taking Advantage of Your Team REAL

The next several pages are critical in your journey to put together a real estate investment team. Remember, all the professionals I refer to ply their trade in investment real estate, where the purchase and rental action is. Their expertise in the practice is invaluable, so be like a sponge and soak up as much of their knowledge as you can. Don't be afraid to let them know you would like to take notes or record any advice they dispense.

There's another challenge you'll probably encounter when assembling your investment real estate team: you are going to develop friendships or social relationships with your lawyer, accountant, banker, investment advisor, and perhaps even a real estate agent. As a result, you will inevitably find it difficult to move away from those professionals. If you choose team members who are only experienced with primary home purchases and don't understand investment real estate, this presents a problem. That's why the rule of thumb, as I advised you earlier, is that assembling a team of individuals experienced in investment real estate is your key to success. If someone does not have investment real estate in their personal investment portfolio, even if you've worked with them in the past and liked them, they cannot give you the best advice on your investment real estate journey and should therefore not be part of your Team REAL.

Making smart choices when assembling your Team REAL will lead you to the best possible outcomes for your investment real estate journey, now and into the future.

Identify the members of your Team REAL.

People will either make you or break you. I cannot think of a more important phrase when you begin your journey to purchasing and renting your first investment real estate property. Throughout the book, I refer to your Team REAL. If you pick the correct people for your team, their advice and counsel can ensure your success.

The cost of entry for investment real estate is higher than for most investments, and the right team members can save you from costly mistakes.

The first attribute of your team members should be that they have a background in investment real estate. Make these your first two questions: What is your experience regarding investment real estate? Do you own investment real estate?

Investment real estate is a specialized area of investing. With just 4 to 8 percent of North Americans owning investment real estate, access to investment real estate service professionals is low. Asking questions can save you from partnering with the wrong professionals.

⇧ Identify members of your investment real estate team and their duties—your bench strength. (I will start your list of core members; finish the challenge by adding who else you think should be on your list and the duties of each of these professionals.)

Role	Duties	Investment Real Estate Background	Investment Real Estate Owner?
Mortgage Broker			
Real Estate Agent			
Lawyer			
Accountant			
Coach			

Day 19 Key Recap

Record your key learnings and actionable items in your notebook or the workbook and planning guide. (Optional)

- ⇧ The first question to ask when assembling your Team REAL is: Does each member own investment real estate?
- ⇧ Review the skill set required by each core member to meet the criteria of purchasing and renting a successful investment property.
- ⇧ Use your core Team REAL members to identify other non-essential members of your Team REAL.

DAY 20 ENTRY STAGES OF TEAM REAL: BEFORE PURCHASE, AT PURCHASE, AND AFTER PURCHASE

Use this day to build your team in each stage of purchasing your first investment real estate property. The coaching challenges will help you understand the value each team member brings and at which point on your journey they'll enter the picture.

Your investment real estate journey consists of three stages: before purchase, at purchase, and after purchase. Today, we're going to go through those stages, so you understand precisely what to expect at each stage.

Before the Purchase:

Before the purchase is a critical time, and you mustn't waste the team members' time. One typical example of wasting Team REAL members' time is asking to view any investment real estate until you are ready to purchase. Real estate is fluid, and looking at real estate without any intention of buying is an inconvenience for the seller, the seller's agent, and your agent. Another example is setting up a meeting with your bank to borrow money when you have not put your finances in order.

Before purchase, you generally aren't required to invest or spend any money—you can get the first meeting with a potential team member for free. In these meetings, the professionals are investing their time with you because they see you as a potential client.

The Purchase:

The purchase stage is where the rubber meets the road, and you will be required to invest or spend money for services rendered.

After the Purchase:

After the purchase, there are certain Team REAL members whose services you will continue to use year after year. Your accountant is one of those team members you will need to use for each year-end, and their advice will be critical to help ensure you get full tax deduction benefits and protection in the future against a larger capital tax bill.

My goal is to give you the big-picture overview of the purchase process and then drill down to specifics.

In each stage, I will discuss each team member and their specific role. Remember, some team members may be with you through all stages and will be folks you have fairly regular contact with, while other team members will almost be a one-off with minimal contact. The onus will be on you to maintain your contact list and make sure the team members you use infrequently are still in business and should continue to be on your list.

As we build your list, my goal is to introduce the team member as they enter the transaction with you and talk about their specific role. I am adding a chart so that you can see exactly how many stages these professionals will be with you through the purchasing and renting process.

Assembling Your Team REAL

Throughout the book, I have discussed the importance of your investment real estate team—Team REAL (Real Estate Advisory League)—and how critical these professionals are to your purchase. But at what point in the purchasing process will you need each member, and when should you recruit them?

The Three Stages of the Purchase:
- Before the purchase
- At purchase
- After the purchase

Some team members are essential for the entire purchasing and renting life cycle of your first investment real estate property: before the purchase, at the purchase, and after the purchase.

Let's review an example.

First, we'll outline the Team REAL members you'll need for acquiring investment rental real estate, and where they belong in the life cycle of the investment rental property.

Purchase and Rental Life Cycle Stages of Team REAL Members

Team REAL Members	Stage(s) of Life Cycle (Before, At Purchase, After)		
Team Real Members	Before Purchase	At Purchase	After Purchase
Mortgage Broker	X	X	X
Real Estate Agent	X	X	X
Lawyer	X	X	X
Accountant	X	X	
Coach/Educational Institution/Organization	X	X	
Coach/Educational Institution/Organization	X	X	
Partner/s		X	X
Levels of Government (Municipal, State, Provincial, Federal)	X	X	X
Property Taxation Department			X
Trades	X		X
Cleaning and Restoration		X	X
Utilities		X	
Condominium Board	X	X	X

The list does not stop here. On Day 19, I defined the roles and duties each Team REAL member plays; the list can grow depending on your personal situation and needs.

The importance of your Team REAL cannot be understated. It can be the make-it-or-break-it piece of your real estate rental property's success. Your piece of heaven can go to hell very quickly. Your tenants are paying rent and expect a seamless, carefree place to live. If you cannot respond to their concerns quickly, it can get a little uncomfortable for you. A good Team REAL can help ease the burden.

 **Determine when your Team REAL members come in.**

Filling in the chart below will give you a visual cue to understand that all members of your Team REAL will come in and out of your real estate investment life. You'll have lifelong relationships with some, and others, not so much. Even though each member plays an essential role, it will be up to you to keep up the relationship with them. You can never know when you might reach out to them in the future. A call or a quick coffee once a year might be enough to keep your team together.

⇧ Use three different columns (Before Purchase, At Purchase, and After Purchase) to check off the team members you'll require in each stage. Remember that some team members will need to be placed in more than one column.

STAGE II: SET I DAY 20 ENTRY STAGES OF TEAM REAL: BEFORE PURCHASE, AT PURCHASE, AND AFTER PURCHASE

(Refer to the chart in the Purchase and Rental Life Cycle Stages of Team REAL Members below and in the appendix portion of the book or workbook and planning guide.)

Team Real Members	Before Purchase	At Purchase	After Purchase
Mortgage Broker			
Real Estate Agent			
Lawyer			
Accountant			
Coach/Educational Institution/Organization			
Partner/s			
Levels of Government (Municipal, State, Provincial, Federal)			
Property Tax Department			
Trades			
Cleaning and Restoration			
Utilities			
Condominium Board			
Other			

COACHING CHALLENGE 40

Dig deeper with your Team REAL.

On Day 19, we identified a list of your Team REAL members, and in the exercise above, we charted the stages of your investment real estate journey each of your team members would be involved in. Some of these team members will be with you for life, and these folks must be a good fit. In this coaching challenge, it is going to be all about interviewing and digging a little deeper to find out if you will have lifelong relationships with these folks.

We've gone over the importance of prospecting for the right person for each role on your Team REAL. Ideally, you're looking for someone who will understand and feed your aspiration, and engage in discussion and brainstorming. Both of you will benefit from this arrangement.

In the beginning, your Team REAL members will take on more of a mentorship role, and you'll be the learner. As a learner, you need to prepare questions for your mentors and ask these questions in advance.

That's what this exercise is all about. For each mentor or team member, create a list of questions to ask when prospecting. I will start you off. Use your notebook, the workbook and planning guide, or the extra lines below to add some of your own questions that are important to you in this process.

What has worked for me in the past?

What will I be responsible for?

Do I know what I want to accomplish?

What can I learn?

What's possible?

Day 20 Key Recap

Record your key learnings and actionable items in your notebook or the workbook and planning guide. (Optional)

- Your Team REAL members will come in at different stages of the purchase journey: before purchase, during purchase, and after purchase.
- Not all members of Team REAL will be involved in all stages of your purchase.
- Understanding precisely what to expect at each stage will ensure you have a smooth journey.

 **DAY 21** WHICH LENDER IS RIGHT FOR YOU?

Use this day to research your lender and identify your needs for financing. Today's coaching challenges will help you identify different financial lenders and determine which options will work best for you.

We've talked about the basics of financing in a few chapters. Today, we're going to review some of the essentials, then dive deeper into the numbers associated with borrowing so that you are fully prepared to secure the investment real estate mortgage or loan that's right for you.

Sandbox Lending Rules

Throughout the book, I've talked about the fact that borrowing money means you're "playing in someone else's sandbox." The reason is simple: if you are playing in someone else's sandbox, you must play by their rules.

When you borrow money, never forget that it is the lender's money, and for the privilege of borrowing it, you must play by their rules.

Lenders are generally looking at your ability to service some or all of your monthly payments, including the new investment mortgage debt. Many lenders want to know you can service all debt should you not have a tenant paying rent.

Each lender has its own rules, and this is another reason to have a mortgage broker—the broker knows each lender's rules and can find you a lender that aligns with your current financial situation.

Your mortgage broker can also help you look into your investment real estate future. If you plan to have only one investment real estate property in your financial portfolio, the lender you might use might be different than if you are planning to make multiple mid- and longer-range investment real estate property purchases.

A good example of sandbox lending rules is the recent mortgage deferral programs offered to investment real estate owners who wanted to help their tenants by either forgiving all or part of the tenant's rent during the COVID-19 pandemic or deferring the tenant's rent. I took advantage of this program and found out that some banks would only defer up to four investment real estate mortgages. I was fortunate that my lenders had no restrictions.

Recap: The Types of Lenders

Mortgage Broker: A mortgage broker acts as an intermediary who negotiates mortgage loans on behalf of individuals or businesses. Traditionally, banks and other lending institutions have sold their own products. As markets for mortgages have become more competitive, however, the mortgage broker's role has become more popular. In many developed mortgage markets today, mortgage brokers are the largest sellers of mortgage products for lenders.

Bank: A bank is a financial institution that accepts deposits and recurring accounts from individuals and creates demand deposit. What does this mean for you as an owner? If you deal with a tenant directly, you can offer them the option of direct rent deposit to your account. You need to check the state or provincial legislation to see if this is allowed. You can also set up automatic withdrawal of many of your expense items, such as monthly property tax payment or condo fees (if applicable). Remember, making your deposits and withdrawals automatic makes your business life easier to administer.

Lending activities can be performed either directly or indirectly through capital markets. Due to their importance in countries' financial stability, banks are usually highly regulated.

Credit Union: A credit union is a member-owned financial cooperative, controlled by its members and operated on the principle of people helping people. Credit unions provide members with loans at competitive rates compared to other financial institutions.

Insurance Company: An insurance company is a for-profit, non-profit, or government-owned company that sells the promise to pay for certain expenses in exchange for a regular fee, called a premium. For example, if one purchases health insurance, the insurance company will pay for (some of) the client's medical bills, if any.

Private Lender: A private lender is not affiliated with a bank or traditional lender, and may or may not normally be in the business of providing loans. Private lenders are not as constrained by regulations as traditional lenders are and can approve ventures that traditional lenders cannot.

Family: A family loan, sometimes known as an intra-family loan, is any loan between family members. This can be tricky, and my personal belief is that there should be a legal document produced, like there is for any mortgage, with transparent terms and conditions. These funds are not a gift, and that should be clear right from the start.

Which Lender Is Right for You?

In most cases, it's best to start with a mortgage broker. I start with a mortgage broker for a couple of reasons. The first is flexibility. Brokers will get to know you and your financial situation from an income and net worth position. From your financial position, they will be able to help identify which lender might be the best fit for you. The second reason is that the mortgage broker will do much of the groundwork for you.

Traditional financial institutions tend to have lower interest rates but tougher conditions to qualify for funding.

Understand the traditional lenders' terms and conditions, and don't get upset if you cannot qualify through these lenders.

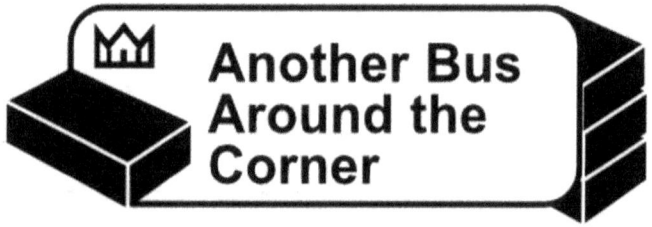

Remember, There's

The fact is, not everyone will be able to qualify through a traditional lender, like a bank. This is why we have listed several lending options; as I indicated earlier in the book, if a 1 percent higher interest rate creates a positive cash flow problem, don't purchase the property.

Understanding Mortgages

The main objective of this book is to help you purchase and rent your first investment real estate property. To do that, most people will need a mortgage.

The mortgage rules can differ widely by lender, state, province, and country. The United States and Canada have different mortgage rules.

On Day 19, we'll focus on identifying and assembling your Team REAL (Real Estate Advisory League), and on Day 20, we'll discuss at which points in your purchasing cycle you need to bring your team members onto your team.

Financing is a critical component of purchasing your first investment real estate property.

The purpose of the information below is to get a sense of the big picture—the view from thirty thousand feet. I don't profess to be an expert on financing in the area you plan to invest in. My goal is simply to give you enough knowledge so that you can talk to the people you would like on your Team REAL—whether they're a mortgage broker or a bank lending agent.

What Is a Mortgage?

A residential mortgage is a legal agreement between you and your bank or lender. The bank or lender lends you funds in exchange for taking the title on the property, with the condition that the bank or lender remain on the title until the payment of the debt is complete.

There are many different types of mortgages, including fixed-rate, variable, and adjustable, and each of these has a repayment period of a different length.

Conventional Mortgage: In North America, the down payment to purchase a residential home or investment real estate property is 20 or 35 percent of the total purchase price for a conventional mortgage.

High-Ratio Mortgage: Many options make it possible to get a mortgage when you have a lower down payment amount, including what is referred to as a high-ratio mortgage. For a high-ratio mortgage, you'll make a down payment between 5 and 19 percent. High-ratio mortgages come with higher costs, insurance, and higher interest rates. You may also be required to have a higher credit score. The lower the percentage of the property's value you initially invest as a down payment, the more challenging it is to get mortgage approval.

I am not suggesting you should not try and make as low a down payment for an investment real estate property as possible. I'm just saying that the numbers need to work, covering all operational costs, including mortgage principal and interest payments.

Mortgage Rules: Financing is an integral part of purchasing your first investment real estate property. Rules regarding financing not only differ by country, but by bank and lender. The mortgage rules can be different for investment real estate, as well. This is why I suggest you have a mortgage broker on your Team REAL. Let these folks do the research and bring you the options best suited to you.

Differences Between Canada and the United States

I've mentioned that 8 percent of Americans own investment real estate compared to 4 percent of Canadians. At the end of the day, I believe that investment real estate should be part of your investment portfolio, no matter which side of the border you live on.

My goal is to give you a broad overview and some examples of financing in the United States and Canada. For the specific details, you'll need to work with your Team REAL to find out what best suits you.

In the United States, mortgages are most commonly granted in fifteen- or thirty-year terms.

The biggest difference between U.S. and Canadian mortgages is that Americans have a financial mortgage staple called the thirty-year fixed-rate mortgage; Canada doesn't have anything that comes close to this mortgage vehicle. The longest-term mortgage Canada provides is an amortization period of twenty-five years, but you have to renew your fixed-rate mortgage every two, three, four, or five years.

Canadians can't count on a loan interest rate to last any more than five years.

Differences in Tax Deductibility

The other key difference between the United States and Canada is that mortgage interest is tax-deductible in the United States but not in Canada.

The tax-deductible rules for investment real estate are the same on both sides of the border.

In Canada, you can use the equity in your home to borrow through a home line of credit (LOC), and as long as the funds are used to purchase an investment real estate property, you can deduct the interest on the line of credit. In a way, this makes the interest on your primary residence tax-deductible. (Please discuss this with your accountant before attempting it on your taxes.)

Since the financial crisis in 2008, both American and Canadian banks have changed, and mortgages have become much less risky.

As an investor, you should not be concerned about tighter loan guidelines; these practices help keep you on track to ensure you invest in a property that makes economic sense.

Listed below are an American mortgage example and a Canadian mortgage example. This illustrates the differences between conventional mortgages versus high-ratio mortgages and gives you a five-year window into costs and equity growth.

In the American example, I will focus on the fifteen-year and thirty-year terms, the difference in interest rates charged for a fifteen-year and thirty-year term, and what higher interest means.

American Example:

In this example, we will look at two scenarios for a $200,000 mortgage. In Scenario #1, we compare a 1 percent rate difference; in Scenario #2, we look at a difference in term length of fifteen years.

Scenario #1	30-Year Term	30-Year Term
$200,000 Mortgage/Loan	3.5% Interest Rate	4.5% Interest Rate
Principal and Interest Costs – Total Payout Dollars	$323,000	$365,000
1% Interest Rate Costs $ Difference		$42,000

Scenario #2	15-Year Term	30-Year Term
$200,000 Mortgage/Loan	4.5% Interest Rate	4.5% Interest Rate
Principal and Interest Costs – Total Payout Dollars	$275,000	$365,000
Additional 15 Years on 30-Year Term		$90,000

In Chapter 8 of her book *Money Honey: A Simple 7-Step Guide for Getting Your Financial $hit Together*, author Rachel Richards discusses mortgages, focusing first on the impact of interest rates and then on the impact of shorter-term mortgages.

The book is a great read for everyone, but Rachel's book puts a little more meat on the bone for my American readers when outlining American mortgage scenarios.

The information I have provided will give you a great base for starting the discussion with your appropriate team members.

Canadian Example:

In Canada, there are many similarities to the American mortgage system and some key differences. Use the example below to help you understand mortgage costs.

To give you context, let's review the difference between a conventional and high-ratio mortgage. We will use this example of purchasing an investment property for $300,000, with a twenty-five-year amortization period and an interest rate of 2.5 percent with a five-year closed term.

	Conventional Mortgage 20% Down Payment	High-Ratio Mortgage 5% Down Payment
Purchase Price	$300,000	$300,000
Down Payment	$60,000	$15,000
Mortgage Principal	$240,000	$285,000
Mortgage Default Insurance	$0	$11,400*
Total Mortgage Amount	$240,000	$296,400
Monthly Mortgage Payment	$1,075	$1,328
Principal Paydown	$37,022	$45,722
Interest Payments	$27,485	$33,444
Total Payment	$66,507	$79,666
Mortgage Balance	$202,978	$250,678

As you can see, there are higher costs to purchase a property with a high-ratio mortgage, including where your mortgage paydown amount is at the end of five years. These are all factors you need to be aware of to make the right decision for you.

Remember, starting to invest with a down payment of less than 20 percent gets investment real estate in your financial portfolio.

You can lower the cost of mortgage default insurance for a high-ratio mortgage by increasing your down payment amount. Most mortgage default insurance is on a sliding scale and can be significant as you increase your down payment percentage from 5 percent to 10 percent to 15 percent. Most lenders have mortgage payment calculators built into their websites for you to plan out different scenarios.

Doing some research on different scenarios can save you tens of thousands of dollars over a period as short as five years.

Free Resource: Mortgage Loan Calculator

MORTGAGE LOAN CALCULATOR		MONTHLY LOAN PAYMENT $1,074	
LOAN DETAILS	VALUES	KEY STATISTICS	TOTALS
Purchase Price	$300,000	Monthly Loan Payments	$1,074
Interest Rate	5.0%	Total Monthly Payments*	$520,679
Duration of Loan (in months)	360	Total Loan Payments	$385,679
Loan Amount	$200,000	Total Interest Paid	$185,679
Loan Start Date	2020-11-05	Monthly Property Tax Amount	$375

*Total monthly payments = loan payments plus property tax payments   Go to Amortization Table

If you have access to Microsoft Excel or the iOS Numbers program for Mac, both these software programs offer a free sample mortgage loan calculator that you can access through the "Templates" section.

The mortgage loan calculator in Excel, pictured above, takes only moments to personalize with your information.

How to Use the Mortgage Loan Calculator

Let's discuss each area of information on the worksheet and how you can utilize the mortgage loan calculator to view different scenarios under the Loan Details Column, Values Column, Key Statistics Column, and Totals Column.

This free spreadsheet allows you to use the different scenarios and, in doing so, notice how the Monthly Loan Payment box will change in value. You may have a number in mind that you would like to see as your monthly loan payment, and it only takes seconds to see what would best suit your circumstances. The scenarios and the financial information are only as reliable as the information you use, so be realistic.

Remember, you can influence and negotiate at all levels of these transactions—don't be afraid to ask. As a first-time investor, you can use ignorance to your advantage. Most professionals, when dealing with someone new to investing, expect these questions.

Purchase price: You might start with the list price of the property. The list price is the price the sellers would like to receive. It is determined by the sellers and the real estate listing agent. The listing agent brings what is referred to in the real estate industry as the comparables. The comparables are the sales of the same type of house sold in the sellers' community. Often, the sellers think their piece of paradise is worth more than the comparables, and in many cases, the sellers' price is overpriced for the market.

Your real estate agent will have pulled the same comparables as the sellers' agent and will recommend to you what she believes is the right price to offer for the property. In many cases, the buyers now try the same trick as the sellers, but instead of going high, they go lower than the market says the price is worth.

The negotiations go back and forth between the seller and the buyer. At some point, there is a compromise, and a price is agreed to. As a buyer, you have a good idea of what your final offer is going to be. As a buyer or a seller, you should always have a range you are willing to work within, and you should have a bottom-line price. My advice for buyers is that there is another bus around the corner, so be prepared to walk if the price is not going to work for you.

This is why we are going through this exercise. If you have a range of pricing and mortgage payments you can afford, loan start date, and loan payment frequency, you give yourself more flexibility to bargain.

Interest Rate: Please refer to the chart above. I mentioned earlier in the book that if a difference in the interest rate of 1 percent or less will force you from a positive cash-flowing property to a negative cash-flowing property, walk away from the deal or the lender, or renegotiate the price or the terms of the loan. You need to start with a positive cash-flowing property from the get-go. Don't subsidize your first investment real estate property yourself. Taking money from your own pocket each month is a recipe for disaster.

Let's dig a little deeper with the example above. You will notice that a loan amount of $200,000 at 5 percent carries a monthly loan payment of $1,074. Move the interest rate up by a quarter of a percent (.25 percent), and your monthly loan payment increases to $1,104, or an increase of $30 or $360 a year. If this amount changes the dynamic from positive to negative cash flow, don't you think you are cutting your income-to-expenses ratio too close for this property?

Each quarter of a percentage point takes your payment up around $30 more per payment; the difference between 5 percent ($1,074) and 6 percent ($1,199) is an increase of $125 per month for the loan payment.

Right now, we have a very low-interest-rate environment, and this is great. However, the reason I used 5 percent as an example is that the mortgage rules are continually changing. Over the last few years, governments have been using higher interest rates as a stress test to see if you can make your payments if the interest starts to move up in the future.

Duration of Loan (in months): Some governments and lenders are constantly playing with the amortization length; we have seen these range from twenty-five years to thirty-five years. Fifteen-year and thirty-year mortgages are prevalent in the United States, while twenty-five is common in Canada.

I would suggest you check into the current lender rules and find out what the average amortization length is in months. Again, play with this variable on the worksheet and see the number it produces.

Loan Amount: This can vary. Many lenders offer loans of 80 percent of the purchase price, meaning they'll ask you for a 20 percent down payment. Again, this all depends on the lender you are using and their requirements.

Loan Start Date: If you can delay your loan start date, this savings could help you offset other costs such as moving, repairs, legal fees, and other professional fees. It never hurts to ask your lender if there is any wiggle room for your first payment to start; remember, the worst the lender can say is no. I would be specific on what time frame you would like. The answer may be a no to your date but a yes to a later date chosen by the lender.

Key Statistics (The Real Costs to Borrow):

On the Excel chart under *Free Resource: Mortgage Loan Calculator*, the first line is your monthly payment over thirty years, or 360 monthly payments. It is important to remember this is a mathematical exercise. In the United States, if you can secure a thirty-year amortization length like in the American example as a first-time investment real estate owner, this is fantastic.

In Canada, with the mortgage rules always in flux, I would be more comfortable if you use a twenty-five-year amortization length, with a five-year term and a fixed rate.

Never forget that you are generally tied into a term between one and five years. The term is the part of the mortgage process that guarantees you your interest rate for a certain period of time.

The term can be hot, cold, or warm. A prime example is the coronavirus pandemic and how this virus changed the entire economic world.

Before the pandemic came on full-force throughout the world, many financial experts were talking about the interest rates moving back up to higher levels in 2020. How wrong they were. Now we should see low interest rates, lower than we started with in 2020, through until the end of 2021 or longer. If you are reading this book at the end of 2021, you might have better insight.

What does this lower-interest-rate environment mean? It means you may never see five-year term interest rates much lower than they are today.

As I mentioned above, a .25 to 1 percent difference should not cause your investment property to have a negative cash flow. Don't create expense conditions this tight.

In *Money Honey: A Simple 7-Step Guide For Getting Your Financial $hit Together*, Richards discusses her five-year rule when purchasing an investment property. The premise behind Richards' rule is simple: don't buy a property unless you plan to own it for five years. Richards explains that you won't pay off much of the principal over the first five years. If you sell too early in the process, you might break even or lose money after paying commissions and other associated selling fees.

Having a five-year term or plan for your first investment real estate property keeps an important part of your costs locked in for the next five years. This time can really work to your advantage as you learn more about the investment real estate market. Besides your mortgage payment, your next highest monthly cost is the property taxes, and I can say from plenty of experience that property taxes rarely go down—count on them going up every year.

In the first five years of owning and renting, two important factors will work in your favor. The first is the positive cash principal paydown on the mortgage; even though it is small initially, it helps you grow equity. The second is appreciation. If the property appreciates in value, it adds to the equity growth you have seen through principal paydown. Remember, you can't spend or easily access the equity growth in the property. There are ways to access these funds, but I would recommend you wait until the end of the mortgage term.

In the American example I provided, you will pay $185,679 in interest over a thirty-year amortization period, while your original mortgage amount was $200,000. Think about this for a moment. Imagine if I, as a friend, lend you a buck, and you have to pay me back two bucks for the pleasure of borrowing a buck. I am sure this friendship would not last long. Remember, the lender is in business to make money.

In a positive cash-flowing rental property, the rent covers all of your costs, including principal and interest. You are not allowed to claim principal paydown, just interest. Remember, principal paydown is coming back to you as value in equity growth.

Equity not only builds in value each time you make a mortgage payment (the tenant is making this payment), it grows if the market values are increasing. Equity is visible on your net worth statement (current market value), but remember, whether you see equity growth through your payments to principal or value growth in your real estate market, you cannot spend this equity unless you sell the property.

Having Your Equity Cake and Eating It Too

This book aims to have you purchase and rent your first investment real estate property, not to chase your next property.

Even so, it does not hurt to understand some of the potential benefits of owning investment real estate and having your first investment lay the foundation for perhaps purchasing a second investment property.

If you are in an excellent real estate market, your tenants are paying your principal mortgage amount plus interest, property values are increasing, and the rental rates are going up, you might want to consider remortgaging your property sometime in the future.

You have to feel good when you receive your rent checks because you have someone paying all of your costs, including interest and principal paydown. If you can increase your rents year after year, and your expenses to operate your rental property have remained the same, you could take the additional rental payment increase and Uberize the additional amount to your principal paydown.

In five years, your equity could be substantial, and you could remortgage this property and access some of the equity for a down payment on another investment real estate property.

Investment real estate opens up so many possibilities. Now that you've started your journey, who knows what the future may hold?

 **Pick your path of financing.**

We've reviewed the different financing sources in-depth, and now we need to look at what path works for you.

Financing can be stressful, especially if you have never secured a principal residential mortgage or a mortgage for an investment property. It is a critical arm of your investment strategy, and I want you to use this challenge to think about who you will source the funds from, where you will source them from, and how.

Do you have a long-term relationship with a bank or a credit union?

Have you ever thought about using an insurance company for a mortgage? Did you even know that insurance companies issue mortgages?

Have you thought about a third-party, private, or family investor as your lender? How would borrowing from these options even work?

The purpose of this challenge is to brainstorm; like always, you are not locked into your answer. With that, let's rank your lender choices below (1 being your top choice and 7 being your last choice).

Your Choices:

Mortgage Broker

Bank

Credit Union

Insurance Company

Third Party

Private Lender

Family

Your Ranking

1. _____
2. _____
3. _____
4. _____
5. _____
6. _____
7. _____

 **Use a mortgage loan calculator to explore your options.**

Learning to use and navigate a mortgage loan calculator only takes a moment; it's easy to get the hang of it. Under the Resources tab on the Vault to Investment Real Estate Success website, you will find a mortgage calculator, or you can use your online banking account. All major lenders will give you access, free of charge, to their mortgage calculator tool. Each lender might post up to four different calculators. These are outlined as follows:

1. Payment Calculator – use this to find out your estimated mortgage payments and options in just minutes.
2. Affordability Calculator – when you are looking to buy, you can use this tool to find out how much mortgage you can afford.
3. Prepayment Calculator – get estimated costs for prepayment amounts and options (here's where you'll use your Uberizing).
4. Insurance – each lender will give you options for mortgage, life, and other insurance coverage costs. (On Day 16, I mentioned that you might find using term insurance a much better low-cost option. Lenders make a ton of profit

selling you mortgage insurance; in most cases, you get more insurance coverage than you need.)

5.

 Compare the lenders you listed in Coaching Challenge 41.

Play with the numbers by lender. Your mortgage broker needs to help you get the costs for you to do this comparison between lenders. It is important to get your broker involved because you can easily go to the lender's website and pull their published information, but this information is going to reflect numbers that are higher than the rates your mortgage broker can acquire for you. I can tell you from multiple mortgages and mortgage renewals that your mortgage broker can negotiate rates a quarter to a full percent lower than the lender's posted rates.

Itemize by lender the length of term and amortization, variable or closed, interest rate, conventional or high ratio, etc. When you know the best terms you can get by lender, you can list them side by side and see which lender works best for your situation.

Put the lender on the left side of a blank sheet, and list the mortgage rate for closed or open variable rate. You might also want to compare length of years for the term or amortization length.

If you decide on a high-ratio mortgage, what are the insurance costs? Remember, high-ratio mortgage insurance is due upfront as a cost, and many times, it is added to the mortgage balance and impacts your payment amounts.

Use this analysis as a guideline to determine which lender might be right for you. (For more on the factors involved in determining the lender you may settle on, see the workbook and planning guide.)

Day 21 Key Recap

Record your key learnings and actionable items in your notebook or the workbook and planning guide. (Optional)

- ⇧ The resources and rules of lenders can be used to identify your financing needs to meet the criteria of a successful investment property.
- ⇧ Review the potential lender types for maximizing equity growth, positive cash flow, and principal paydown—the trinity of ROI.
- ⇧ The lowest interest rate doesn't always mean the best overall financing strategy.

DAY 22 THE OFFER: DEFINITION, STRUCTURE, AND PROCESS

Use this day to reach out to a potential seller and let them know you are presenting an offer. You'll learn the definition of an offer, how to structure the offer, and how to make an offer for your first investment real estate property. At the end of the chapter, complete the coaching challenges to try a "making an offer" practice run.

You've made it all the way to Day 22, and this is where the fun begins. It's time to make your first offer on an investment real estate property.

Today, we are focused on the basic elements of the offer. The goal today is not to confuse you with the more complicated parts of an offer. These additional elements are called conditions and can vary greatly depending on your experience, your real estate agent's experience, and your circumstances. We'll worry about them later.

What Is an Offer?

In simple terms, an offer is a formal document that lays out the terms and conditions under which you propose to purchase a property. The title of the actual offer form can vary by municipality, real estate board, state, or province, but you'll often see it referred to as an Offer to Purchase.

The basic elements of an offer are as follows:
1) Title of the Form (e.g., Real Estate Purchase Contract)
2) Subtitle – Offer to Purchase and Earnest Money Deposit
3) Property
4) Purchase Price
5) Settlement and Closing

In the book's appendix, I have added a couple of samples of a blank offer so you can familiarize yourself with these forms.

Since it's your first offer, you are probably a little nervous. By this point, you should have reviewed the potential investment real estate properties you're interested in, and today, in the coaching challenges, we're setting the stage of practice before you do the real thing.

If you have also spent time with your Team REAL getting all the elements of the offer together—the date of the offer, the initial deposit amount, the exact required details of the property, the address and legal description, the price you are prepared to pay, and the closing date and where the balance of funds to purchase will come from—then the coaching challenges will seem easier to complete.

Day 22 is one of the most important days in this book. Understanding all the elements of making an offer increases your investment real estate knowledge base exponentially and can get the blood flowing.

Remember, the price you offer and the price agreed to by the seller tend to be different. You need to know the bottom-line price you are prepared to pay before walking away from the deal. There will also be other restrictions your real estate agent adds to the offer before it is a done deal.

Once you have your initial offer price in mind, you need to think about an initial deposit amount. When making an offer, you also have to give the sellers a deposit. This amount should show the buyer you are serious, but it does not have to be such a large amount that it ties up your funds. I have seen many different scenarios, but the strategy I recommend is using 1 percent of purchase price. If a home is listed at $300,000, then $3,000 would be a good start. Remember that your real estate agent may have their own advice. The money you give as a deposit is kept in trust with a lawyer until the deal is completed. The funds, of course, are part of the agreed-to final selling price.

You will need to disclose your down payment amount, state the financing terms, and address the possession date in detail. It may be a good idea to wait to discuss the possession details until the counter-offer comes back so you can negotiate. You also need to be clear on who pays what fees, buyer or seller.

Special Reports, Including Maintenance

The reason I mention special reports, including maintenance, is centered on understanding the property you are purchasing. For example, we have discussed single-family homes. In single-family homes, you may add a revenue suite in the basement or over the garage. Or, if you purchase a home in a multiple-unit complex like a condominium building, these homes come with different rules and regulations.

You might request special reports, such as zoning bylaws to allow income suites in single-family homes, or the owner may have kept records on furnace, fireplace, or air-conditioning maintenance.

Also, if you purchase a condominium, the structure's age can be a good clue to what reports you might request. You should ask for the current Reserve Fund Study to ensure the condo owners and board have kept the study current and are funding the total maintenance of the building properly.

Remember, the bylaws are always changing, and what was standard or legal in the 1970s, for example, may not be now. The expiration of your offer is another element. You need to double- and triple-check your offer; don't take anything lightly.

Once you are confident everything will work out, you can submit your offer, and in anywhere from a couple of hours to a couple of days, you will know if your offer has been accepted.

Your real estate agent can be instrumental in helping you get started on your offer. This is where your investment real estate education truly begins. Make sure your agent has reviewed a blank offer form with you before you ever fill an offer out. It is important you understand this form is a legal contract, and you should be aware of what you are signing and what you are committing to. Your real estate agent is there to help; they may have been involved in handling dozens or even hundreds of these offers, but this offer could be the first one you have ever signed.

Make sure you're honest with your agent about that. They should know this is going to be your very first offer on an investment real estate property. Don't be embarrassed or stay silent because you lack experience; your agent is there to educate you. You are paying for these services when you purchase the property, so take advantage of this education.

Before you start to fill out the offer form, you should write down, on a separate piece of paper, what you are thinking in terms of price, closing date, possession date, and a deadline for accepting your offer. In the next section, we'll talk about how to determine these different elements of the offer.

How to Structure an Offer

When you present an offer, it needs to be structured properly. The offer should have the following key components:

- seller's details
- buyer's details
- price
- closing date
- possession date
- deadline for acceptance

From the Big Picture to the Fine Details

Now that you know the parts of an offer, it's time to learn the process. As I mentioned earlier, writing down the details of your offer in advance is critical. Make sure your real estate agent is clear on your goals. This is why it's so essential that you get to know the offer form before you write anything down. No question is stupid—your understanding is paramount. This is your first offer for your very first investment real estate property. How you start can set you on the road to financial freedom or create a financial burden, so let's get this right the first time.

Seller's Details: Information about the seller and the property. This should include their name, contact information, the property's legal description (lot and block number), other legal descriptions required, and other legal matters attached to the title. An example is a right of access, where the state, province, city, or town has the right to enter your property to do work (e.g., utility upgrades).

Buyer's Details: Information about you, the buyer. You will need to provide your legal name, the price you are offering (more details below), the items other than the home that you wanted included (e.g., appliances, window dressings, etc.), the amount of your deposit, the closing and possession date you would like (see more details below), the date when your offer is no longer valid, and any other conditions you want met (e.g., home property inspection, approval of your financing, etc.).

Price: This is the price you are offering to pay for the property. Remember, the price is what you feel comfortable with, and the numbers must work to create a positive cash-flowing rental property. Bear in mind that, in most cases, the seller will counter the price you offer. Again, know your walk-away price. This price needs to keep you in the positive cash-flow zone.

Closing Date: This is when the ownership and title to the house are transferred, and the funds given to the buyer's lawyer or notary are paid to the seller's lawyer or notary.

Possession Date: This is the date the buyer can take possession of the house. As part of your offer, flexibility can work in your favor. Some folks need to move right away; in other cases, they may be building a new home and their possession is a little further out, or their kids are in school and they want them to finish out the school year. A later possession date could work to your advantage. It gives you time to find a renter before you even take possession of the property. The details of you wanting to show the home to potential renters or take pictures to put online must be worked out in the offer. These details are handled by the seller's and buyer's agents and should be written into the offer, setting days of the week, times to show, and how much notice the current residents need for you to show the property. The pictures could be handled in two ways; the easiest would be to get permission to use the existing images the seller's agent is using to sell the property, or again, set up a time and date when you can go to take more current pictures.

Deadline for Acceptance: This is the date by which the seller must agree to your offer. It is important you are reasonable in the time given to the seller to accept your offer, but don't make it too far out. Remember, the seller has already given this process a lot of thought, or they would not have listed their home for sale. The buyer has a bottom-line price in mind, so it should not take long to make the decision. A reasonable amount of time might be forty-eight hours; the sellers may come back to you and ask for a longer period of time. Be careful—a delay in accepting the offer might be a negotiating tactic because the seller and the seller's agent might think more offers are coming in. The longer you give the seller to accept your offer, the greater the chance of losing the property.

Knowing the basic elements of an offer means you're almost there. The biggest moment in your investment real estate journey—the actual purchase—is not so far away!

COACHING CHALLENGE 43: Complete the big-picture details for your "making an offer" practice run.

Think not of practice making perfect, but practice making you aware and more knowledgeable. A practice run for making an offer will help you feel more comfortable when the time comes. Imagine you're about to make an offer on your desired investment real estate property. What are the big-picture details required for the offer?

Ask your real estate agent for a blank copy of the offer form used in your area. Using the real-deal form will better prepare you for the real thing.

If you don't have a form from your agent, fill in the blanks in Coaching Challenge 44 and in the big-picture details line below, or write them out in your notebook or the workbook and planning guide.

Big Picture Details, Sellers and Buyer's details, price, closing date, possession date and deadline for acceptance.

COACHING CHALLENGE 44: Drill down on your "making an offer" practice run.

Building on the big-picture details you provided in the last coaching challenge, it's time to drill down and get more specific. Let's fill in the fine details.

Even though this is a practice run, try to use realistic details based on the area in which you would like to purchase, regarding a property close in value to what you would like to purchase, with a closing and possession date close to a real offer, and a deadline for acceptance you can live with.

Drill-Down Details:

Seller's Details:

Buyer's Details:

Price:

Closing Date:

Possession Date:

Deadline for Acceptance:

Day 22 Key Recap

Record your key learnings and actionable items in your notebook or the workbook and planning guide. (Optional)

- ⇧ When creating an offer, your terms and conditions must be totally outlined. Don't rush this process.
- ⇧ Review all key areas of the offer and know where you can add the terms and conditions.
- ⇧ Use the resources of your real estate agent and lawyer to identify and meet the criteria you have set to a successful investment property purchase.

DAY 23 THE OFFER: ADDING CONDITIONS, INCLUDING PROPERTY INSPECTION

Use this day to focus your efforts and prepare to make an offer. There are some standard components, and some creative components. These ideas will help you to make an offer that stands out from the rest of the pack. At the end of the chapter, complete the coaching challenges to get creative with conditions for your offer.

On Day 22, we learned about the basics of an offer. The offer is what gets the process of purchasing a real estate property in motion. It is the framework that identifies the property, the purchase price, the general terms, the deposits, the land title, and the basic conditions that need to be met in order for the offer to go through.

An offer is a standard form provided in your local jurisdiction. This is why, on Day 22, I asked you to get a blank offer form for the area where you are going to purchase your first investment real estate property. Day 22 was to get you comfortable with the standard offer form in your marketplace. It is important that you have a firm grasp of the basics of an offer before we elaborate on the conditions of an offer and talk about how and why you should think outside the box and get creative when you can.

What Are Conditions?

Simply defined, in a contract, a condition is an issue that must be resolved within a certain amount of time. Conditions are common to real estate purchase offers, which are, as you know by now, a type of contract.

There are many different ways you can present an offer. Understanding the seller's situation can create favorable purchasing conditions you may not be aware of. This is important because your goal is to purchase and rent your first investment real estate property. The conditions can be very basic, following the standard offer format, and dealing primarily with a home inspection and your ability to secure financing. Home inspection and financing tend to be the only things addressed in most offers.

With most offers only including basic conditions, the door is open to set your offer apart from others by applying creative conditions that get the seller's attention.

Getting Creative with Conditions – Seller's Market

Every seller has a reason to sell, yet most buyers don't ever find out why. If you and your real estate agent can dig a little deeper into the seller's why, this can be a treasure chest of opportunity. Knowing this information gives you an edge in creating an offer that stands out from competing offers if you are in a seller's market, where we are seeing multiple offers being thrown at the sellers.

Remember, you can tailor the offer in the conditions section.

When it's a sellers' market—meaning there are multiple bids coming in—smart folks and their real estate agents get creative. The first place people go is the price. Money, possession dates (shorter or longer), and waiving some conditions are all standard methods buyers use to try and make the offer more appealing to the sellers. Everyone does this. But it's hard to get truly creative with numbers like price and possession.

You need your offer to do more; you need it to capture and pique the seller's interest. To do this, you need to try and dig into the seller's motivation. Ask your agent to talk to the seller's agent and find out why they are selling, where they are moving, or even their hobbies or interests. Also, looking at the seller's public social platforms can give you great insight into them as people. (Note: don't be a stalker—make sure you are forthcoming if you use information you came across this way.)

For example, if you find out the sellers love Italy or Italian cooking, what if your offer includes a trip to Italy or cooking lessons with the city's top Italian chef? These may sound like wild ideas, but if it is legal and gets your offer accepted, why not?

What if you found out the sellers are retiring? Maybe they love their home but need the money to live in their retirement. What if you said you would purchase their home and give them a two-year or three-year lease at $200 below rental market value? This would allow the sellers more time to enjoy their home and think through what they might do next. You could end up with renters for life. They are happy with the condition of the home, and you didn't have to do a thing to market the house or get it ready to go on the rental market—it's a win-win.

Some other creative ideas could include memberships, introductions, or subscriptions. Again, if it's legal, why not?

The purpose of all of this? To give the seller an incentive to sell to you beyond price, possession dates, and waiving conditions.

Talk to your Team REAL—your lawyer, accountant, and real estate agent—and see how an offer can be enhanced.

Getting Creative with Conditions – Buyer's Market

If it is a buyer's market, meaning homes are harder to sell, sellers are often the ones getting creative with conditions. They often throw in furniture, draperies, appliances, electronics, or even vehicles to get you to buy their home.

If there are visible signs that a seller is trying to encourage you to make an offer with various items, think about what might bring value to you and your tenants. Furniture and draperies might be a way to rent your investment property as a furnished home. Is there a market for this type of rental in the area you are purchasing your first investment real estate property?

Also, in today's real estate marketplace, most appliances are left with the home. This is not much of an incentive to purchase if all sellers are offering appliances with the purchase of their home.

More Creative, Expand the Box – Buyer's Market

In a buyer's market, you have some leverage to make requests with the conditions.

For example, what if the property needs a fresh coat of paint, new flooring, plumbing work, a new furnace, or an air conditioner? The list of renovation items to have this house show great as a rental property might be considerable. Either ask for all of these items to be done by the seller, or get prices for this work to be done from the members of your Team REAL. Take the quotes, add the items together, and have the seller's real estate agent show their clients the list along with a price reduction to the house to match. You then control the renovations, picking the color of the paint, the type of new carpet, etc.

Again, check with your lawyer about the rules for adding incentives to your offer, and don't be afraid to stand out with some creative conditions if the property is right for you as an investment.

Remember, the worst that can happen is the seller says no or they come back with an alternative.

 **Create some conditions.**

Where do you need help when it comes to making your offer for your first investment property? Is it the renovations, is it financing, is it appliances, is it furniture or mechanical upgrades, or is it window coverings? What creative components would make your investment real estate property a success?

Review the list above, brainstorm, and build your own list of what you would feel comfortable asking for in your offer.

⇧   Using your notebook, the workbook and planning guide, or the boxes below, write out some creative items to utilize in your offer. You can add as many or as few as you'd like.

1)	7)
2)	8)
3)	9)
4)	10)
5)	11)
6)	12)

Present your creative conditions.

Once you have decided on the items you would like to add to the offer, you need to brainstorm with your real estate agent about how the offer should be presented to stand out.

One method might be to write a letter by hand to the sellers detailing why you have added these items to your offer. It might be as simple as telling them how this property could help your family in the future.

In today's video-oriented world, you could also video-record yourself and talk directly to the sellers, explaining how you understand why they need to sell and how proud you are of having the opportunity to own this property. If you are sincere and your video message is viewed this way by the sellers, how different would that be to most offers?

- How will you make your offer stand out? Will you write a letter or record a video?

In your notebook, the workbook and planning guide, or using the lines below, write down what you have in mind and how it would get delivered to the sellers as part of the offer.

_____
_____
_____

Day 23 Key Recap

Record your key learnings and actionable items in your notebook or the workbook and planning guide. (Optional)

- When creating your offer, understand what conditions in the offer are and how the conditions protect both the buyer and the seller. Don't be afraid to address all your concerns until they have been resolved to your satisfaction.
- Get creative with conditions as a buyer to lower the purchase price or address property deficiencies. The conditions should be a win-win for both buyer and seller.
- Knowing the differences between a seller's and buyer's market can help you present the best offer for your situation.

DAY 24 THE PURCHASE: PROPERTY INSPECTION DONE AND CONDITIONS REMOVED

Use this day to make your first investment real estate purchase and get to know your product. At the end of the chapter, complete the coaching challenges to write a home inspection list.

Now that you've made the offer to purchase your first investment real estate property, it's time to make good on one of your conditions: the home inspection.

You should have made sure to mention in the offer paperwork that the offer is conditional to a home inspection. If any issues with the home arise during the inspection, the inspector can give you the approximate costs to repair. Based on this information, you can make a more educated decision. You may walk away from the home, or you may negotiate to get the price of the offer lower to deal with the cost of repairs.

What Is a Home Inspection?

A home inspection is usually limited to a non-invasive process to examine the condition of a house and is generally done in connection with the sale of the house.

Why Do a Home Inspection?

As the purchaser, you should know about what you are buying. You have heard the saying, "Beauty is only skin deep." As an informed buyer, you need to use the home inspection information to gain knowledge about the inner workings of the home.

What Is a Home Inspector?

A home inspector is a professional with certification and training in the home inspection field that allows them to perform this inspection. A home inspector will determine the condition of the house or structure and identify problems with the home.

A home inspector is not a real estate appraiser. An appraiser determines the value of the house, and an inspector determines the condition.

A couple of examples of items that a home inspector might examine are the furnace, air conditioning, or hot water tank age and how much life is left in the units. They might also look at the fireplace and determine the last time it was cleaned.

A home inspector can give you real insight into work you might have to address the moment you take possession of the house. By knowing the issues, you can price these items out and, in many cases, get the seller to do the work before you take possession or take the price of doing this work off the original purchase price.

Hiring a Home Inspector

When you hire a home inspector, the process should be just like it is for any other member of your Team REAL: do your research and find a professional home inspector who is also an investment real estate investor. Make sure the inspector understands that you are looking to purchase this real estate as an investment property, and ask them to think about the use of this property as they conduct the home inspection.

Your real estate agent should have a couple of suggestions of who to hire and why. They should have used the home inspector with other clients. Ask for a couple of referrals from the home inspectors suggested and give them a call.

Today, most home inspectors are certified. Ask about their certification.

What Happens During the Inspection?

During the home inspection, the inspector will be looking for any issues that need immediate attention. If the home is neglected, you will be made aware of this; on the other hand, if the home has been well taken care of, you will be made aware of this, too.

Ensure you know what the home inspector is looking for in advance, before the inspection occurs. Ask the inspector to outline the information they'll collect and what type of report you will receive. Ask for a blank copy and develop any additional questions for the home inspector you feel should be addressed before and after the home inspection. I would also ask your real estate agent for guidance and questions to ask the home inspector.

The home inspection can take up to several hours to complete. It is conducted by the professional, and the home purchaser is usually not involved. One of the reasons for this is that the home inspector may carry special insurance while on business in case of any issues; there might be liability issues related to this that prohibit you from attending the home inspection.

Make sure you set time aside for a debriefing to review the home inspection report with the home inspector once the job is done. I would encourage your real estate agent to sit in on the conversation, as the agent will be the one to negotiate any changes to the offer to purchase should items need to be price-adjusted or work needs to be done before you take possession of the home.

The key areas viewed by the inspector are the exterior, interior, plumbing, and electrical.

Let's discuss these key areas in depth.

Exterior

The exterior starts right at the curb. Think of your list as you make your walk up to the house.

- ⇧ Sidewalks to house, driveway, and patios
- ⇧ All exterior doors, including garage door
- ⇧ Garage and/or carport
- ⇧ Wall coverings, siding, and trim
- ⇧ Eaves, fascia, and soffits
- ⇧ Drainage, grading, plants/trees, and retaining walls

- ⇧ Downspouts and gutters
- ⇧ Balconies, decks, steps, porches, and railings
- ⇧ Roof (house, garage, and shed), including chimneys and other roof penetrations like skylights

Interior

The interior is defined as any area within the home and garage.

- ⇧ Cabinets and countertops
- ⇧ Doors and windows
- ⇧ Kitchen appliances
- ⇧ Walls, flooring, and ceilings
- ⇧ Ductwork
- ⇧ Garage door operators
- ⇧ Foundation
- ⇧ Fireplace and stoves

Plumbing

Plumbing is described as the installation and maintenance of systems used for drinking water, sewage, and drainage in plumbing systems.

- ⇧ Sump pumps
- ⇧ Water heater

- ⇧ Fixtures and faucets
- ⇧ Drain, vent, and waste systems

Electrical

Electrical is the wiring of the home and related equipment. The electrical work might include the installation of new components or the maintenance and repair of existing electrical infrastructure in the home.

- ⇧ HVAC (heating, ventilation, and air conditioning), including vents, distribution systems, thermostats, access panels, insulation, and vapor retarders
- ⇧ Service equipment, drops, grounding, and main disconnects
- ⇧ Service cables, entrance conductors, and raceways
- ⇧ Light fixtures, receptacles, and power switches
- ⇧ Overcurrent protection devices
- ⇧ Circuit breakers

Remember, the list I have provided is a guideline and may not include every item that a professional home inspector would have on their checklist. If you don't understand any of the terminology they use, just ask. No question is stupid.

You also need to understand, in general terms, what a home inspection or inspector is not including or looking for:

- ⇧ Areas that are not easy to reach

- ⇧ Low-wattage electrical systems (alarm systems and phone lines)
- ⇧ The general landscaping
- ⇧ Drainage of the property or tree roots impacting foundation or drainage lines. (Depending on what part of the country you live in, you might ask the home inspector to add this to their work or suggest a specialist to review)
- ⇧ Insects, including carpenter ants or termites
- ⇧ Rodents
- ⇧ Airborne hazards

Make sure you are clear on what you are paying for in a home inspection. Some inspectors like to upsell products and services, such as testing for mold, carbon dioxide, or asbestos.

Don't purchase any unnecessary services. An example would be checking for asbestos. Canada banned the use of asbestos in homes in 1979, but up until 1991, you could have found materials with asbestos being used. If a home was built in Canada after 1991, I would not spend money checking for asbestos. Check your municipal, state, provincial, or federal regulations around asbestos.

Ask yourself if these funds could be better used to help create a better rental home for your tenants.

The Costs of Home Inspections

Home inspections are generally paid for by the homebuyer. This is a good idea, as the home inspector is working for you and giving you their advice and insights. Pricing generally varies from $350 to $500. As recommended above, ask around and see if there is any certification of home inspectors in your area. If so, find out what it is, and whether your inspector has it. Home inspection is an investment and is one of the best ways to start your investment real estate journey. The knowledge you will gain going over the home inspection will be invaluable. You will learn so many details about the property you are purchasing, so there will be no surprises.

Remember, each area in which the home inspector finds a deficiency comes with a cost to repair or bring up to current code. In many cases, you can ask the home seller to spend the money to bring things up to code before you take possession, or you can ask for the price to be reduced by the cost of the deficiency.

I am more in favor of getting the current homeowner to do as much of the work as possible before you take possession. After all, you are going to have enough on your plate—financing and banking, getting the property ready to your standards to rent, marketing it, and finding a tenant. The less you have to do before taking on ownership, the lighter the load on your shoulders.

Acceptance

Once the home inspection is complete, if everything is up to speed, or the offer is revised and agreed to by the sellers, the conditions are removed from the offer and it's time to make the purchase. Everything has led up to this exciting moment: agreeing to buy your first investment real estate property. Congratulations!

Conclusion

I talk a lot about your financial foundation, and how you use this information from today can give you that extra boost to a great start in putting your best foot forward with your future tenants. Knowing all the aspects of your property are in the right condition will ensure you end up with a great investment property and a wonderful home for your future client-tenants.

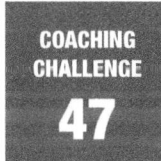

Write your home inspection list.

The home inspection is an essential step toward the purchase and one of the key conditions on an offer. Having the right items on your list is necessary so that you can rest assured the home is in great shape before you buy.

The type of property you purchase as your first investment real estate property will determine what should be on your property inspection list. Let's work on building your list according to your ideal investment property. Use the space below, or write in your notebook or workbook and planning guide.

⇧ What items should be on your list to check when conducting a property inspection?

Day 24 Key Recap

Record your key learnings and actionable items in your notebook or the workbook and planning guide. (Optional)

- ⇧ Your home inspector can help you understand the costs involved in purchasing a particular real estate investment property.
- ⇧ The key areas viewed by the inspector are the exterior, interior, plumbing, and electrical.
- ⇧ If necessary, use the findings from the home inspection to revise your offer to address unforeseen concerns not captured in the original offer.

Stage III:
Goal

Days 25 to 31

STAGE III: GOAL

CROSSING THE FINISH LINE, ARMS IN THE AIR

Congratulations for making it to Stage III! Our final stage makes it clear that investment real estate is not a get-rich-quick scheme and that it takes time to realize the potential in investment real estate. This section is all about what happens after you make the purchase of your first investment real estate property with vigor and enthusiasm.

From the moment you get the keys, there's much to prepare. We'll walk you through the process of readying your new investment property for rental, finding ideal tenants, dealing with the financials, and completing your year-end paperwork at the end of your first year as an investment real estate owner.

On Days 25 and 26, we will spend time marketing your property to renters, then screening, acquiring, and retaining renters.

On Day 27, we will discuss the move-in checklist.

On Day 28, we will review your revenue and expenses monthly and on a rolling year-to-date.

On Day 29, we will look at how your funds are working for you, and Day 30 will get you thinking about growing your investment real estate portfolio with this process, should that be something you desire.

All good things come to an end, so on Day 31, we will discuss your exit strategy, as there will be many ways to view your exit from investment real estate.

You'll learn how to use the legacy of inheritance while you are alive and have a say on how your legacy is used to make a difference for your family and/or community. The neat thing is being involved in the decision-making and getting to enjoy improving people's lives now instead of waiting until you're gone.

Building a strong real estate foundation can have positive effects for generations of your family and community—effects that live on long past your time in this world. This final stage will help you become the third little pig and set in motion clear strategies to build your own brick investment real estate house that can't be blown down.

Whether you are new to investment real estate and looking for a system to take you from the sidelines and onto the playing field, or you have done some investing but aren't happy with your progress, this section will help you bring your dream to fruition and achieve great results.

Once you've worked your way through Day 25 to Day 31, you'll have achieved your investment real estate goal.

If you're still hungry for more, you can read the many supporting blogs, podcasts, and resource-rich website that supplement this book. These materials are regularly refreshed with helpful information you can rely on to support the development of your investment real estate portfolio. Remember, you don't have to be in acquisition mode to keep yourself engaged in the fundamentals of your small business; this is the base of entrepreneurship.

In addition, the book is supported by an online course and my workbook and planning guide. I encourage you to check out these great resources if you are enjoying this book and wish to take things a step further. Visit my website, vaulttorealestateinvestmentsuccess.com, for more details.

As I say during many of my podcasts, let's get on with the show . . . or should that be Goal!

DAY 25 MARKETING YOUR PROPERTY TO RENTERS

Use this day to structure your marketing materials to promote your property in the rental marketplace and understand some of the external factors affecting how you market. You'll find some traditional elements and some ideas about using the internet, partner websites, print materials, and video. At the end of the chapter, complete the coaching challenges to identify your unique selling proposition, build your brand, and make your property stand out from the pack.

Attracting your perfect tenant—the one you defined back on Day 7—can mean the difference between your own personal heaven and hell. The correct approach can go a long way to increasing your level of happiness in your investment real estate business and how financially secure and profitable your experience can be.

If you adopt a customer-and-client philosophy rather than a landlord-and-tenant mindset, you will find your investment real estate business will be kinder to you.

The Immigration Connection and the Why for North America

We, as a global society, are seeing certain parts of the world's population growing dramatically. Meanwhile, many countries do not have high enough birth rates to offset the population decline. In Canada, deaths are expected to start outnumbering births by the year 2030. From that point forward, immigration would be the only growth factor for the Canadian population. What do you think this means to the rental market in countries that will rely on immigration as the backbone of their population growth?

UNICEF estimates that an average of 353,000 babies are born each day around the world. The birth rate is 18.9 births per 1,000 population, equating to 255 births globally per minute, or 4.3 births every second. Our current world population, which passed the 7-billion mark in 2011, is now approximately 7.2 billion and growing. It is expected to reach between 8 and 10 billion by 2050. These numbers are calculated using the current medical and health-care paradigm.

Once you have determined what type of renter you would like to have rent your property, you need to do your homework. By going above and beyond and properly vetting your tenants, you can turn these folks into long-term clients who will pay for all of your operational costs, including mortgage principal paydown. A credit check, employment verification, salary verification, the last place they rented (talk to the property manager), or even something as simple as meeting them at your property and seeing how clean and tidy they keep their vehicle can give you a glimpse into who these folks are.

But before all of this, you have to prepare the property for your new renters. Then, you have to attract some prospective client-tenants.

Preparing Your Property for Renters

Many homeowners will hire a staging service when they sell their homes. Unless you are renting a furnished apartment or condo, I recommend you don't pay for a staging service. Few apartments or condos are staged for rental purposes.

Cleanliness should be your number-one priority when showing; this should include ensuring there are no funny or nasty odors. If your unit is in a building, make sure you know how the building is maintained. Fresh paint or touch-ups are paramount, and you should keep the paint colors neutral.

Your Unique Selling Proposition

If you think back to Day 12, when we focused on the FOCUS (Follow One Commitment Until Success) concept, you can put all your energy into the positive aspects of your investment real estate property and create what many marketers call your unique selling proposition (USP).

The unique selling proposition is your positioning statement to a tenant; this is the online or print description of the property, and should include pictures. Your USP helps your tenant quickly categorize what type of property you have—one-bedroom, two-bedroom, single-family home, etc.—and the amenities that set it apart from others of a similar type. The potential renter should be able to choose you above the competition through what marketers call your point of difference (PoD), so challenge yourself to turn your PoD into your USP.

Creating your unique selling proposition doesn't require you to outspend your competition by a large amount. Simply ask yourself the following questions:

- Why is our rental property unique?
- What is the proof of that?
- What benefits will our tenants enjoy?
- What problems will our property solve for our tenants?

If you are struggling with answering these questions, you will have a hard time developing your unique selling proposition.

To help make this easier, in the next section, I will share some of the USP techniques we have used in our rental units. Remember, if you don't highlight these in your marketing, they don't have any value.

I am not suggesting you use all of these ideas at once. Do your market research and determine what will bring the most value to your potential tenants.

It's possible to implement several of these ideas for under $100, and you'll have created your own unique selling propositions. In the future, should you decide to own multiple investment properties, you could even develop a signature USP to use in all your rentals.

Making Your Investment Property Stand Out with USPs

Standing out from your competition takes a little trend-watching, some elbow grease, and a small financial investment.

We use a six-point improvement strategy for our investment real estate properties: exterior, entrance, kitchen, living room, bathroom, and bedroom. The goal is to make at least one improvement in each of these six areas.

- **Exterior:** Install a motion light at the front entrance or the garage. You could also put in a built-in camera doorbell at the front entrance for extra security. Make sure the front door to the home or condo is freshly painted and the hardware is in good shape.
- **Front Entrance:** These areas tend to be small. Install mirrored sliding closet doors, which make the area feel more spacious. Plus, people love to check their appearance before they leave home. You could also install a closet kit to maximize space. Most closets generally come with a top shelf on which to place hats and personal wearable small items, and a hanging bar. Imagine a closet with a built-in shoe-and-boot rack, and a couple of sliding drawers for small personal items.
- **Kitchen:** Add a dishwasher or a microwave built into the range hood. We have found we get a higher rental rate for the same type of unit in the same building on the same floor with a dishwasher. Or, put in a range hood with a microwave. Most kitchens tend to be small with not much counter space; putting a microwave above the stove as part of the range hood is a feature folks love, and the investment is reasonable. Appliance retailers like Home Depot, Lowe's, and others have a great selection and reasonable prices.

Putting shelf lining into the kitchen cupboards is another affordable and attractive option.

- **Living Room:** Install curtains. Again, go to Home Depot, Lowe's, or other big-box retailers and purchase curtain rods and curtains for a modest investment. These are easy to install, match to your paint color, and use as an accent. You only get one chance to make a good first impression! Or, offer to paint a feature wall.
- **Bathroom:** Install a new inner and outer shower curtain. Again, this is a modest investment that can make the bathroom look awesome. Match the color to the paint scheme in the bathroom, use to accent, and don't be afraid to purchase new shower curtain hooks if the existing ones are rusty, don't match the color scheme, or look worn or broken. Also, put in an additional bathroom storage unit if the space can benefit from more storage.
- **Bedroom:** Just like I recommend in the entranceway, install mirrored doors on the closet. If there's a wide opening to the closet, go with sliding glass doors; use a bifold for smaller openings. Put in closet organizers to maximize space. Install blinds if it's within your budget.

These recommendations are not carved in stone. Use your own personal flair; just remember to keep on-trend, cater to your ideal client-tenants, and watch your budget.

Know Your Competition

With online services like PadMapper.com, Kijiji, Craigslist, and Apartments for Rent, you can easily drill down to the area you have purchased in, the type of property, and the rental rates. Find some properties that compare to yours and review the pictures of current properties. What USP are they offering, and how does your property measure up? Can you take any inspiration from these properties to make improvements that will make your property more marketable and competitive

Creating a Marketing Structure

Creating a marketing structure is all about building your brand as an investment real estate investor.

One of the real estate educational groups I belong to, Real Estate Investment Network (REIN), has been in business for over twenty-five years. A few years ago, they asked us members to pivot from calling ourselves landlords and rebrand ourselves as rental housing providers. At first, many of us thought this was a cute marketing ploy. But for REIN, the change ran much deeper.

Patrick Francey, the CEO of REIN, talked to us about moving from a tenant mindset to a client philosophy and creating a value-based relationship with our renters.

He explained that, for our clients, it is all about trust. The four dimensions of trust are truth, reliability, competence, and heart (caring). We, as owners, can take action upon and control the four dimensions of truth. This trust is an integral part of REIN's brand.

At the beginning of this book, I wrote out my vision, mission, and value statements. My vision, mission, and value statements are part of my brand.

Have you thought of yourself and your investment real estate business as a brand?

Building Your Investment Real Estate Brand

In today's set of coaching challenges, we will talk about tools you can use to market your brand. But first, we need to discuss what a brand is and how you build your brand.

You might be thinking, "Rick, this is one property I am branding." But answering just a few simple questions gets you to think about your investment real estate property as a small business and helps add to the element of success.

Think about what you bring to the rental market. What are your strengths? What makes you unique? How do you build on your uniqueness and strengths? Think of your uniqueness and strengths as part of your brand-building.

You identified your values through your value statement way back in the first part of this book, and now it is time to set your priorities.

It is important you use the areas you control to set your business apart in this competitive environment. Create the little things that most landlords would not think of doing for their tenants. Paying attention to the small details can be low in cost but high in return, numbers of prospective tenants to choose from, and rents. Make sure you are speaking directly to your audience—your ideal tenant. Don't let looking at every other investment real estate owner in your rental market suck you into mediocrity; crush the noise and look at ways to stand out. I have outlined seven simple methods on how to do this.

Building your brand starts at the beginning of your investment real estate journey, when you have the most energy. Create a brand you are proud of, that you will love, and that will showcase your rental property personality.

How are you going to build your brand and personality? Through higher quality, customer focus, lower price point, great value, and differentiation for price? Select one of these ideas and focus on that. The more your rental unit can stand out from similar rental units, the more memorable you become. Learn to be the industry leader.

Investing time and building value into your strategy early can save you time and lead to more revenue down the road.

Early in the book, we talked about financing, expenses, and understanding rents in your area of investment. If you have done a good job on your expenses and understanding rents in your area, you may have left yourself enough room to spend a little extra on the seven key ways to create your uniqueness.

7 Key Ways to Build Your Brand through Your Uniqueness and Strengths:

1. Treat others how you want to be treated. Many of us start out life as a renter—anyone whose parents were in the Armed Forces is a prime example. My dad was a member for twenty-five years; he started as a young adult. My parents didn't purchase their first home until his last posting. Over the years, we often lived in the Department of National Defence housing, but my parents rented at least half the time. We were good tenants, and if it was not for having a landlord with good housing, we would have had nowhere to live. These landlords left a strong impression on our lives. By treating your tenants well, you'll leave the same sort of good impression with them.

2. Get to Know Your Tenants. Your tenants are your customers and clients. Remember, investment real estate is a business, and companies are successful because they know their customers.

For example, if you want to rent to couples with small families, a swing set in the backyard—a small investment—adds value and shows that you are family-friendly without saying a word. If your ideal tenant is a senior, have safety railings installed in the bathtub or shower area for easier access. It's not an expensive investment, but it says a lot about your concern for your clients' well-being. Or, if you are marketing to singles, security might be a concern. Having motion lights installed over each entrance to the home can show that you care about making the home safe.

Remember to showcase these improvements when showing or marketing the home. Otherwise, the investment is for nothing.

We reward our current tenants in many ways, including ensuring they have a safe, clean, and reliable place to live. In the past, we have gifted our loyal tenants with movie passes or grocery and restaurant gift certificates. With the onset of COVID-19, we have offered rent relief to get folks through the government help or their return to work. In this way, we build our reputation as a rental housing provider who knows and cares about our tenants.

3. Look for Small Technological Ways to Stand Out. In today's technological world, we all have smartphones, tablets, e-readers, and other devices. Simply putting in some plug-ins with built-in USB ports is a small investment, but it can be a major selling point to a tenant and set you apart as a rental housing provider who is on the cutting edge.

4. Welcome to the Neighborhood. Create a list of local businesses in your neighborhood. Approach these businesses and see if any are prepared to welcome new folks to the neighborhood with a discount at their establishment.

5. Celebrate Birthdays or Move-in Anniversaries. You don't need the year someone is born, just the day of their birth. Send them a card—yes, a physical card, not an e-card or text. Or, send a card on the tenant's move-in date and thank them for being a tenant. Make sure you personalize the message by adding a nice compliment on why you are happy to have them as a renter.

6. Fix Something or Upgrade Something. Can you imagine showing up and fixing something out of the blue that needs repair, or upgrading something without being asked? This applies to everything from the creaky door to a board or two in the fence that needs replacing. Make sure you give the tenants adequate notice according to the laws in your local area. They'll appreciate your efforts to make their lives more comfortable, without having to ask.

7. Return Phone Calls, Texts, or Emails Promptly. The person on the other end might need you more than you realize. By doing so, they'll see you as reliable.

Using these tips, you can strengthen your brand as an investment real estate investor and ensure your tenants see you in a positive light.

Marketing Your Rental Property

When you start the search for a tenant, you can take numerous approaches. One of my favorites is through the online apartment hunting platform PadMapper.

Back on Day 11, you used this site to gather information on rental rates and the types of properties in the market. Well, you can also use PadMapper and many similar services to rent and market your property.

PadMapper (www.padmapper.com) improves the apartment-hunting experience. This platform, which is free for users, plots apartments on a big map, and allows users to filter for properties that suit their preferences. **PadMapper's goal** is to make apartment hunting something that people don't dread.

In addition to PadMapper, there are many other online rental websites; visit the different sites and look at their services. Each service and how they receive compensation is rapidly changing. Don't get caught up in monthly fees; look for a flat-rate service fee that can be extended month-on-month. If you are going to pay a monthly fee or a percentage of the rental fee, you are better off working with a local property manager. (See more information on property management services below.)

- www.Apartments.com
- www.Forrent.com
- www.MyNewPlace.com
- www.Hotpads.com
- www.Padmapper.com

Making Your Property Stand Out in a Print or Online Ad

The biggest undertaking you have when listing your property for rent on the sites I mentioned is providing high-quality pictures and ensuring the description you provide to these services is complete and reflects the property's true nature. You can do all the work from the comfort of your computer. You only have a few seconds to make a good impression, so make sure you have the most current pictures of your property, and that they are high-quality.

With the quality of modern cellphone cameras, getting professional-quality pictures might not be as difficult as you think. Lighting tends to be the most important element of getting good photos. Try and take pictures on a bright, sunny day, and don't be afraid to bring additional lighting. Even a good table lamp without its shade can create great lighting.

Make sure you don't have dust in the pictures. The only downside of good lighting is that it can show the dust easier. Bring cleaning supplies, and get scuff marks off the walls and counters. Yes, when it comes to taking pictures, cleanliness is next to godliness.

Try and create a story. People love the bathrooms being close to the bedrooms; take an angled shot to capture this. Also, if you have sliding patio glass doors opening onto a patio or deck, create the effect of someone coming home from a long day at work and being able to open the patio doors and sit out on the patio or deck, enjoying a drink and a quiet moment outside.

There are so many devices you can purchase to help you take incredible pictures. I have purchased an Osmo Mobile handheld stabilizer that holds your cell phone and helps you take incredible pictures as you move around your property.

Recently, a company named Pivo created a cell phone pod that works with a free app called Pivo Tour. By combining the Pivo Black Pod and the Pivo Tour app, you can capture 3D spaces for marketing and business purposes. Users can create immersive virtual tours in a matter of minutes with a smartphone and the Pivo Pod, which comes with a remote control and a regular tripod.

Please note I am not asking you to spend a ton of money. If you feel comfortable taking pictures with your smartphone alone, no problem. One step up, for under $100, is the handheld stabilizer, or for between $200 and $300, you can go all-in with the Pivo solution.

The Description

Once you have at least ten quality photos, view them as you write your ad. We'll discuss writing the ad below.

You should create a detailed rental property description that includes the basics about the bedrooms, bathrooms, storage, dining area, living areas, and kitchen. How many bedrooms and bathrooms are there? You should highlight the upgrades (e.g., USB ports, feature painted wall, etc.) and any other desirable features.

Clearly list rent price, lease duration, and required fees (e.g., damage deposit, pet fees, etc.). Ensure you mention parking and pet restrictions (e.g., size, weight, number of pets). Be upfront about your rental policies and any shared amenities. Finally, make sure you don't forget to market the rental's proximity to transit, dining, shopping, etc.

Last but not least, proofread your ad. Get someone else to review it, just in case.

Your Own Website

The internet gives you multiple choices; creating your own website might be an option. I am not sure if you will attract enough traffic or the right clientele to make this a viable option, but it could be of interest to some.

Property Management Websites

Another great option for attracting and securing potential tenants is a property manager's client website. This is generally a free service that includes taking pictures, offered by a property management company to help secure your business. If you are dealing with a good-sized property management company, this may be all the internet exposure you need, and the service has not cost you a dime.

Using a Property Management Service Instead of Self-Managing

When we purchased our first investment real estate property, we decided to take on the job of property manager. We learned a lot in this role. My suggestion is to take on this task at the beginning of developing your investment real estate portfolio. You will soon realize that it takes time, patience, and a certain level of skill to be a landlord.

Let's start with understanding the roles of a property manager and a landlord, and how these roles have everything to do with effectively marketing your investment real estate property.

A property manager is a professional who serves two primary roles regarding investment real estate. The property manager works for the owners of a single property or multiple properties; these properties can vary in type from single-family homes to multiple-unit apartment blocks or condominiums. Property managers are also heavily involved in commercial real estate, but for the purposes of this book I will focus on residential real estate property management and landlording.

Property management can be defined as the operation, control, maintenance, and oversight of the investment real estate property. Management also takes care of and monitors the real estate, with accountability for and attention to the property's operational life and condition.

A good property manager needs to be much more than an operational company; they need to understand the real estate market—the big picture—in your town or city. They are also fully aware of the desirable areas to live in. There are several factors driving peoples' needs and wants. For renters, rental rates, safety and security of the property, and proximity to work, transportation routes, shopping, banking, and numerous other services have an impact on decisions made by renters. The property management company needs to be aware of all of these conditions and how to market to potential tenants.

A property manager can manage two parts of multi-family complexes. First, they can manage an apartment or condo unit that has one owner within a complex of multiple apartments or condo units. Second, they can also manage the entire apartment or condominium complex. This means the property manager could manage the unit for an owner but not manage the entire complex.

When we first started investing, we purchased several condominium units in different complexes; a different management company managed these complexes. Over the years, we first changed our property management company for our single residential units. As we learned more about investing, we decided it was also much easier from a marketing, communications, and operational side to align the property management of our units to be the same as the property management of the complex. When you have one property manager handling the tenant side (your single residential unit) and the entire complex, it makes your life much easier. The property management company is producing the communication of what is happening operationally in the complex, and they are also responsible for communicating this to your tenants they are managing. Think about how easy this will be for you. You won't have to contact your tenants about any operational or maintenance issues; this is your property manager's responsibility.

Sit on the Board

Whether you self-manage or have a property manager, you should sit on the board of directors if you own property in an apartment, townhouse, or condominium complex.

The board of directors is not responsible for the day-to-day operation of a complex but makes the decision on who to hire as the property management company.

Again, you might be wondering what this has to do with marketing your property to potential clients. Everything! You might own the nicest, cleanest, safest, most secure unit in the complex, but if the complex is mismanaged, you will never realize the full rental and return on value. By being on the board of directors, you can influence how the appearance, maintenance, and operation of the entire complex is handled. All these building factors lead to curb appeal, and with great curb appeal, the job to market your residential rental home becomes easier and more attractive.

Hidden Gems

You should look to present your property as one with small hidden gems—neat little features that folks will remember right away. One way to do this, as mentioned, is to install several wall plug-ins with USB ports; with technology driving our lives, all these electronic tools need to be charged, and potential renters will appreciate that attention to detail.

Even a simple investment into a programmable thermostat or programmable lights can give an impression of convenience in one's life. Programmable light bulbs can be very reasonably priced, and your tenants can download a free app to work these lights.

As always, don't forget that you need to market these features.

Web Partners

I have spoken about using a property management service, and if you pick the correct property manager, they will manage all of the marketing of your unit, including taking pictures and writing the description. Most good property managers have their own websites showing all the properties they rent, and these property managers will link their sites to other major rental sites.

I love our property management company, but I still check up on how they are marketing our vacant homes for rent. I find that, from time to time, we do new upgrades, like painting countertops or adding newer appliances, and the property manager is still using old pictures of the unit. Make sure they are showing your best side.

Print and Signage

You might find great tenants by creating a nice one-page flyer of your rental unit and posting it on community information boards. These boards provide great visibility.

Make sure you first understand the rules for posting a flyer, and make sure your flyer has a great picture of your unit and includes contact information.

Video

In today's video-crazed market, a great video can go a long way. A great type of video for introducing your rental space is a walkthrough, in which you feature the property, room by room, just as if the prospective tenant were having a tour in person.

You don't need a lot of fancy equipment for this—a modern smartphone will do just fine. Most folks can purchase a handheld smartphone holder to take smooth, stabilized video that won't be shaky like a regular handheld video. An example of such a device is a gimbal handheld stabilizer. Check out sites like Amazon.com or eBay.com to find different models for various budgets.

Make sure you record the video with lots of natural light pouring into the home. Try and create a bright and cheerful feeling from the moment you drive up to the property, as first impressions and curb appeal are critical. Describe the area in which your rental unit is located. Because you have identified your ideal tenant, focus on the features they would like to see. It might be about the parks, pathways, schools, shopping, and services nearby; include these in your video.

As you create your video, a simple welcome as you open the door to your rental home is a great way to introduce your unit. Make sure you are videotaping each room in sequence; it is crucial that people get a feel for the home, just as they would if they were entering in person.

One area people often neglect in their real estate video is giving a sense of storage space. Make sure you give people a look at the front entranceway, kitchen storage, washroom storage, bedroom closets, and any additional storage space, like other closets. Should your unit be a condo, if there is extra storage external to the condo that renters will use, ensure you take the time to show this space.

Don't forget about any amenities with the building, either; it might be as simple as the laundry room or parking space, but it provides a fuller picture of your home.

Should you be renting a single-family home, duplex, or townhouse, ensure you show the storage in any garage or storage shed on the property; describe how someone's tools or lawn appliances can be stored.

Resources to Attract Target Renters

We have discussed how much thought you should put into who your target renter is from the very beginning, even before you purchased the property. To attract and retain these renters, you need to think outside the rental box.

When you go to rent your first investment real estate property, you may not think you have a lot of resources to attract your target renter. But getting creative can make a big difference in how attractive your property is to prospective clients. Below is a suggested list you can build a resource around:

- Offer first or last month's rent free
- Give your potential client a voucher for a moving company
- Ask your family, friends, and neighbors for referrals
- Ask your property manager, if you have one, if they can think of any past clients who would make great tenants
- Network with other investors
- Search for businesses who might need housing for their employees
- Seek out businesses that specialize in welcoming new people to the area
- Participate in community events and get to know your rental marketplace
- Focus on your unique selling propositions

Have you noticed that most of the list comes at no or little cost? It is your time and efforts that give you the biggest returns on these ideas.

What Should I Start With?

When it comes to deciding where to start marketing your property first and how many methods to use, the answer depends on whether or not you use a property manager. As I mentioned earlier, using a property manager can keep your marketing costs low as they have their own internal system for the properties they manage.

You should price out the cost of marketing services in your rental area.

When starting with one property, you might be able to find free services that will work great for you in the beginning. A prime example would be community bulletin boards. The community bulletin boards tend to be free; one caveat is that you need to monitor your posting regularly as you might have competition and find your information goes missing.

A simple sign in the window of your rental home can attract clients. Make sure you use a phone number on which you don't mind receiving these inquiry calls, or have an answering mechanism as part of this phone's service. Remember, most people are impatient and will move on to the next rental if they don't receive information promptly.

Marketing your property properly will take a lot of the stress out of the rental process. So, make sure you are putting the property's best foot forward by following the tips in this chapter.

COACHING CHALLENGE 48

Build your brand and determine what it should say about you.

Like in any business, good marketing is all about building your brand. So in this challenge, that's exactly what we're going to do. Take the following steps to build your investment real estate brand:

⇧ 1. Declare to your world, including your social media audience, that you are now an investment real estate investor.

⇧ 2. Take great pictures and videos of your investment real estate property. Make sure you take these pictures before any attempt to rent your property. Develop a story with your video.

⇧ 3. Think about your brand philosophy. The type of property you purchased may help you, as will the type of clientele you are trying to attract. I mentioned I was part of an Armed Forces family—could this be your space?

⇧ 4. Create your value statement about your brand, referring to the section in the book's Introduction about value. Read your value statement out loud. Does it sound natural? Is it in your voice?

⇧ 5. Decide what personal social media platforms fit your brand. People today are very visual; social media requires not only great photos but videos, too.

⇧ 6. Remember that building your brand doesn't happen overnight.

Choose your ideal marketing mix.

When you put a marketing plan in motion for your investment real estate property, it's important to determine your marketing mix—or set of tools—for your needs.

In the beginning, you might want to take a hands-on approach and self-manage and self-market your property. Doing everything yourself is a great learning experience, but it can be time-consuming and challenging. Or, if you don't want the headache of showing the apartment, collecting rents, or evicting a tenant for nonpayment or non-compliance with maintenance, you can hire a property manager. Another option is to take a hybrid approach where you take on a portion of the marketing yourself.

What is the best marketing mix for you?

- **You.** In this scenario, you do all of the work, take care of the property, ready it for renting, set the rent, list the property on a rental marketplace, and find ways to get the word out through websites, social media, print advertising, or video.
- **Property management company.** This is a one-stop shop that involves little work on your end. They do all of the marketing, take care of the property, set the price, create and manage the listing, and promote it.
- **Website partner.** This is more of a hybrid approach. You use their social media and website platforms (promotion), but you handle the product (your rental unit), the price (rental rate), and the place (information on your rental marketplace).

 **Determine how you'll deal with last-minute challenges.**

Dealing with any last-minute issues in getting the property ready to rent can be a challenge, and the problems seem more amplified when it is your first property.

In your current phase of the process, you have gone through the home inspection and addressed everything on your list. You are moving from the eye of a home inspector to the eye of a tenant—a tenant who is looking to make this a home. Make sure your rental home is delivering on the brand-building we discussed.

This is when you should be living by the adage "under-promise and over-deliver."

When you are dealing with prospective rental clients, remember any issues that might pop up. If you feel it is important, you can deal with it before your next showing. You have control over your property, but if the transit stop or a park is not as close as the prospective client would like, you can't change that situation.

How do you deal with any issues in getting the property ready to rent?

Take a deep breath and put yourself in the shoes of the tenant. Do a thorough walkthrough of the area and your home. Make sure you are looking through the eyes of your potential tenant, not your own eyes. You have identified the type of client you would like to rent your property to; if you are renting to a generation younger than you or someone who is single when you are married and have a family, your tenants' needs will be much different than your own.

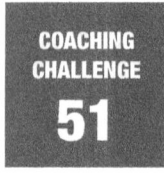 **COACHING CHALLENGE 51 Transform your investment values into differentiation points.**

When you analyzed your first investment property to purchase and rent, you thought about the reasons you were attracted to this property. Some of your reasons were business-related, such as that the property would be a good cash-flowing and equity-growing property. The other reason you purchased it was to attract great tenants. Make sure you kept track of the reasons you believed this would be a great home for your tenants. These reasons should reflect points of value and differentiation, and you should have your list ready to complete the coaching challenge below. Write your answer in your notebook, the workbook and planning guide, or in the space provided.

How do you apply your investment values to your investment real estate property as points of value and differentiation?

_____

 **Determine how you will attract your target renters.**

When you made your decision to purchase your first investment real estate property, you were thinking about your target renter. Do you have the pollen to attract your ideal worker bees to create your rental revenue honey? Write your answer in your notebook, the workbook and planning guide, or in the space below.

How do you attract your target renters?

_____

 **Determine how your USPs will retain your clients.**

We have talked about how your client-tenants are your most important asset in purchasing and renting your first investment real estate property. These tenants will ultimately provide you with all your revenue and pay all of your expenses. Remember, the more often you turn over tenants, the greater the chances of having no revenue but increased costs. You'll not only have to cover the normal expenses to operate your rental but the increased costs to market your property to attract a new tenant. Therefore, you want to design your USP to retain your clients.

How will your values and differentiation points keep your clients?

Take five minutes over a coffee to work out a tenant retention strategy. With today's technology, you can simply put a reminder and a date in your smartphone calendar and stay on top of tenant retention.

We'll go into retention more on Day 26, but each time a tenant leaves, you'll need to pay for a complete cleaning, decide if there are repair and maintenance items, pay to have the home show better, pay for utilities, pay to have the doors rekeyed, and pay for advertising. The investment in tenant retention is more than worth it when you consider all the prospective costs of losing them.

Day 25 Key Recap

Record your key learnings and actionable items in your notebook or the workbook and planning guide. (Optional)

- ⇧ Building your brand will help you meet the criteria of a successful investment property.
- ⇧ Use your unique selling proposition to attract your ideal renter.

DAY 26 SCREENING, ACQUIRING, AND RETAINING QUALITY RENTERS

Use this day to learn how to screen, acquire, and retain high-quality renters. You'll find ideas on getting great renters and what you can do to keep them. At the end of the chapter, complete the coaching challenges to write the interview questions you'll use when screening your prospective tenants.

It would be hard to understate the importance of getting great renters for your first investment real estate property. After all, they're the ones who will be paying your mortgage for you, and without them, none of this would be possible. So, you want to ensure that they're the right fit.

Back on Day 7, in Coaching Challenge 16, you created your ideal client-tenant profile. Yesterday, on Day 25, we determined your rental property's unique selling proposition (USP) and how it fits your client-tenant profile, and we learned how to use your USP to attract your ideal renter. And today, we'll learn about how to qualify, acquire, and retain those ideal tenants who are willing to pay fair or higher rents for your property, so that your investment real estate journey is as smooth and hassle-free as possible.

Screening Quality Renters

The first step in finding a quality client-tenant is to screen them. This way, you ensure that you won't be engaging with people who waste your time.

Over time, my wife and I have learned not book appointments through email or text. Instead, we have a phone conversation with all potential tenants.

Stage One of Screening

A phone call helps you to get a feel for the person. You will be surprised how many time-wasters and bad tenants you will eliminate from this simple act alone. During this conversation, we ask two qualifying questions: 1) Do you have pets? 2) When are you looking to move in?

I know these two questions might seem innocent, but they provide you some insight into the person. First, did they read your ad closely? You may state "no pets allowed." How far out are they looking for possession? Remember, people looking for a great property may try and push your limits to see how desperate you are for a tenant and hope you will take their pets or hold on to the property for several months until they're ready to move in.

Hidden Nugget

Also, there can be a real nugget in the second question: When were you looking to move in? You might assume people always want to move in on the first of a month, but this is not always the case. We have had vacancies where the tenant wants to take possession immediately. Getting a partial month's rent is much better than no rent.

If the person passes this screening to your liking, arrange an appointment to view the rental property. Advise them that, if they are interested in the property, they will be required to fill out a rental application form, drop off or email the completed form to you, and provide a deposit. (In our situation, we ask for $600, but you can make this amount whatever you want.)

Asking for a significant amount is helpful because if they have trouble coming up with the deposit, it is often an indication that rent will be difficult to obtain moving forward.

If you get a sense at the initial viewing that you will not rent to a particular individual, tell them they are not right for you and do not give them a rental application. Trust your gut and, eventually, your experience.

In the appendix of this book, you will find a sample rental application you can use and modify to suit your purposes. If you'd like, you can refer to it while reading this section, as I will give an overview of the rental application and the process.

Remember, deviating from the rental application or the process can cause headaches down the road, and this is where most owners create their own bad experience with tenants. Follow the rental application form and the process and you have every chance of being a happy landlord.

The Rental Application

The rental application is a great mechanism to weed out potential bad tenants. It includes the following important sections in the first part of the form:

- Header (your name or company's name, address, phone number, and website)
- The email address you would like the rental application emailed to
- The full address of the rental property, including the town or city and unit number (if applicable), the rental amount, and the security deposit amount
- The requested move-in date, length of the tenancy period (six months or a year), number of occupants (over the age of 18), total number of children (including date of birth), pets (including breed and size), how they heard about the rental, and who showed them the unit
- The following statement: "Please fill out all information, including phone numbers. Everyone over the age of 18 must fill out an application."
- The following statement, highlighted: "Incomplete applications **will not** be processed."

As you review the rest of the application, keep the following in mind:

- ⇧ How is the application filled out?
- ⇧ Did they complete all fields?
- ⇧ How quickly did they return their application form after the viewing?

The rest of the rental application will address the following:
- full legal name
- date of birth
- phone numbers
- email address
- present landlord and their information
- one previous landlord and their information, plus the previous rental information
- monthly income, plus a current paystub or letter of employment
- information of current employer
- information of one previous employer
- bank with address
- auto makes and license plates
- emergency contact (not residing in the unit)

On your application, include a minimum of four statements that the tenant must agree to:
- for you to conduct an ongoing credit bureau history of them;
- to provide the credit bureaus with information about them on an ongoing basis;

- to co-operate with local, state, provincial, or national authorities with unlawful or improper from fraudulent activities (each jurisdiction has different regulations; what might be lawful in one area may not be lawful in another area. The rules around marijuana are a prime example: growing a single plant in one's home is okay in one place but unlawful in another)
- to disclose your personal information where necessary to protect your interest and theirs.

Also, you should add a section entitled "Frequently Asked Questions." These questions generally include things like:

- How long does the application process take?
- What are the requirements to rent from us?
- Why do I need to pay a $600 application deposit?
- How can I pay the application deposit?

After the frequently asked questions section, you will outline that once you start collecting the first month's rent and security deposit, you will not be able to accept cash as a form of payment. You can then outline several options for payment forms you will accept and indicate your preferred form of payment (ours is automatic bank withdrawal).

The last two areas on the rental application are:

- the date signed, and
- the potential client's signature.

Developing Your Interview Questions

This is by far the most important section when getting ready to rent to a tenant. You will find owners and landlords get into the most trouble because they skip or don't pay enough attention to this part of the process.

First, you are only to do your initial screening over the phone. Phone, text, or email should never be the primary interview. (Even during COVID-19, we adopted the health department protocols for meeting in person, and met our prospective clients in person.)

Second, in the rental application section, we have the potential renter fill out the rental application form and drop the form off or email it back. On the rental application, it clearly states that incomplete applications will not be processed; this is another safety check to screening the applicant.

Third, once you have done the initial screening, including the review of a completed rental application, you can schedule an interview at the property.

The rental application asks most of the interview questions I have outlined below. Remember, though, that this is your rental application and you need to do your own research for your area of rental.

Relying on your Team REAL members, consult a lawyer who specializes in knowing which questions are discriminatory and which are okay to ask. Your real estate lawyer may have to recommend a lawyer who specializes in human rights law.

Each state, province, and federal government may have different mandates and laws, so be aware. Government websites may have clear guidelines and sample questions; a simple Google search can give you more specific insights.

Interview Question Do's

Generally speaking, the following questions are permissible. Again, check before you ask, and see if your real estate agent has access to a tenant interview form.

- Are you currently renting? Where?
- How long have you lived there?
- Why are you looking for a new place?
- Date required? What kind of work do you do?
- What is your estimated income?
- How many people will be living with you?

- Do you smoke?
- Do you require parking?
- Do you have any pets?
- What are your references?
- Have you ever been evicted?
- Can I do a background check for screening the rental application process?
- Have you ever filed for bankruptcy?
- Can you pay a security deposit?

Interview Question Don'ts

Generally, do not ask questions about the following:
- Race and ethnicity
- Skin color
- Religion
- Sexuality (including sexual harassment and stereotyping genders)
- National origin or ancestry
- Family status (e.g., pregnancy)
- Disability

Check the laws in your area and with your Team REAL members. Even asking someone if they can pay the rent can be viewed as discriminatory. It's far better to be safe than sorry and ensure you're asking the right questions.

Visual Tricks to the Interview Process

When you meet the prospective tenant at the rental property, stay in your vehicle until they arrive. You should try and arrive at least thirty minutes early. This is, first, to ensure the property is completely presentable, and second, to gauge their promptness; if they arrive a little early or on time, it gives you a little insight into their character. Also, try and meet them at their vehicle and do a quick scan of its cleanliness, especially the interior; the cleanliness might be a subtle clue into how they might handle your property. (Don't make this visual check too obvious.)

Acquiring Quality Renters

After you've screened your prospective renters and have one or more potential candidates who have handed in rental applications, it's time to go through the acquisition process.

It's important that you have clearly stated you will not process an application if the form is not filled out completely. Make sure you do your job and verify the entire application form. Only pull a credit check if you are moving forward with the application. Once you have processed the entire application, have completed a credit check, and feel this is a valued tenant, then call them and let them know they are approved.

Go over the possession date and lease terms. Advise the tenant by email of the necessary information about tenant insurance, utility hookups, payment of the remainder of the funds required (give them three business days to comply), and book their move-in date. Make them aware of any condominium documents, bylaws, and pet approval process, if applicable.

Remember, with COVID-19 protocols in place, in most jurisdictions you may use a DocuSign system for signing leases and other documents. The world is changing quickly and no one knows when things will return to the old normal or the new normal; each area will have different requirements.

When the tenant is ready to move in, conduct a thorough property inspection (covered on Day 27, tomorrow). Have the tenant sign the inspection form, and note any work that you have agreed to that needs to be done. Also, you will need to confirm that tenant insurance is in place and all applicable utilities are in the tenant's name. Only then do they receive the keys.

Retaining Quality Renters

After carrying out the screening and acquiring process, you should have a wonderful client-tenant who calls your property home. The trick is keeping your client for years to come. How do you do it? Remember, you have purchased your investment real estate property for long-term buy-and-hold. If you have developed a five-year plan for your property, why not build a five-year strategy for your tenants?

Why Strong Client Engagement Is Essential

To help clients feel at home and give them a reason to stay in your property, it's vital to cultivate a good relationship with them.

Getting to know your tenants is critical. When you build questions to acquire tenants, make sure you use some simple but effective questions to learn who they are and what their interests are. These are little things you can build on and use to market to their personalities.

Please keep in mind that you need to work on these items throughout the entire year. Don't just drop niceties on the tenant at the last minute a week before the renewal date—they can see right through this. If you are engaging with your tenants all year long, there will be no surprises should they not renew.

Simply caring can go a long way toward keeping and cultivating a great tenant.

Tips for Cultivating Strong Tenant Relationships

You don't have to do anything extravagant to show your tenant you appreciate them and make them feel welcome.

Gift baskets or gift cards around Christmastime, a birthday card, a simple thank-you card for a small deed done, a night out at the movies, or a stay-home digital movie . . . the list of ideas for tenant engagement is endless, so let your imagination go wild. Remember that retailers like Costco sell discount cinema packages, and going to your local automobile association (CAA and its provincial affiliates in Canada, and AMA in the United States) also gets you discounts for gift cards.

Being clear on what your property has to offer can also contribute to customer retention. The unique selling proposition you created yesterday can help you get clarity.

A Great Guarantee

Marketing experts often suggest you have a guarantee. A guarantee is a great approach to take in investment real estate, too. Your guarantee could be as simple as letting your clients/tenants know that, when it comes to an emergency call, they will hear back from someone in an hour, and if it is a general inquiry, someone will return their call within twenty-four hours. Make sure you are prepared to deliver on your guarantees. Guarantees are valuable, but not worth much if your guarantee is weak or you don't deliver on your promises.

A great guarantee is a super way to keep a good tenant, and a weak guarantee is a quick way to lose one.

Last Word – Legal Issues

In over fifteen years, we have never had a legal challenge. As long as everything is documented, you stand a good chance of winning the case.

Your hard work building an ideal client-tenant profile on Day 7 will pay off today, as you are using the personas or avatars you created to represent your ideal client-tenant to get aligned with the real-life client-tenant you put in your rental home.

COACHING CHALLENGE 54 Write your interview questions for your ideal target renters.

It is almost time to interview your renters! What questions will you be asking? That's what we are going to decide in this coaching challenge. This is where you need to almost take on the role of a human resources manager, be sensitive to people, and understand the law behind the questions you ask.

In the appendix, you'll find a sample interview form with room to add your own questions. During this exercise, please ensure that all questions, including the ones on the sample form, are legally allowed in your rental marketplace.

Day 26 Key Recap

Record your key learnings and actionable items in your notebook or the workbook and planning guide. (Optional)

- ⇧ Screen your renters carefully to avoid wasting time.
- ⇧ When screening for a great renter, collect all the tenant information permissible in your area.
- ⇧ There are several ways to identify the ideal tenant, and it takes multiple steps to ensure you've found the right renter.
- ⇧ It's better to take time to acquire a good tenant than to get your first renter as quickly as possible. Be totally relentless in completing every step necessary.
- ⇧ The small effort it takes to retain a good client pays dividends in your investment real estate business, saving you significant time, money, and effort.

DAY 27 THE MOVE-IN/MOVE-OUT INSPECTION CHECKLIST

Use this day to create move-in and move-out inspection checklists for your rental property and let tenants know about the benefits of doing the checklist together. If you are using a property management service, make sure you share your checklist with them. Valuable ideas on what makes a checklist complete will be shared both ways. At the end of the chapter, complete the coaching challenges to do a move-in/move-out walkthrough practice run.

The day your tenant finally moves in is a big milestone in your investment real estate journey. You'll want to be ready for it. That's why, today, we are going to discuss what happens on the tenant's move-in day and prepare some documents that will make your life—and your tenant's life—much easier.

I have created blank forms for you to use to create your own move-in and move-out inspection checklists; you'll find them in the book's appendix. In today's digital world, you might take these sample forms and develop your own forms for an iPad or other digital hardware that you can use upon move-in or move-out. You need to gauge your new tenant's comfort level and what they might feel most at ease with.

Remember, the form is a formal document, and each party is required to sign it.

The Move-In/Move-Out Tenant Policy

Communication is critical when working with a tenant. By having a clear move-in tenant policy, the expectations will be clear on both sides, right off the bat. The policy should be in writing, as part of a handout.

With today's technology, you can, for under twenty dollars, create a tenant's policy binder. Office-supply companies like Staples carry binders that allow you to insert a title sheet into the front of the binder. Setting up print tab sections of the binder has never been easier. We create one of these for each of our investment real estate properties. It contains not only the move-in tenant policy and move-in checklist (more on that in a minute), but other sections as well, such as a move-out checklist that will help tenants when it's time to leave; contact information such as phone number, email, and website list; and a list of services and retailers in the area. The tenant's policy binder is another part of your brand experience with tenants, so feel free to get creative here.

A checklist is a fluid document that can evolve every time you change tenants. You'll learn lessons from tenant to tenant, and these can be incorporated into the checklist.

Remember, if you are renting a single-family home, it is your sandbox, and you can control the rules. If you are in a condo, an apartment, or a townhouse complex and you only own one of many units, you and your tenants must comply with the complex's rules.

Completing the Move-in Walkthrough with the Tenant

The tenant and the owner or owner's representative should complete the move-in walkthrough together, before the tenant moves in, and fill out the move-in checklist. (In the appendix, you'll find a sample move-in inspection checklist you can modify to suit your own needs.)

Below, we'll review the major parts of move-in inspection checklist:

On the top left-hand side of the form is the landlord's information, including name, address, phone number, and email address. On the top right-hand side of the form is an area for tenant information, including tenant name and phone number. (I suggest you have two lines for two tenant names and phone numbers, in case there will be more than one tenant.)

The next portion of the move-in inspection checklist has an area for the address of the property being rented, the unit number (if applicable), and a forwarding address.

The next area is the main body of the checklist. The first portion is the keys: How many keys are handed out? There is also an area for each type of key; this could be an outside lock for a building (if applicable), the rental unit, a mailbox key (if part of the building), storage, garage, and possibly a garage remote (if applicable).

The next portion of the move-in inspection checklist covers each area of the rental unit. This includes entranceways, storage rooms, kitchen, dining room, living room, study, family room, all bedrooms and bathrooms, and a general area for all other items like furnace, balconies, and garage.

On the left-hand side of the form is the specific name of the area under review. Under each major area, you are looking at the following: doors/locks, closets, walls, ceilings, flooring, fixtures/lights/windows, blinds, and screens. Each item has a column to the right with a tick box: OK, Needs Repair, and Needs Cleaning. There is also a line for each item entitled Description, with room for you to add details. In the Description line, you may put details of the approximate time it will take to address the issue.

At the very bottom of the form is the date of the move-in inspection, the landlord or agent's printed name and signature, and then the tenant's portion, which has details on who was present but would not sign the inspection, the number of attempts made for the inspection, the tenant agreeing to the report even if not in attendance, if the tenant does not agree with the inspection report, and the tenant or tenant's agent's printed name and signature.

It is important that both parties get off on the right foot. As an owner/landlord, work your hardest to ensure that all areas of the unit are addressed in advance of turning it over to the tenant. You made up the checklist, so put yourself in the other person's shoes.

Also, if work or cleaning needs to be done, under-promise and over-deliver. Give yourself a little time to complete the agreed-to work and then do it in advance of the original date, if possible, but ensure this is acceptable to your tenant.

Explaining Rent Expectations

After you've completed the walkthrough and filled out the checklist, explain to the tenant how the rent check gets handled. With online banking, the process should be easy; see if they are willing to automate the rent payment directly to your bank. You need to explain that the rent check is due on the first of the month; ensure they understand that the rent check goes into an account and you have payment obligations to the bank and others, including your mortgage payments.

There should be penalties if the rent is late, even by one day. Explain these penalties and let them know that this can also lead to a notice to vacate the property. The penalty should be predetermined by you. Your bank will charge you a fee if you are one day late with your mortgage payment, and this might be a good place to start. Our bank, for example, charges forty-five dollars for a late payment. You also have to take your time into consideration. Start with a flat fee of one hundred dollars for the first day; after that, you might find out the daily amount of each day's rent as a penalty. Do your homework and find out the state, provincial, municipal, or national regulations around the late fees; most jurisdictions address this issue.

It's crucial that you don't allow any leeway on late payments. Explain to the tenant that the bank doesn't allow you any grace time. Being transparent with the tenant will help them understand your rules.

After you have gone over the checklist, ask them if they have any other questions.

You can hand over the keys during the move-in inspection. The keys are part of the move-in inspection and can be addressed when you come to this area on the form. You may allow for two keys, but have no objections to the tenant making duplicate keys if they choose to. Your rental unit might be in a multiplex building with special entranceway keys and only a finite number of keys allowed per unit. These keys may have to be signed for, and any requests for more keys might come with a cost. Since they can be pricey, ensure your tenant is aware of this and that they'll be responsible for the new key charge should they lose theirs.

An Example of a Move-In/Move-Out Tenant Policy

Below, you'll find a sample move-in tenant policy handout. Use it for inspiration when creating your own move-in and move-out materials.

⇧ MOVE-IN/MOVE-OUT TENANT POLICY HANDOUT

Kindly be advised that we have ensured that you have a neat, clean residence to occupy. This assurance is due to the landlord and tenant's mutual commitment that each will be responsible for the proper maintenance of the property.

The landlord is responsible for any maintenance that is not created by the tenant, and that the tenant is unable to do.

The tenant is responsible for:

1. Yard upkeep: cutting the grass and shoveling snow from the sidewalks.
2. Treating utilities and facilities (e.g., washer, dryer, fridge, and stove) with respect.
3. Cleaning the residence thoroughly upon vacancy. Please see the checklist below.

MOVE-IN/MOVE-OUT INSPECTION CHECKLIST

Refer to these forms in the appendix and feel free to modify them to your property and circumstances.

(Note: The items below give you an excellent feel for what the move-in and move-out might look like. Please refer to the more complete move-in and move-out inspection checklist in the book's appendix for further detail. Each checklist is going to differ depending on the type of property you are renting. That's why I have included a couple of different checklists: one for a single-family home, and one for a home in a multiunit complex.)

- ❏ 1. Check that the fridge and stove are clean, both inside and out.
- ❏ 2. Check that behind and under the fridge and stove are clean.
- ❏ 3. Check that all cupboards (kitchen, bathroom, hallway, bedroom, etc.) are clean.
- ❏ 4. Check that all linoleum floors are washed.
- ❏ 5. Check that all carpets are shampooed (if applicable).
- ❏ 6. Check that all bathroom fixtures (tub, shower, sink, vanity, mirror, toilet) are clean.
- ❏ 7. Check that all light bulbs are working.
- ❏ 8. Report any damage that needs repair.
- ❏ 9. Ensure the landlord has given you all the keys.

We look forward to an enjoyable association with you and are thankful to have you as tenants.

Some Notes About the Move-In Process

When you spend time taking a new tenant through a move-in checklist, you verify the tenant is moving into a reliable, safe, and secure property while addressing any concerns that may have been overlooked. With the tenant, you review any deficiencies, and it gives you a list to follow of work that needs to be done to bring the property up to par. You can create work orders from this list to address these concerns.

The move-in checklist protects both the tenant and the owner, and it goes a long way to establish a good relationship. The tenant can see that you care, and when you follow up and have the deficiencies addressed promptly, you hope this leads to a long and mutually respectful relationship.

Many landlords overlook a critical part of the move-in process: the move-out policy. I highly recommend that, after the move-in review is done, you do a quick review of the move-out policy. Even though you may not want to remind the new tenant they will be leaving someday, it is part of the tenant–owner relationship, and it should not get lost that this relationship is a two-way street. This stage, along with the others I'll share with you, is critical to establish expectations.

The Primary Differences between a Move-In and Move-Out Inspection Checklist

The major differences between the move-in and move-out inspection checklist are the header title, the closing portion, and the signature box of the forms.

You might consider using a different color for each form because the body content of the forms is so similar. It is also important to bring a copy of the original move-in inspection checklist when doing the move-out. That way, if the tenant says, "That damage or issue was there when I moved in," you can refer to the form.

Creating Your Own Move-In/Move-Out Inspection Checklists

The objective of the move-in and move-out checklists is to ensure they are specific to your rental home. Each property has its own characteristics.

Remember, even though I encourage you to create your own, I am not asking you to recreate the wheel. Simply use the blank copies in the appendix and modify these documents to suit you.

The final thing you should say to the tenant, in a friendly manner, is, "How we have given the property to you is how we would like it back."

Practice the move-in/move-out walkthrough using your checklists.

This exercise will help you gain confidence when completing a move-in and move-out checklist. Do a practice move-in walkthrough of your property. If possible, take a friend or relative who has not seen the property and ask them to have a watchful eye and pretend they are a tenant. Explain to your friend or family member that you want to start off on the correct foot with the tenant and you would like them to err on the side of concern; let them know you want a happy tenant in your Happy Place.

Doing a practice move-out inspection will be harder to do, but you might give it a go at the same time. Your first real move-out inspection might be your real practice!

Turn to the appendix of the book, where you'll find the base sample move-in/move-out inspection checklists. The form can be the same for a single-family home and a condo, apartment, or townhouse. You can simply mark non-applicable (N/A) on the forms if there's a section you don't use.

We have left you a couple of blank spots to add your own items to the checklist, as not all properties are the same.

Day 27 Key Recap

Record your key learnings and actionable items in your notebook or the workbook and planning guide. (Optional)

- When creating your move-in and move-out inspection checklists, capture all details specific to your investment real estate property.

- ⇧ Address all issues in advance of tenant move-in.
- ⇧ Do a practice move-in inspection with someone who has not seen the property and can give you an honest appraisal of how it looks.
- ⇧ Work with the tenant throughout their stay and address issues you may have missed right away. Your investment real estate property is a long-term investment, so keep its best foot forward!

DAY 28 BREAKING DOWN THE RENT CHECK AND THE MONTHLY AND YEAR-TO-DATE INCOME STATEMENT (MICRO VIEW)

Use this day to understand the elements of your rent check and what expenses the rent check needs to cover, including a contingency fund. In the coaching challenges, you'll complete a sample income statement to understand why you are an entrepreneur and how it creates the basis for owning a small business.

As an investment real estate investor, the rent check is ultimately what allows you to do what you do. It's what pays for your property and sets you on the path to a strong financial foundation, sustainable wealth, and a living legacy.

Since rent is so important, make collecting rents as easy and painless as possible; with online banking and technology, collecting rents immediately when due has never been easier. My suggestion is to ask your clients/tenants to allow you to set them up on automatic withdrawal for the rent. You will have to make sure this is permissible in your marketplace. For investment real estate investors, e-transfer is a very reliable way to collect rents.

Some folks may wish to give you checks or cash; I would be very hesitant to take cash. Taking cash does not give you an instant paper trail; with cash, you may have to chase your tenant for the funds, and this can add time to your administering of the rental property. If you decide to take cash, make sure you have a receipt book and get the tenant to sign the receipt. Also, since most everyone has an automatic banking card, this is also a good way to receive the rents, but it means you have to have a system in place to accept this form of payment.

At the beginning of this book, we talked about setting up one bank account for your investment real estate property to receive revenue and pay your bills. I would again remind you to automate most of your payments, property taxes, mortgage payments, etc. With online banking and automating most revenue and expenses, it will not take you long to create your monthly income and expense statement.

Collecting your first rental income is unlike any other feeling in the world. When you produce your first income and expense statement, all expenses have been paid, and you have some extra cash in the bank account, you will think you have died and gone to heaven.

Keeping Track of Rental Income, Expenses, and Revenue

An easy way to keep track of your rental income, expenses, and revenue is by using a workbook in a computer program like Microsoft Excel.

A workbook is composed of several worksheets. For each property, I create a workbook consisting of twelve months' worth of monthly income and expense statement worksheets and a linked year-to-date summary sheet. You can find an example in the appendix. The idea behind the worksheets and workbook is to measure expenses that are pertinent to the investment real estate property so you can understand your revenue.

A worksheet is the grid of columns and rows into which information is inputted. In many spreadsheet applications, such as Microsoft Excel, one file—a workbook—can contain several worksheets, as I describe above. Worksheets can be named using the sheet tabs at the bottom of the spreadsheet window.

Parts of the Monthly Income and Expense Statement

The monthly income and expense statement workbook consists of worksheets divided into four main sections: rent, expenses, mortgage (principal/interest), and net revenue.

Rent is a little more dynamic than you as a landlord might think. Rent is not only the amount you collect for the home you are renting; it can also include other elements. You may allow for pets in your rental property, and I would suggest adding a charge monthly or, at the very least, a non-refundable amount. Even good pet owners cannot prevent unforeseen damages from the pet. (From my experience, at the end of a lease, you as an owner tend to break even on this revenue.) Also, any rental deposit you collect will need to be returned at the end of the lease. Finally, as mentioned on Day 27, if the rent is not paid on time, you need to charge a late charge immediately. If you are unsure what to charge, look at the banking fees if you are late with a mortgage payment, or any other fees associated with missed payments.

Expenses are all costs associated with the rental unit. Should this rental unit be part of a larger piece of property (e.g., a basement, upper floor, or garage suite), you need to know the exact square footage for tax purposes to prorate expenses.

Expenses include things like bank charges, utilities, credit card transaction fees, property taxes, condo fees (if applicable), insurance, property management fees, professional fees, cost of repairs, maintenance and renovations, other, and state or provincial goods and services taxes.

Net Revenue

Each month's statement will reflect net revenue. Because you receive your income monthly, it is important to set up all of your expenses to occur monthly. In most towns and cities, you can arrange to pay your property taxes monthly. After your original purchase, you should not have any legal expenses. The one professional expense you will pay yearly would be for your accounting services. When you complete today's coaching challenge, a trial sample of the monthly income and expense statement, please ensure you add a monthly fee for your accounting services.

Also, remember that your monthly income and expense statement will take all revenue and expenses into consideration.

Mortgage (Principal and Interest)

When completing the year-end worksheet, you will find your mortgage principal and interest listed separately. It's necessary for income tax purposes to separate the mortgage principal annual total and mortgage interest annual total on the year-end statement. You are only allowed to claim the interest at year-end, not the principal. The principal is the portion that is yours for equity-building.

I will go into a little more depth about your year-end statement in the next section.

Follow the Money

You may have heard this saying before: follow the money to determine why people do the things they do.

This is important for you to remember. Follow the money—the rent check—and how it trickles down the worksheet to the monthly bottom line.

Please refer to Day 28, where I suggest you have one bank account per property. I made this suggestion for a good reason: the easiest way to follow the money is to ensure the money you are following is for one property and one property only. Don't get caught up having all your apples (properties) in one basket (bank account), where one bad apple pulls the other good apples down with it. By monitoring each property separately, you will see any cash-flow issues immediately and can take action.

The only time I recommend that you use one bank account for multiple properties is when you incorporate and have multiple revenue properties under one company name, or when you are in more than one joint venture partnership with the same joint venture partner. It is still important to create an income and expense worksheet every month for each property, even if they are part of the same corporate ownership or joint venture ownership.

"Figures don't lie, but liars do figure" is a saying that has been around for years. The essence of this saying is that if you follow the figures, you can get to the truth, but you can also play with the numbers and create your own distorted reality. This is where you get in trouble with your rent checks if they don't cover all of your operational costs.

An example I have witnessed is when owners of investment real estate say that the rent check covers all the costs but the mortgage principal. These owners will tell you they are getting principal paydown—their equity—and they will recapture these funds when the property is sold. I have two issues with this thinking. Firstly, they are taking money from their own pocket each month to help subsidize the property's monthly payments. Secondly, we are talking a long-term buy-and-hold strategy; if the owners hold on to the property for ten or fifteen years or longer and cover the monthly principal paydown for the duration of that ten or fifteen years, it can get awfully expensive and drain you of any funds you might have saved to purchase another investment real estate property in the future.

Earlier in the book, I gave you a strategy to build a contingency fund into the rent expenses, serving as a rainy day fund. You never know when the hot water tank might go, or when a patio door screen will need repair; these are a few examples of costs I have had to cover over the years. This is a reminder that you can't sidestep this expense. If you don't have a contingency fund, you will have to cover these expenses from your own pocket.

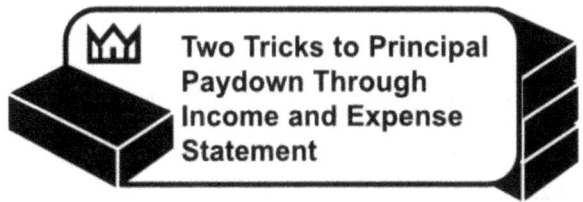

Value Brick – Two Tricks to Principal Paydown through Your Income and Expense Statement

When it comes to investment real estate, I recommend living by the following philosophy: "You can pay me now, or you can pay me later, but you will pay."

A good practice is to budget 5 percent of each rent check and set these funds aside as a contingency fund. By setting these funds aside, nothing can throw you off your game, and you'll be able to cover any unexpected expenses that may arise.

If you don't use these funds by the end of the year, I suggest the following strategy: take half the funds and roll them over to the next year, and take the other half and use them as a one-time payment to your mortgage principal.

For example, say you collect $1,000 rent, of which 5 percent is $50, times 12 months, for a total of $600. Roll $300 over into the next year's contingency fund and use $300 as a one-time payment to the mortgage. I recently did this and took four weeks off the end of my mortgage amortization period.

A Word About Cash Flow

I have heard some owners say they are averaging $500 a month in positive cash flow. This is an exception, not the rule.

If you can average $100 to $150 a month in positive cash flow after all expenses are covered, including a contingency fund, this is a nice monthly return. The objective is to have the consistency of positive cash flow over time.

My recommendation is, at the end of the year, not to dip into the positive cash flow. Your annual build is between $1,200 to $1,800. Just like you do with the contingency fund, take half the annual funds you have built, put half the amount into your next year's operating budget, and take the other half and pay down your mortgage principal.

Do these two simple tricks with half of the savings from your contingency fund and positive cash flow, and your positive rental income will be very significant. Plus, the number of years you'll take off your amortization period will astound and amaze you.

The great thing about principal paydown is this: the more you pay down the mortgage, the more of your payment goes to principal paydown. In most cases, the bank is more than happy to accommodate extra paydown to the principal, and some banks will let you pay down as much as 20 percent in one year.

Controlling Costs Versus Revenue

Investment real estate puts your capital to work for you, and one of the most critical factors in doing this successfully in investment real estate is balancing costs versus revenue. There are many expenses involved in residential property. Buying a primary residence comes with many costs: mortgage, property taxes, utilities, cable, internet, maintenance, repair, and, if you buy in a condominium complex, there are also shared costs. The money for all of these expenses comes from your income after tax, and very few, if any, of your residential costs can be used as tax deductions.

Sometimes people affectionately refer to their home as a money pit. (There was even a movie called _The Money Pit_ starring Tom Hanks, which took the costs involved in purchasing residential property to an extreme!). The point is that a residential home costs money. It is a negative outflow of cash, no matter how much wishful thinking you do. When folks buy their first home, they hope for equity growth, which will help their net worth. First-time homebuyers think that, down the road, they will sell their home to reap a cash payout. But the reality is, all homes need upkeep over time, and this takes money. I hope to show you how to find a balance to enjoy your home and create a strong financial base.

The truth is, many folks have used their equity and mortgage paydown to create an ATM. That's right—just like the regular automated teller machines, money comes out. And though that idea seems great at first glance, it's very, very bad.

How do people turn their homes into ATMs? They will put on a second mortgage, line of credit (LOC), or later, a reverse mortgage (a mortgage vehicle that becomes available when you turn fifty-five and don't have a mortgage on your home). These folks tend to spend the funds on lifestyle and daily living expenses. For the most part, you end up with new debt and suck every last cent out of your home with nothing to show for it and no legacy to leave.

As we get further into the book, we will address good debt and bad debt, and how bad debt cripples and ties up your financial foundation and future security.

The Dangers of Negative Cash Flow

Negative cash flow occurs when all of the operational expenses of an investment real estate property, including the mortgage payment, total more than the rental income.

Do I advise you to purchase negative cash-flowing investment properties? No!

Too many investors believe they can offset some of their costs through mortgage principal paydown. Remember, your mortgage payment is broken down into two pieces: your principal paydown and your mortgage interest. Principal paydown is the funds that belong to you as you pay down the mortgage, and mortgage interest is the amount the lender takes as their fee for lending you the money to purchase the investment real estate property.

You should never, ever invest in any property that requires you to take money out of your own pocket to pay the principal paydown amount; it doesn't take many of these properties to cause financial hardships. This is why I talk about purchasing a bungalow with an income suite or a duplex as your first investment real estate property. If you are going to need to do unexpected repairs or upgrades, you have your income and that of your tenants to help offset costs. If the tenant moves out, the money you are using is at least helping you benefit. You might be able to adjust your own personal budget to support these expenses as you search for a new tenant.

There are enough ups and downs in our state, provincial, national, and global economies, and having negative cash-flowing properties should never be part of your investment real estate strategy.

The coronavirus pandemic is a prime example. Millions of people lost their jobs, were left with no income, and had a hard time paying their rent. If you had an investment property that was already a negative cash-flowing property and suddenly you were receiving little to no income, where do you think the pressure would move? To you.

In the recent pandemic, a few of our tenants gave us one month's notice and were gone. We had other tenants ask for 50 percent rent relief forgiveness. All of our properties were positive cash-flowing, but I can assure you that a vacancy or a 50 percent rent reduction was not covering our costs. Luckily, there were government programs through the banks to help those affected by the pandemic, and we were able to take advantage of mortgage payment deferral programs.

Over the years you own an investment property, there is lots of positive news, such as principal paydown, positive cash flow, and equity appreciation, but life also comes with adverse situations. You need to use the positive times—the good times—as your hedge against any downturns—the bad times.

To borrow a gambling analogy, don't bet against the house. Start your first investment property with positive cash flow, including a 5 percent contingency fund built into the rent.

When I first started purchasing investment real estate twenty years ago, I underestimated our first property's expenses. I learned a lot from that experience. That's why it's vital to put together a rental income budget, plan for the worst, and expect the best.

COACHING CHALLENGE 56: Complete a dry run of your monthly income and expense statement.

Your monthly income and expense statement is a critical document for your investment real estate business. That's why, today, we're going to do a dry run on your income and expense statement.

At this point, you have completed your research on the rental rates in your area and should have a rental rate in mind. You should also know all the approximate costs on the expense side. Using this information, fill in the different lines of the form below and get a feel for your monthly income and expense statement.

Don't be afraid to adjust the numbers should you see an opportunity to increase revenue (e.g., pet or garage rental income, or lowering costs in a certain area).

Remember, all utilities should be handed off to the tenant. From time to time, when you have a vacancy, you might have to take on the responsibility until a new tenant is secured.

Debt service simply means the mortgage principal and interest.

As mentioned at the beginning of this day, mortgage principal cannot be claimed for the year-end statement and income tax purposes. Mortgage principal paydown is part of your equity growth in your property and will come back to you should you sell the property.

Also, the column on the right-hand side of this form is only used at year-end. Once you have received the year-end mortgage statement from your bank or lender, be sure to only use the mortgage interest amount for income tax purposes. Remember, as an investment real estate owner, running a profitable small business requires you to cover the mortgage principal and interest and still show a positive cash flow.

The government, however, does not allow you to claim the mortgage principal for tax purposes. The government views the paydown of the principal amount as your money, and when you sell the property, you as the owner will receive the proceeds of the sale less any mortgage principal balance left.

The monthly sheet below can be found under the Resources tab on my website, vaulttoinvestmentrealestatesucccess.com. This is free for you to download or create your own copy using this as a guideline. This workbook has a tab for each month and is tied to a year-to-date summary sheet.

Below is a monthly sample; the type of property for the purposes of this example is a basement suite. Research these numbers to reflect your own circumstances.

Address of Property – 202_ Income Statement

	Month	January 202_	Details of Expenses
RENT:			
	Rent	1150.00	Two-bedroom
	Additional Rental Income (E.g., Pet, Garage)	25.00	Pet fee
	Refunds	0	
	Total	**1175.00**	
EXPENSES:			
	Bank Charges	6.00	
	Utilities (Electricity)	0	Paid by tenant
	Contingency Fund (5% of Rental Income)	48.75	Set aside in bank account
	Taxes	112.00	Prorated based on square footage and assessed value and town or city's calculation
	Fees (Includes Gas/Water/Sewage, etc.)	125.00	
	Insurance	22.75	Addition to homeowners
	Property Management		Self-managed fee plus part of personal income tax charge. If you are tracking, charge could be minimal
	Legal/Accounting Fees	25.00	
	Repairs/Maintenance/Supplies	0	
	Renovations	0	
	Other	0	
	Telephone	0	Paid by tenant
	Cable	0	Paid by tenant
	GST/Tax	0	
	Total Monthly	**339.50**	
	(Before Mortgage Principal and Interest)	**835.50**	

Mortgage Principal/Interest	537.00	Prorated based on square footage of home. Payment on a $240,000 mortgage, 25-year amortization at 2.49%
Revenue	298.50	
TOTAL REVENUE		

(after debt service and principal repayment)

Day 28 Key Recap

Record your key learnings and actionable items in your notebook or the workbook and planning guide. (Optional)

- ⇧ For total revenue, include rent, additional rent for pets, garage rental, shed rental, etc.
- ⇧ For total expenses, include bank charges, all administration expenses including accounting, tax preparation, utilities, property taxes, repair, maintenance, renovations specifically for the portion of the rental suite, and insurance.
- ⇧ Ensure you have a clear square-footage calculation of the portion of the rental income property if it is part of a house. Seek professional help from a home inspector or real estate agent and review with your accountant—you don't want the taxman to come a-knocking.
- ⇧ Use your revenue and expense totals to determine whether this property can meet the criteria of a successful investment property.

DAY 29 RATE OF RETURN ON INVESTMENT: MONITORING REVENUE SUCCESS ELEMENTS (MACRO VIEW)

Use this day to learn about the three components of investment real estate ROI and why they are integral to investment real estate. At the end of the chapter, complete the coaching challenges to think about your return on investment.

Having a tangible asset like investment real estate can bring more financial certainty in a turbulent marketplace like we're experiencing right now.

Investment real estate creates wealth through three primary means: positive cash flow, appreciating asset, and mortgage paydown. The thing I love about investment real estate is you only need one of the three major factors for you to outperform the returns in the stock market, mutual funds, ETFs, and a multitude of investment vehicles on the market today.

When you look at most investment vehicles, including investment real estate, you can see your investments go up in value. If you purchase dividend-paying investments, you can have positive cash flow for reinvesting. But the crucial element that has investment real estate standing out above every other investment is that your tenants are making your mortgage principal and interest payment and covering all other operational costs. Beyond your initial down payment, you don't have to use any more of your own money for this investment.

If you want to buy more of a stock or another type of financial vehicle in your portfolio, you can use your dividends or cash returns, but if there is a real opportunity because of the stock's performance, you will have to dig into your own funds to purchase more stocks.

The return on your real estate investment starts the moment your tenant makes their first rent payment. You start making your mortgage payment using the rental income proceeds, and a portion of each payment pays down your mortgage principal.

This is a reminder of why your tenant is your most valuable asset.

Even though money for mortgages will be inexpensive for several years due to interest rates and you might be thinking cheap money will take renters out of the rental pool, the fact is, there is very little chance we will see a downturn in North America for the foreseeable future.

Through the United States and Canada's aggressive immigration policies, there will always be a need for good rental real estate. In North America, our birth rates are not producing enough people to fill the job vacancies created by retiring and aging boomers.

Up until the pandemic hit, the United States was taking in over a million immigrants a year, and Canada was taking in an average of 240,000. These folks need housing. Most North American banks will not lend new immigrants funds for mortgages until they have been in the country for a minimum of three years. And remember, this is a new set of people every year.

North America will have to play catch-up, and we will see larger immigrant numbers coming. You don't need to own a crystal ball; what you need to own is investment real estate.

There is a good chance rents will be higher because there will be a shortage of good investment real estate properties to rent.

As investors, many of us have seen the volatility in the stock market, and unless you have the stomach and the luck to time the market on the way down and on the way up, your stock, pension, 401K, or RRSP investments are going to take several years to reach the value they had in February 2020 at the height of the market.

However, investing, purchasing, and renting good, affordable housing will fill a need for decades to come.

Reviewing Capital Return Streams

The return on your initial investment (your down payment) is where the real magic begins.

As I mentioned earlier, when you are making the decision to purchase most investments, you have to come up with 100 percent of the capital required to buy the stock, mutual fund, ETF, or other investment vehicle.

The magic of investment real estate is that there are banks and other lenders who are willing to give you the majority of the working capital to purchase an investment real estate property. These banks and lenders are prepared to lend you up to 95 percent of the investment real estate's total purchase price. Most often, your investment is between 5 and 20 percent.

Why would the lenders take on a greater risk to do this than you? It's not for the good of their health. It is all about wealth creation. Their lending institutions earn a ton of money on the borrowing process of mortgages. As we alluded to on Day 21, in Coaching Challenge 42, the interest you can pay over the fifteen to thirty years of your mortgage can add up to tens or even hundreds of thousands of dollars in interest payments.

The banks and lenders have legal documentation linking them to the security of your property until all of your financial obligations are met. The risk for your lenders diminishes over time. If you have a fifteen-year mortgage, the lenders know you are not only paying down the mortgage principal but, over fifteen years, they can be assured of equity growth in the property.

If you default on your mortgage at any time, the lenders know their loan amount becomes more and more secure each year. The lenders are concerned about their original investment; they earn their return on interest charges, not taking over your property by default and selling it.

Earlier in the book, I mentioned we purchased a couple of foreclosures. The price we paid to the bank was considerably lower than these homes' market value. The bank sold these properties to us at an amount closer to the outstanding mortgage balance.

The major capital return stream is the mortgage principal paydown. Like I said earlier, the magic begins the moment you receive your first rent check. It is important to remember the mortgage principal paydown is for the bank or lender's funds invested; you are not going to see the return on your funds until your lender's exposure has been completely paid back. Once the mortgage obligations are taken care of, you own the entire property and all the equity in the property. If you sell the property after there is no mortgage balance, all the sale funds are yours.

This being said, if your financial investment is 5 to 20 percent of the purchase price of the property and the value of this property holds through several years, the mortgage paydown funds become yours, and this is where I suggest you measure your return. The process of your return on capital is a little different than it is for the bank or lender. The bank or lender sets the mortgage repayment schedule up to have the interest repayment be the most significant portion of your mortgage repayment; as the years of repayment take place, it begins to equalize, and at the end of the mortgage, your repayment amount is more to the principal than the interest.

The funds you invested come back to you a little more slowly as a return because the principal paydown amount of the mortgage needs to be equal to or larger than your investment. In the beginning, as stated, more of the mortgage payment is going to the lender's interest payments.

You might be a little concerned about how slow the process might be; let's go back to Day 21's examples. Over five years on a $240,000 mortgage at 2.5 percent, you have paid down $37,022 in principal and $27,485 in interest. This equates to a nearly 62 percent return on your original investment of $60,000.

Take a moment to look at most banks or other financial institutions. They would like you to deposit your money in their savings accounts and promise you a return of 1 to 2 percent annually. If you were to compound these funds over five years, you would be hard-pressed to hit high single-digit returns on your investment.

Throughout the book, I have stressed the importance of positive cash flow, including building in a contingency fund for repairs and incidentals. I have recommended that you carry over half of these funds at year-end for the following year's operational budget and use the other half for principal paydown.

On Day 28, we talked about breaking down the rent check, revenue to expenses. We discussed the specifics of building in a contingency fund; in our example, the fund added up to $600 annually, and the positive cash flow added up to $1,200 annually. The idea was to roll half of each of these two funds ($900) into the next year's operational budget and to take the other half and pay down part of the mortgage principal ($900). Over five years, this equates to $4,500; remember, this number of $4,500 is a bit higher over five years, as you are putting the $900 against the mortgage principal annually, and more of your payment is going to principal paydown, not interest.

Let's take this $4,500 and add it to your principal paydown over five years; as mentioned earlier, it's $37,002. This totals $41,522, or over 69 percent return on your original investment of $60,000.

I have not yet talked about any equity growth in value over the five years. Humor me for a moment, but please don't run to the bank with these funds. If you used a 1 percent equity growth number each year for five years on the original value of $300,000, this would give you growth of approximately $15,300.

If you added the $15,300 to the $41,552 amount mentioned above, this would give you a total of $56,822, or almost 95 percent return on your original investment of $60,000.

Measuring Your Annual Return and Completing an Annual Property Check-In

Back when we were children, most of us were excited to take our report cards home and show off our best grades. Our teachers prepared these report cards. Your investment property annual assessment is like a report card for your property, but you are the person grading your return.

To help put your annualized return into perspective, let's take a quick glimpse into the world of the stock market. I use the S&P 500 index as it shows an annualized dividend percentage. The S&P 500 also has a long history of annual returns for review.

Often, when you make an investment, you can look at your year-end statement, and the report includes the calculation of your percentage of return. Today, most traditional investments in the finance world are lucky to show mid-single-digit returns. The S&P 500 index shows annual returns over the last thirty years of just over 2 percent. The last time the S&P 500 had an annual return over 3 percent was 1991, thirty years ago.

Take a moment to review Day 13 in this book and look at the mortgage paydown amount made in the first year of your ownership. Whether you used the minimum down payment amount of 5 percent and added the default insurance amount, or you went the conventional mortgage route and put down 20 percent, you would have seen an annualized return of over 53 and 66 percent, respectively.

To get to these annual return percentages, you need to do your own calculations as your returns are not on a year-end statement. You need to have your year-end mortgage statement to calculate your annual return.

Also, I mentioned in the introduction that investment real estate can provide returns in three ways: mortgage paydown, as discussed above; positive cash flow from excess funds above all costs left over from the monthly rental amount; and equity growth. In the next section, I am going to discuss the annual return in detail.

We also need to do an annual property check-in. The annual property check-in should evaluate two major components: first, ask your real estate agent if you could do a comparable analysis of your property value in today's current market (with this number, you can calculate your percentage and approximate dollar value growth over the year), and second, look at the capital costs for any improvements that need to be done over the coming year. Remember, these are costs over and above the normal wear-and-tear maintenance you are doing throughout the year. It is one thing to replace a few roofing tiles as maintenance instead of replacing the entire roof.

If you have not put a contingency fund aside to cover roof replacement, you could have to invest additional funds to keep the property current.

Capital Costs and Your Rental Property

When it comes to owning real estate, you are going to have wear and tear. Some of the wear and tear is more about maintenance and some requires large amounts of spending. These short-term repair and maintenance costs tend to be expensed in the year you make the expenditure. Large expenses, such as a new roof, vinyl siding, interior painting, driveway repaving, and new windows are more commonly referred to as capital costs. Your accountant can advise you best. The capital costs may be amortized over several years, and you may even remortgage or finance these capital costs over a longer period of time.

If you have been running a positive cash flow on the property and have accumulated funds in the bank, you are not likely to draw on this money to spend because you know it is earmarked for capital cost work. Replacing the roof might increase your investment property's value, but it's not possible to easily access these funds.

Setting funds aside each year from some of your yearly positive cash flow may be a less stressful and more prudent way to fund these costs. Hopefully, when you had your home inspection done before you purchased your property, you were given a list of items that would need to be addressed in the future. Therefore, you shouldn't be surprised when some capital cost work is required.

The Annual Return

Let the excitement begin! This is why you purchased your first investment real estate property.

Now that we have done a quick financial and physical assessment of your investment property, let's bring all the pieces together. At the end of this chapter, the coaching challenges will help you work out a complete annual return statement of your own.

This annual return will give you your first of many yearly snapshots that give you a look at your investment's health.

Once you have completed your first annual assessment by following the process below, I would love to hear from you. This is why I do what I do. This assessment can be life-changing, not only for you but for your family and future generations.

When I did my first annual assessment, it changed everything. It was the first time I was involved in an investment where I wasn't giving my money to someone else to manage, and I was involved directly in the financial results.

It was the first time I ever realized that my investment funds could show me more than one way of earning returns on the same money. I saw the mortgage principal paydown, positive cash flow, and equity growth, and I was amazed by the results.

The potential to have multiple returns showed me that I could grow my future wealth in ways I never knew were possible through the power of compounding, and how this additional wealth could help my family in the future.

Why I was doing this was becoming clearer: there was going to be sustainable wealth creation through paying off the investment property and realizing increased yearly positive cash flow. These funds could pay for future generations' education and other needs, creating a lasting impact I couldn't yet even imagine.

By starting the investment real estate journey as soon as possible in my life, the financial results could begin immediately and last through my lifetime and beyond.

And to access this potential, all I needed to do was purchase and rent my first investment real estate property. Just like you.

Using Your Annual Mortgage Statement to Calculate Your Return

When I first started my investment real estate portfolio, we had to wait for our annual mortgage statements to appear in the mail. In today's technologically advanced environment, most banks now post your annual mortgage statements to your account overview. This account overview, the personal summary, is divided into different sections. Below, I will discuss the areas I believe are most important when calculating your annual return.

Summary:
- Bank accounts (e.g., checking, savings)
- Credit cards
- Loans and mortgages
- Investments

How to Read Your Mortgage Statement

Your year-end mortgage statement is available days after the end of the calendar year. If you have been keeping your monthly income and expense statements up-to-date, your year-end mortgage statement will be the last piece of the puzzle, with your mortgage payments broken out into principal and interest amounts. Remember, mortgage interest is an expense you can claim, while mortgage principal paydown is funds building as equity in your property. Equity funds are usually accessed in two different ways: selling the property and receiving the equity funds, or refinancing the property down the road and accessing the funds.

The year-end mortgage statement is usually divided into two parts. One part shows your **mortgage account details**. These include:
- the type of mortgage product for the current term
- the lender's posted fixed rate (at setup or last renewal)
- your rate discount (if applicable)

- your fixed interest rate (compounded semi-annually, not in advance)
- the maturity date (your remaining actual amortization date)
- the amount of skipped principal and interest payments (if applicable)
- any other details, such as mortgage cash account balance (if applicable)

The second part of your year-end mortgage statement gives you the important part for your year-end accounting purposes. This area details your **mortgage account transactions**:

- opening balance from the previous year (funds disbursed)
- interest charged for period (including prepayment charges)
- payments received
- principal and interest
- principal prepayments
- prepayment charges
- closing balance at year-end and interest adjustment or pre-paid interest (not included in interest charged for the period)

Capital Appreciation

Capital appreciation is a tricky number that many folks overstate when calculating their net worth.

My first exposure to capital appreciation, which is the value or price growth in assets, came from selling my first home and buying my second home. I bought my first home and sold it eight years later for double what we had initially paid. Remember, we could not access this capital appreciation amount without selling the home.

Other ways some of us see appreciation is through company stocks or bonds you purchase, which increase in value over time. Items like jewelry, collectibles, artwork, and gold can also appreciate over time, but again, in most cases, you can't access this capital appreciation unless you sell these items or put them up as capital to borrow against these assets.

Capturing your true capital appreciation number can be done by paying for an appraisal, but an appraisal is only a report at a specific point in time that is determined by comparing sales of similar properties in your area. Only when you actually sell your investment property will you know the actual capital appreciation.

Lenders will refinance your property if there has been enough capital appreciation since you originally purchased your property. This is another way to access the capital.

With a long-term buy-and-hold philosophy, you are not rushing out to sell your property anytime soon after purchasing. You have created conditions to make this a positive cash-flowing investment, and many of these conditions come with costs if you try and exit too early.

Capital Appreciation Challenges in the First Five Years

I have included the Investment Real Estate Magic Annual Return Review form in today's final coaching challenge. Even though I am asking you to complete this form at the end of your first year of owning and renting your first investment real estate property, and I know the excitement it will bring, I cannot emphasize enough the importance of the long-term buy-and-hold strategy. It is a cornerstone to your financial foundation.

Earlier, I mentioned how author Rachel Richards, in her book *Money Honey: A Simple 7-Step Guide for Getting Your Financial $hit Together*, recommends a five-year rule when purchasing investment property. The rule? Don't buy a property unless you plan to own it for five years. In the first five years, the funds mainly go toward interest payments, so you don't add much to your principal paydown.

As a new small business owner and entrepreneur, you must not forget any of your original investment expenses. Ensure you capture all associated costs: legal costs, appraisal fees, home inspection, and all other expenses associated with the purchase of your investment real estate property. Please ensure you take time with your accountant to review all the expenses you incurred in purchasing your property, and ask your accountant if there are any expenses you may have overlooked.

Cash flow: One of the key pillars when purchasing investment real estate is to ensure you have sufficient cash flow to cover all costs, including a built-in contingency fund.

Do your market research. Make sure you have competitive rental rates for the type of property you are renting. Ensure you maximize your rental amount, including reasonable charges for items like pet fees. If you are going to allow pets, you need to charge for each pet. I love my dog, but pets tend to create a small amount of damage, such as scratches on walls or baseboards. There are generally two ways to handle pet rental income: a flat fee for the lease duration or a monthly fee. I have used both methods and have found a flat fee works best.

We learned about the need to charge for pets the hard way—after damage occurred. Please note we didn't let the pet damage deter us from having pet owners as tenants; we simply got smarter. Most people love their pets and are prepared to make a small investment to have a nice home for them.

Total Annual Return: Your annual return is the total of your mortgage principal paydown plus capital appreciation. If your marketplace is seeing substantial value increases, ask your real estate agent once a year to give you a quick value assessment. Remember, your agent—a key Team REAL member—should have the pulse of the real estate market. If they are prepared to do a comparative marketplace evaluation for you, great. But if the media has been talking about market values increasing over the last year and is reporting a 1 to 3 percent increase, go in the middle and use 2 percent. Don't waste your real estate agent's time, though. This is a nice-to-know, fun-to-calculate, feel-good number, but until you sell the property, you cannot access these funds. And don't forget—as quickly as a market can heat up, it can cool down. Don't just reflect the good news; this a long-term buy-and-hold commitment.

Original Dollars Invested: This is the down payment, legal fees, appraisal fees, home inspection fees, and any other fees associated with the purchase of your first investment real estate property.

Percentage Annual Return: The annual percentage rate of return for an investment real estate property is the total percentage of change of the total dollar amount from one year to the next. I recommend you track each year you own the property separately. Having a running percentage from your original purchase date done with the annual percentage will give you a better feel for your total funds invested. As I mentioned, market conditions can impact the property's value growth from year to year. If the real estate investment made a profit, the percentage is positive. Don't forget, if you have to invest funds out of your pocket for the year or the real estate values take a downward trend, your investment losses give you a negative percentage.

By ensuring you have positive cash flow and that the positive cash flow is covering all costs of the mortgage, including principal paydown, you are going to be happy with your percentage of return from one year to the next.

The most exciting thing about mortgage paydown is that, each year, a higher percentage of your total payments goes to paying down the mortgage principal. As the percentage of your return grows year after year, this simple mathematical fact makes you wish you had paid more attention to your math teacher.

The Annual Property Check-In

Throughout the duration of your real estate ownership, it's vital to conduct an annual check-in of your investment. This will ensure that when it comes time to sell, you are primed and ready, and so is your investment property.

When you purchase your first investment real estate property, your first annual check-in is exciting. You'll get to see the impact owning your property has had on your yearly income and expense statement and your net worth statement.

Elements of the Annual Check-In

Return on Investment (ROI)

What to do: Find the positive or negative cash flow (sourced from your monthly and annual financial statements), property value increase or decrease (sourced from your real estate agent providing you with comparable values in your real estate marketplace), mortgage principal paydown (sourced from your annual mortgage statement), and capital cost expenditure (sourced from a member of your Team REAL who can give you a quote for the work in this area). Add all four factors together and divide into the original investment (the total resulting from your down payment, legal fees, appraisal fees, high-ratio mortgage insurance, and any other one-time fees that you paid in the initial purchase of the property) to realize the annual return on investment.

The best time to do your annual review is when you have access to your most complete financial information. The annual mortgage statement is a critical piece of information, and you generally receive this information at the end of the year. The statement itemizes the year-to-date spending on mortgage principal, mortgage interest, and any other incidental expenses related to the mortgage that your year-end statement needs to reflect.

Timing it right also means not duplicating your efforts. If you have to prepare for the income tax season and must produce the majority of your financial records at tax time, don't recreate the wheel—use this information to do your annual review, too.

Personal Financial Situation

What to do: Review your personal income and expense statement and net worth statement (refer to Day 3). If you have been using a software program like Quicken to track your daily spending and you have downloaded all of your assets and liabilities into this software, it should only take moments to print your year-end income and expense statement and net worth statement. Make sure you have captured all the necessary financial information (e.g., mortgage interest separated from mortgage principal), ensuring this information is as accurate as possible.

But these two statements aren't the only tools in your financial toolbox. You can reflect on the amount of your positive cash flow, as we discussed on Day 28. Can you roll over part of these funds into your operating budget for the upcoming year? Are there funds to help pay down the mortgage principal? How did your contingency funds work out—did you have to access any for expenses you didn't see coming? If there are funds left over, can you roll some into your upcoming year-end operating budget and put a portion toward your mortgage principal?

When you're doing your annual fiscal review, it's a great time to check your credit report. After all, you have taken on new financial obligations. This should not impact your score negatively; it should actually strengthen your credit score. (Some inquiries about your credit are viewed as positive, a sign you are actively building your credit.)

Once you've completed the financial review process, including your return on investment and your personal financial situation, how do you feel about your assets and liabilities? Did you achieve your financial goals as planned (in terms of positive cash flow and contingency funds)? What lessons did you learn, and how do you intend to use them to improve for the upcoming year?

If the strategy you employed worked, give yourself a big high-five and don't change a thing if you are satisfied with the result.

Physical State of the Property

What to do: Assess the outside (curb appeal), including paint, roof, overall exterior, lighting, yard, fence, garage, pathway, etc. Assess the interior, including paint, plumbing, electrical, flooring, hardware, cabinets, doors, appliances, etc.

Before deciding to roll any funds from your contingency fund or excess funds from rent over on to your mortgage principal, complete your annual review of the physical state of the property. It is much easier to use the funds for needed repairs or upgrades when you have them in hand, rather than after giving them to your lender for mortgage principal paydown.

Also, make sure that, if you have purchased a condo or townhouse and you are paying into a shared reserve fund for the building, these funds cover all the capital costs, and there are no surprises coming. Most reserve funds have a capital spending plan, and this plan is tied to funds already paid by you and other owners.

Some boards don't do a great job communicating with the owners, and capital spending projects frequently pop up that are only revealed at the annual general meeting. This is information you can request at any time, but you are the one who needs to ask.

The question is simple: ask the board if there are any capital spending projections not in the reserve fund spending plan that you should be aware of. One quick phone call to the property manager or a board member can help.

I know you might be saying, "Rick, I have a contingency budget for the upcoming year," and I know and love it, but if work needs to be done now and you have the funds, don't put off the repair issue waiting for funds in the future.

Tenants

What to do: Review the payment history, issues, positive indicators that your tenant has taken care of your property (e.g., planted trees, bushes, or flowers; painted interior or exterior parts of the property with your permission; etc.), and renewal dates. When a tenant renews (their renewal date is when they first moved in), send a thank-you; I also recommend setting up a Christmas or year-end gift of appreciation (e.g., treat them to a dinner out, a grocery store gift certificate, movie passes, or groceries in the cupboard). You can plan these in advance and put them in your calendar—know your tenant and what type of gift would be most appreciated.

It's important to do an annual review of your tenant experience as well. Are you happy with the tenants? Have their rent payments arrived on time, every time? How have they treated your property? Have there been any unexpected repairs? Have they asked for things that are not included in their lease? When is their renewal date, and will they want to renew? Should you renew with them? Have you shown your appreciation for these tenants throughout the year, and if you have, what have you done?

Remember, your tenant is your most important asset. You should be checking in on them from time to time and doing little things to recognize they are good tenants. An annual review is more a recap of key contact points throughout the year.

Team REAL

What to do: Review all the professionals, service tradespeople, and vendors who are on your team. Year-end is the best time to make any changes to your Team REAL contact list. Keep this contact list in a folder with other relevant property information, so you can do an easy review of each member's contact information, the work they provided, etc.

Making sure your Team REAL is still intact and ready to be part of your investment real estate journey is important each year. For example, keeping up the contact information is critical. Addresses, phone numbers, email addresses, and contact person of a company can all change in a year. A quick email to your main contact person once a year is the simplest way to reconfirm the information.

It wouldn't hurt to talk in person, if possible, to the main folks on your Team REAL; your lender, lawyer, and accountant would be great places to start. A quick hello keeps you visible, as you never know when you might need their services.

Marketplace

What to do: Assess changes in value, rental rates, job growth, and service additions to your investment real estate property's area (e.g., transit routes, shopping or entertainment facilities, restaurants).

Just like anything else, neighborhoods can change. If you have not made an effort to drive around your rental marketplace lately, noting any positive or negative changes, this would be a good time. I suggest you treat yourself to a meal at the end of your tour. Try a local restaurant and ask the service staff questions about the area; you will be pleasantly surprised at the information you will receive.

Even a quick stop at the local community center or recreational facility can be revealing. Talking to the folks at the front desk can give you a feel for the neighborhood and any changes they have seen, or you can find out if they know of any changes coming.

Also, note any changes to the transportation routes, and any new bike paths or walkways.

You never know when your tenants might move on, and the more you know about your rental marketplace, the easier it is to find tenants for your rental property.

Conclusion

The work you are doing on Day 29 is the culmination of your efforts in completing the coaching challenges outlined in this book.

You didn't start out on your investment real estate journey to help support me; you started this journey in the hope of answering the question, "What's in it for me?"

By creating your own investment magic and using your annual return and annual check-in, you are taking time to enjoy the fruits of your labor, reflect on lessons learned, and think about the year and years ahead.

You are breaking down each line on your way to a lifetime of building a strong financial foundation, unlocking sustainable wealth, and creating a living legacy.

 **Think about your ROI.**

You made your choice—you're not going to sit on the sidelines waiting for the ideal moment to purchase and rent investment real estate. Instead, you took advantage of low interest rates and are ready for plenty of clients for years to come. And what do you get out of it? Return on investment.

⇧ What are the three components of the return on investment in purchasing and renting your first investment real estate property?

1. _____
2. _____
3. _____

Who pays all of your expenses for your investment real estate property after your initial investment?

Coaching Challenge 58: Complete the Investment Real Estate Magic Annual Return Review.

⇧ Capital Return Revenue Streams

Mortgage principal paydown: $_____ (Sourced through tenant rent payment)

Capital appreciation: $_____ (Sourced through market conditions. Only add this number to review your potential return)

Capital investment work: $_____ (Capital spending)

Cash flow: $_____ (Market and purchase conditions)

Total annual return: $_____ (Total of mortgage)

Original dollar investment: _____ (Down payment, legal fees, appraisal fees, home inspection)

Percentage annual return: _____% (Ending value divided by initial value)

Coaching Challenge 59: Do your annual check-in.

Do an annual check-in that includes the current state of your investment real estate. This annual check-in isn't only about the financial performance of your property. You not only made a large investment of capital (cash), but you invested a ton of time in developing your mindset to run a small business successfully. You also grew your knowledge about investment real estate exponentially, including learning how to utilize your employment situation and tap into additional earnings to strengthen your investment portfolio. You spent time learning real estate property types, market and economic conditions, trends and timing, vacancies and rental demand, financing, assembling the right team members, marketing to renters, and maintaining strong relationships with your tenants.

Your annual check-in should take into consideration your short-term and long-term goals. Make sure it takes into account the following:

- How it has impacted your finances. What is your net income and net worth today compared to where you were prior to purchasing your first investment real estate property?
- Any changes in interest rates. Have they gone up or down?
- The physical state of the property. You had a home inspection and corrected the deficiencies. How are the changes holding up, and do you have to address any of the capital work outlined?
- How you can invest in work to help keep and grow the property's value.
- Your tenants, who are making all of your payments on your investment property. What little things could you do to keep them? Are your tenants renewing to stay another year? If they are vacating, why? If they are staying, what is keeping them renting your property?
- Your Team REAL members. How have you stayed engaged? Have you made at least a couple of contacts a year with your core Team REAL members, and who on your list should you check in with to ensure they are still offering the services you used?

- The marketplace. What resources are you using to stay on top? Are you viewing current rental rates for similar properties in your area? What about vacancies in your area? New industries or employers? Can you get an increase in your rents?

Ask yourself your Five W's.

The last question you should ask yourself as part of your year-end review is: What are your five W's?

Many times when people are trying to motivate you, they get you to gaze into an imaginary crystal ball and envision your life five years from now. In fact, we did this back on Day 1!

This book's purpose was to get you to see what is possible in thirty-one days and teach you the processes and methods that will make this a reality in your life.

Purchasing and renting your first investment real estate property is an incredible accomplishment that most people will never have the satisfaction of achieving.

Think about all of the short-term goals you have accomplished in thirty-one days and sixty-one coaching challenges. Wow!

Owning and renting an investment real estate property for one year will be another "wow" moment.

Please take the time to review these five questions. Set a one-year anniversary date in your calendar. You need a starting point, so answer these questions the moment you rent your property. Having a comparison point can help keep you focused.

The "Your Five W's" worksheet is in the appendix. I have given you lots of space to write down your thoughts and reflections.

WHO are you doing this for, and are they the same people you thought of before you purchased and rented your first investment real estate property?

WHAT do you need in order to be able to do this? What has changed for you to move to purchasing and renting your first investment real estate property?

The "what" will change a bit when you check in next year. What do you need in order to keep the property meeting your expectations? What are the personal and financial results for you purchasing and renting your first investment real estate property?

WHEN should you be doing this? When could you look to do this process of purchasing and renting another investment property? Remember, the "when" could be never again. If you are happy with the results and want to benefit from the fruits of your initial labor without adding to your portfolio, good for you!

WHY are you doing this? Is this the same answer as when you first started on this journey?

HOW has your life changed since doing this?

You don't have to be a magician to create your own capital return magic. Simply stay on top of your numbers every year to ensure you don't get off-course.

Day 29 Key Recap

Record your key learnings and actionable items in your notebook or the workbook and planning guide. (Optional)

⇧   Know the return on your financial capital investment.

- ⇧ To get a true understanding of your ROI, review all the elements beyond capital investment, including the physical state of investment real estate property, tenants, and rental marketplace.
- ⇧ Update your "Five W's" once a year at the end of the current calendar year.

DAY 30 ADDING MORE DOORS: CONCERNS AND POSSIBILITIES

Use this day to consider the possibilities for expanding your investment real estate business in the future. You get a day off from the coaching challenges today!

Before we come to the last day of our investment real estate journey together, I would like to reflect on any concerns you may have or possibilities you might consider after purchasing your first investment real estate property.

A Time to Reflect

The goal and focus of this book has been to help you purchase and rent your first investment real estate property in thirty-one days.

With your tenant in place, your first couple of rent checks deposited in the bank, and your income and expense system working great, you might be thinking, "I like this investment real estate side hustle or side hack."

Now what?

Duplicate the Success System, but Don't Chase Doors

If you decide you'd like to expand your investment real estate business, do so responsibly. Making a wrong move can have major consequences and impact your profitability. Each property must go through full scrutiny, so don't skip any steps.

As a long-time and long-term investment real estate investor, I would like to share our successes and failures. Just like many investments outside of investment real estate, the market conditions change, and you need to stay in step with its ongoing evolution.

Lessons

Life Gets in the Way

Today, my wife and I continue to own the majority of the investment real estate portfolio that we acquired through the years. However, we have sold some of our properties because of changing family dynamics.

The importance of joint venture agreements cannot be understated, no matter how tight your family seems. Please note that separation and divorce can affect family harmony and quickly change investment relationships. (A sample joint venture agreement can be found in the appendix.)

Looks Can Be Deceiving

Part of our financial portfolio encompasses joint venture partnerships. Some of our partnerships, as mentioned, are with family, and some of our joint ventures are with folks we vetted and became partners with. We have partnerships that have worked out great over the last twelve to fifteen years.

Not every joint venture has a happy ending, though. Early in our investment real estate career, we had one joint venture partnership that didn't work out well.

This joint venture partner appeared to be in great financial shape. His family was quite well-to-do, as they had sold a family business for millions of dollars.

This joint venture partner decided to invest his money in investment real estate and was looking for joint venture partners on a couple of his purchases.

We knew the family and thought this was a great opportunity. We did our research; each property met the criteria and each was a good standalone property. With everything checking out, we decided to purchase two properties with this partner and signed joint venture agreements protecting both parties.

Within a couple of years, this joint venture partner had purchased twenty-six properties (or twenty-six doors; we refer to each property as a door).

Each month, we would have our financial review and go through each property's income and expense statement. All was great.

After a couple of years of everything going well, this joint venture partner informed us that he had overextended himself and needed to divest himself of some of his properties. He thought that he could carve out a full-time salary for himself by having multiple doors, but this was not the case. Even with positive cash-flowing properties, the monthly income was not covering his living expenses.

He said he was fine from our end, but within a couple of months, he was asking us to buy his share of the joint ownership properties. This was not something we were happy about, but we were concerned that we could be putting these properties in jeopardy. So, we bought him out.

We still own these properties to this day, over ten years later.

Unfortunately, this joint venture partner had to sell off all of his twenty-six properties and go to work for someone else.

One Bad Apple Spoils the Bunch

You have the process working for you, you've purchased your first investment real estate property, you've rented the property, and you have a positive monthly cash flow. You might be thinking, "On to the next property!" and skip a couple of steps because you are now a professional investor.

Wrong.

Make sure you don't skip a step; one bad apple can spoil all of your hard work. You need each property to stand on its own. If they don't, you could end up with a negative cash-flowing property that will drag your investment real estate portfolio down. Stay true to your success, and find a way to turn the negative cash flow positive. You can always work with the lender to lower your payments if your current situation is not working.

Even though I am all about long-term buy-and-hold, if unforeseen circumstances occur and this property will not have a positive cash flow for some time, calculate the net loss you will incur, look to sell the property, and stop the bleeding.

As owners, we had an excellent cash-flowing property in an ideal location with great rents, but the building started to show its age, and the costs began to rise. It took us over five years to read the writing on the wall and sell! Don't let this be you.

Other Investment Real Estate Opportunities

Commercial – Your Professional Practice Pays Your Way

Part of our Team REAL is our lawyer, who has built a successful law practice over the last couple of decades. He has handled all of our investment real estate transactions over the years. We have discussed the value of investment real estate together on more than one occasion.

One of his methods to take advantage of investment real estate was to build a strong client base. He moved his law office three times over the years, and the last time, he did a very neat thing: he relocated to an outside mall location and bought the space he moved his law offices into. Because he owns the commercial space, he also spent a little extra on his interior and has beautiful and functional law offices.

We have had several discussions about his decision to own his own commercial space, and it is working extremely great for him. The tenant next to him is a dentist, and this dentist has done the same thing.

The lessons and learnings my lawyer shared with me are twofold. He mentioned he has set his mortgage to end before he retires from his practice. He also has hired two other lawyers who work for him. His goal is a simple one: at the end of his career, he plans to sell the practice to the other lawyers and rent them the office space. It's brilliant. My lawyer created a monthly income to help support his retirement.

Can you think of other professions that could use the same strategy?

If you are a professional who is starting out, using our lawyer's strategy might fit the bill. Professions like the dental profession, medical, insurance, and many others fit this description. Are you in a profession that will last for decades and could benefit from a stable location that can support a mortgage?

Is this a strategy you can work into your business goals?

Vacation Rental Investment Real Estate Property

Many of you have heard of Airbnb, and you may have even used this service yourself.

My wife and I became vacation rental real estate property owners before Airbnb became a household brand.

In the summer of 1999, I had to work a World Cup mountain biking event. This was the last major race competition before the 2000 Summer Olympics in Australia. The competition took place in Canmore, Alberta, Canada, a small town minutes away from Banff National Park.

This region is one of the most beautiful places in the world and is a recreational heaven for all of Mother Nature's four seasons. It's perfect for skiing, golf, mountain biking, fly fishing, snowshoeing, hiking, and the list goes on and on.

I asked my wife if she wanted to come along and help. She jumped at the chance, and we worked the event together.

During our stay, we had some spare time to look around the area. We even discussed how amazing it would be to own a vacation home here. This all sounded good in the moment, but to make it practical, we would need to have some income from our vacation home to offset all of the expenses. After the event, we thought our idea of owning a vacation home and renting had died.

Surprise

Then, a couple of years later, we were attending a home and garden show, and the last booth on the way out was a beautiful model of a four-building complex that was being developed in Canmore, just off the downtown. This complex was being marketed as a vacation home that came with a marketing company that would rent your vacation home when you were not using it. Wow—we thought we had died and gone to heaven.

What a great concept! We would own the home, and someone would market it to the world's vacation clientele.

Within a month, we had signed the papers. Within less than a year, we took possession of our vacation home and were already starting to get rentals.

I don't want to mislead you; the marketing company renting our mountain vacation home never promised us 100 percent rental, but we took in enough income to offset property taxes and utilities. With both my wife and I working in great professions, we didn't need to cover all costs.

You might be saying to yourself, Rick, this property does not match one of your primary strategies: to not have a negative cash-flowing property. You are correct; in the beginning, our goal for this property was to have a vacation home. We weren't thinking about profit; it was more like, if we could receive some rental income, great.

Over the years, my wife and I gradually transitioned from owning a vacation home in an incredible region that we enjoyed as our primary focus. We eventually began to think of vacation rental as a core part of our business.

Improvements to the Vacation Rental Business Model

Over the years, Airbnb and VRBO started to make their way onto the scene and offer their services to homeowners who wanted to rent their property to vacationers. To make a long story short, we moved away from the marketing company we started with and adopted the VRBO vacation rental model. What an incredible business model! This decision to get serious about owning and marketing a vacation rental property turned into our investment real estate Cinderella story.

Over the years, we went from having an income that supplemented some of our costs to eventually covering all of our expenses and leaving us a tidy little profit every year from cash flow, not including value growth in the property.

We also spent two decades enjoying our vacation home and having our family and friends come to visit and enjoy every minute.

I love this type of property and the vacation rental business. My next book, *31 Days to Purchasing and Renting a Vacation and Recreational Investment Real Estate Property*, will follow the same theme as this book. It will also be supported with a workbook and planning guide, and an online course.

Foundational Strategy to Investment Real Estate Portfolio

"Buy, Invest, Remortgage. Buy, Invest, Re-mortgage."

This strategy helped my wife and I build our investment real estate portfolio.

During the early 2000s, my wife and I acquired several properties, and during this time, like in many real estate markets, the price of real estate took off, and values increased dramatically.

With a couple of our properties, we had made a pretty good dent in paying down our mortgage principals through Uberizing. On several occasions, my wife and I earned excellent bonuses through our jobs, and we used these funds to pay down the mortgage balances.

For several of our investment property purchases, we accessed down payment funds by remortgaging our existing properties. What was great about this strategy was that we could get increased rents from our remortgaged properties and the tenants who paid the new rental rates helped us pay for the funds we accessed for down payments.

Endless Possibilities

If you decide to stop at one investment real estate property, that's totally okay. There's nothing wrong with adding one investment property to your financial portfolio. This one property can help you build a strong financial foundation and create a living legacy. But should you wish to take things further, the playing field is wide open. Whether you want to own multiple doors, join up with joint venture partners, or start investing in vacation rental properties, keep your ear to the ground, and what comes your way can be endless possibilities.

Day 30 Key Recap

Record your key learnings and actionable items in your notebook or the workbook and planning guide. (Optional)

- ⇧ The information you used to purchase and rent your first investment real estate property can be used to purchase and rent other successful investment real estate properties in the future and create successful, positive cash-flowing investment properties.
- ⇧ Don't chase doors.
- ⇧ There are great investment real estate opportunities in the recreational and vacation home marketplace should you wish to expand your business.

 **DAY 31** THE EXIT STRATEGY

Use this day to think about your exit strategy. Has your original purpose been achieved, or was your journey not what you had envisioned? At best, an exit strategy contributes to your strong foundation, sustainable wealth, and living legacy; at worst, it allows you to rethink your decision. On this last day, it is time to look back. At the end of the chapter, complete the coaching challenges to describe your own exit strategy.

You've come a long way from Day 1, when you were just beginning your investment real estate journey. Today, we're going to focus on the final part of that journey: the exit strategy.

The exit strategy is just what it sounds like: an end to your investment real estate career.

Legacy: Giving, Quality of Life, Medical Advances, or Generational Transfer

Throughout this book, I've talked about how investment real estate can help you leave a legacy. When thinking about your exit strategy in the future or your legacy options, you need to look back on the foundation of your investment real estate success. This has been one of the few investments in your portfolio you have gotten to control and drive the results. Has it delivered what you hoped for?

Whether you choose to sell the house and use the proceeds for giving, for quality of life, for health-care and medical advances, or to create generational wealth through your living legacy, your options are bountiful. Remember, you have no say in your government old age and pension programs or your company pensions; you are paid your monthly payments until your death. In many cases, the funding stops when you pass away, and your family sees no more income from your labor over the years. Yes, there can be some spousal or partner benefits that might get transferred, but when this person passes on, that's it. The funding doesn't move on to the next generation.

The funds from your investment real estate don't have to cease, however. If you need the cash for health-care, for medical advances, or to help your family, you can simply remortgage and have your rent cover the mortgage costs as you use the money to improve your life or the lives of your loved ones.

Each generation is living longer, and remember, being classified as a senior by the government at age sixty-five is rooted in a past when most people were not living much past sixty-five. I don't want you to think I am going off on some political tangent, but if we as a society are living much longer than past generations, is it not time to reclassify our retirement age and what age senior citizenship begins? If the governments index our pensions and old age security payments, why should we not as a society reindex our terms for old age?

Let's get rid of the aging stigma and elevate our work or career to allow people to work much longer without being placed in a tidy box.

With many boomers being too healthy for retirement funds, and the leapfrog healthcare and medical advances we're seeing, the aging population can fund better health-care and medical advances to perpetuate a longer and healthier life.

Having sustainable wealth is critical if you live longer and eventually need to fund health or medical expenses.

I don't want to scare the hell out of anyone, but what will be the costs to society to pay for COVID-19? At some point, the world will have to pay for the investment made into our health.

An Exit for the Ages

None of us are going to get out of this life alive.

Having an exit strategy means knowing that you will leave your investment real estate to someone or something at some point. Or, if you're creating a living legacy, are there items on your bucket list you would like to share with your family—

memorable trips, adventure sports activities, charity work, community projects? Being involved in any of these worthwhile ventures while you are living can lead to a more fulfilled life.

Also, if you have educated your family members on the sustainable wealth resulting from investment real estate, your children or inheritors can adopt your exit strategy and let the investment property you left to them live on as sustainable wealth. You will need to plan with your Team REAL members how this will work to preserve as much of this wealth from the taxman as possible.

In this chapter, we'll talk about why an exit strategy is essential. Then, we'll cover each of the four exit strategies in depth so that when you're ready to cash in on your investment, you'll be prepared.

Why You Need an Exit Strategy

By the time you reach this stage of your investment real estate journey, you should have little or no mortgage left. Your investment real estate portfolio has been maintained over the years, and you know that your real estate is at its highest value. You may have just one property, or maybe you purchased more than one investment real estate property over the years.

It's essential to think about an exit strategy early on. How do you feel about your life? Do you want to retire early, or do you see yourself working well into your eighties or nineties, like Warren Buffett? Do you see yourself having a family or having your family involved? Do you exit your real estate portfolio by passing down your investment real estate business? How are you going to communicate your plan to family members for a successful transition?

This type of planning is known as succession planning. You may not have started a family, or perhaps you aren't even in a serious relationship, but you still need to think about people who could be in your world in the future. This book is all about awareness and making sure you are not blindsided down the road. Planning your investment real estate exit strategy is part of good succession planning.

Why Succession Planning Is Important

You have worked hard for everything you have financially accumulated over a lifetime of work and smart financial decision-making. If you are going to leave a legacy, you want to make sure much of your wealth remains intact as this wealth moves on to the next generation.

The taxperson is alive and well with all governments throughout the globe. I am not suggesting you try and cheat the tax system. Rather, you need to be aware of and put in place the options that the tax system allows you to use to protect your wealth.

You should be thinking about estate planning, with firms that specialize in estate planning as one option.

Another option is joint venture ownership with your heirs.

We also talked earlier in the book about different ownership methods. We mentioned joint tenancy and the simple term that ownership passes from one person to the surviving person. This method can be restrictive and cause tax issues. I suggest you work with your Team REAL members to find the best option for you. Whatever method you use, you need to create an exit strategy transition.

Exit Strategy #1: Selling the House

Selling the house may be the most obvious exit strategy. But by now, you may have gathered that selling your investment real estate property is not my preferred option.

You have used a long-term buy-and-hold strategy, paid off the mortgage, and the majority of the rental income is now going into your pocket.

This exit strategy may not need to wait until later in your life. I suggested earlier in the book that you should hang on to a property a minimum of five years, but the real positive impact comes when you pay off the mortgage.

I understand life circumstances. Exiting early is not what I am advocating, but life has a way of getting in your way sometimes. Try not to sell in a downturn in the real estate market.

If you consider liquidating your properties based on the economy over time, sell off at the top of the market. Selling should be part of a plan, not a knee-jerk decision. But how do you know when the selling prices will be right to exit? When will the next sales cycle come along?

When thinking about your family, some members may be interested in investment real estate, and some may not. How do you handle such a situation?

I talked earlier about Rachelle's story; her mother was reluctant to give each child their inheritance early because one child was not good with money. Don't paint each adult child with the same brush. You could give the early inheritance to the child who is more financially savvy with no restrictions, and for the other adult child, you might put on restrictions, such as the distribution of funds in chunks over time.

If you have multiple properties, can you sell them off for more value as a package, or does it make more sense to sell one property at a time?

Some lenders are willing to lend a mortgage as a bundle of properties put up as collateral. Again, discuss with your Team REAL.

Exit Strategy #2: Leapfrog Health-Care and Medical Advances

In the book's introduction, I talked to you about leapfrog health-care and medical advances. To refresh your memory, as we age, health-care and medical advances will help us to be fully functional longer than ever before, in mind, body, and soul.

With the challenges seen in long-term care during the recent coronavirus pandemic, it's a good bet that the aging population will be living on their own much longer. The cost of living on your own can be higher, and you must be prepared to ensure you do not outlive your retirement funds.

There is also a shift with baby boomers embracing technology. With the boomers being able to surf the internet and technology more knowledgeably and skillfully than ever before, the chances are great that we'll spend more time being our own medical advocates, ensuring we live healthier longer.

Exit Strategy #3: Creating Your Own Habitat for Humanity

I have used Habitat for Humanity as my example. The challenge here is to create your own aspiration to make a difference in society. I love the work Habitat does and how it aligns with my personal beliefs. There are many ways to be charitable, so choose your path.

We make a living by what we get. We make a life by what we give. — Winston Churchill

Investment real estate could be your passion, and over the years, perhaps you have benefitted big-time from the proceeds from investment real estate. Your life has been full, and you would like to see others enjoy the benefits of real estate, too. You know good housing gives families a safe, decent, and affordable place to live. The thought of creating your own habitat for humanity could come to life through your investment real estate.

Habitat for Humanity International, generally referred to as Habitat for Humanity or simply Habitat, is an international, non-governmental, and non-profit organization that was founded in 1976.

Habitat has a vision of helping people by building strength, stability, and self-reliance together with families who need decent and affordable homes.

In 1985, the Habitat for Humanity movement spread to Canada, with the first Canadian build in Winkler, Manitoba. Habitat for Humanity's Canadian presence has since grown to seventy-two affiliates in ten provinces and three territories, and it has successfully provided over 2,500 families with safe, decent, and affordable housing.

Habitat for Humanity also operates home and building supply stores that accept and resell quality new and used building materials. The world's first ReStore, as they are known, was opened by Habitat for Humanity Winnipeg in 1991. Shopping at a Habitat ReStore is a socially conscious decision, as funds generated are used to fund local Habitat for Humanity homebuilding projects.

You might decide to donate one of your investment real estate properties to Habitat for Humanity and have them use the funds in your name to build a home or homes through their program. This exit strategy is a great way to give back to the community and make a difference in the lives of underserved and underprivileged families.

Exit Strategy #4: Your Living Legacy

Some of the world's most high-profile folks have used or are using their wealth to create a lasting legacy. I have a strong belief in what I refer to as a living legacy—a legacy you get to enjoy with others while you are still part of this world.

Starbucks has become a living legacy of my dad. — Howard Schultz, CEO and president, Starbucks

Why a Living Legacy?

As I reach out to boomers, Gen Xers, millennials, and Gen Zers, my personal challenge to you is to understand each of our generations, how we think, and how our lives differ from one another's. If you are open to knowing and building relationships with other generations, they become part of your resource base and possibly even joint venture partners.

The internet, smartphones, and many other technical wonders were born after the youngest boomer came into this world; meanwhile, Gen Xers, Gen Zers, and millennials have had a close relationship with such technology, leading them to have different thought processes and views on life.

What ties us all together is that we are all a continuation of past generations. Humankind starts with our family, and at the end of the day, for many humans, our family is our prime driver for wealth accumulation. We know, in many cases, that we cannot spend or use all the resources we acquire over life, and we want to leave our families better off than we were when we came into the world.

Many people would protect their families with their lives, and we spend much of our wealth to help our families. Much of our joy, too, is achieved through helping our children and our grandchildren, and we develop inertia driving us to help future generations—perhaps ones we will never even meet.

We as human beings dominate this world by creating living legacies for multiple generations. You have seen living legacies built around monarchies, dictatorships, businesses, foundations, educational institutions, hospitals, and many other organizations. What you might not realize is that many of these legacies survive and thrive because they are built on a foundation of great investment real estate.

Go back in human evolution. Families have evolved to family and friends; family and friends have evolved to family, friends, and community. Today, we have cities, countries, continents, and the world as large communities. We are seeing many cases of one person touching the entire world and leaving a lasting legacy. Many communities worldwide are using social media and other technological advances to build global communities and legacies; think of Steve Jobs, the cofounder of Apple, and the worldwide community that thrives because of his actions.

Being the richest man in the cemetery doesn't matter to me. Going to bed at night saying we've done something wonderful, that's what matters to me. — Steve Jobs

Through the technology that Steve helped develop, many of us capture and keep records and memories that will live for eternity.

How can you influence your legacy so that others want to keep records and memories of who we are and were?

For most of us, our homes will be our biggest single purchase and financial investment. We protect this home as if it were our pyramid. The Ancient Egyptian pharaohs thought they could take their worldly possessions with them into the afterlife and enjoy these fruits in another dimension. We all know the pharaohs did not take their worldly possessions into their afterlife. Many generations of graverobbers enjoyed the pharaohs' wealth, and if the pharaohs were lucky, their possessions ended up in museums around the world for all of humankind to enjoy.

I believe that the pharaohs would have left a much more fertile legacy if they left their physical wealth to their future generations rather than taking their gold to the grave and allowing someone to steal these future generations' hand-up.

Sharing our wealth and leaving a legacy involves making a plan. We must consider not only our possessions but also how we keep our legacy alive. Earlier in the book, we discussed the parable of the Three Little Pigs and their homes made of straw and sticks. These materials didn't protect two of the three little pigs, but thanks to their third sibling, who built a strong foundation from bricks, the little pigs staved off the big, bad wolf. Having a strong foundation helped the third pig to create a legacy to be proud of and protect the current and future generations.

My Family's Legacy

When my mom passed away, my dad asked me how we could keep my mom's memory alive, and it occurred to me that, thanks to Steve Jobs, the entire world is going digital in capturing memories. Many of my mom and dad's memories were captured on film, slides, and video. We are now converting these to digital and carrying out my dad's wishes.

My dad and I decided to use the website Ancestry as the base where all can see our generations' past lives. Ancestry keeps evolving, and it is neat how someone's life is told as a story with a few strokes of the keyboard.

It is interesting to me how millions and millions of us have a fascination with our ancestors. Think of the number of TV shows, books, movies, and websites dedicated to searching for our roots. As we age, there seems to be more and more interest in our past.

Also, how many times have you watched a successful person being interviewed, talking about the home they grew up in and their many fond memories? It was never about the size of the home; it was about special family memories. Real estate is a bond that ties families together.

I mention my mom and dad's story because, as I was putting my mom's life story on Ancestry, I made contact with a cousin in Britain who had also been building his family tree. I could import part of his family tree into my family tree to learn more about our history. One of the pictures he sent was of my great-great-grandfather's family home.

This home survived both World Wars, the bombing of London, England, and a disastrous short-term modernization in the 1960s that almost destroyed many historical sites. My cousin told me that this home, well over one hundred years old, is now located in one of the most desirable places to live in London, even though it is modest in stature.

Real estate, on an individual basis, can serve as our home for several decades. But clearly, it can be part of a much richer and long-lasting legacy. Think about it: my great-great-grandfather's home has not only endured some of the most pivotal moments of the past century, but it has outlived four generations of my family. Real estate will always provide a financial foundation, sustainable wealth, and a living legacy for generations upon generations. We're all well aware that they're not making any more land in this world, which makes the homes on this land more valuable every day.

Humankind has been built on legacies of current and past generations, and it always will be. I think of my childhood and how family homes are multigenerational. These homes draw the generations together, and we build family memories from them. Thinking about past generations is important to so many of us. The popularity of websites like Ancestry.com is proof, connecting families over the ages.

Our future is always rooted in appreciation of our past.

Think of the legacies of Aristotle, Buddha, Winston Churchill, Mahatma Gandhi, Alexander Graham Bell, Thomas Edison, and Steve Jobs. What kind of impact have their legacies had on the world? What about your own family and friends' legacies? What have these people meant to your life?

No one gets out of life alive. At some point, our mortality takes over, and we can only hope our spirit lives on through the legacy we have created.

What does your legacy look like? Wouldn't you like to be around to develop some of your legacy?

Thoughts about Inheritance

Over the next decade, Canadians will inherit $750 billion, yes, billion, and in the United States, the figure will be around ten times that amount.

My brother and I asked our folks not to leave us any inheritance as we are just fine financially. In our family, the inheritance train jumped a generation and is impacting the second and third generations.

My father, who had six great-grandchildren upon his passing, decided to leave the bulk of their estate to their great-grandchildren through Registered Educational Savings Plans (RESPs).

With my parents' great-grandchildren being young, anywhere from three to thirteen years will pass before the money is invested into their education. Once the great-grandchildren go on to have careers, thanks in part to their great-grandparents' funding, they will be creating their own living legacies. My dad and mom's impact will live on—and that's pretty cool.

> *A family is a place where minds meet one another.* — Buddha

There is a lesson to be learned from my folks: to give some thought to how our vault to investment real estate can impact generations of our family we may never even know.

The end is just the beginning. —T.S. Eliot

 **Describe your exit strategy.**

Is it not great that as you complete your journey of purchasing and renting your first investment real estate property, you get to choose how your story ends and how you can use this as a new beginning? How will you craft your legacy?

- In your own words, describe your exit strategy for your investment real estate. Imagine your living legacy and its story.

Day 31 Key Recap

Record your key learnings and actionable items in your notebook or the workbook and planning guide. (Optional)

⇧ When creating your exit strategy, stop, take a deep breath, and be totally honest with yourself. Ask yourself how things have changed, and how they can change.

⇧ Pinpointing an excellent exit strategy from your investment real estate can take several years to develop. Think about your life stages, from being single, to married, to a family, to empty-nesters, to grandchildren. Think of the two main lessons from *The Lion King*. The first is the Circle of Life. We all make our journey through it, and each moment impacts our thinking at every stage. Our thinking constantly evolves or revolves.

- ⇧ Use the second lesson from *The Lion King*, which is to simply move on from your past. Whatever happened in your past is in the past. As you come to the end of this book, learn from it, grow personally from it, and then move on with your life and don't get hung up on things. You get to write your own story.

CONCLUSION

THE END, AND WARMEST APPRECIATION

In *31 Days to Purchasing and Renting Your First Investment Real Estate Property*, I dive into the long-term buy-and-hold investing philosophy I have embraced for over twenty years. I hope that this vision becomes a part of your life, too.

If you've gotten to the end of the book, there's a good chance you are thinking seriously about adopting investment real estate as part of your financial portfolio. Even before you reached this part of the book, you may have made steps toward purchasing and renting your first investment real estate property.

Life goes flying by. As investors, we are limited by time—and, ultimately, death. I certainly don't want to sound morbid, but none of us get out of this life alive; we don't get a do-over. How we use or spend our time is up to us.

The time it took to read *31 Days to Purchasing and Renting Your First Investment Real Estate Property* was small in the grand scheme of things, but it can have a huge impact for the rest of your life.

Taking thirty-one days can help you make this investment, and your life, unforgettable. By dedicating this time to your investment real estate journey, you can focus on making this financial component important and building value around investment real estate. If you develop investment real estate as part of your financial philosophy, you can find yourself living a life with financial direction and, perhaps, riches that last beyond your lifetime to benefit future generations.

The life lessons I share with you in this book will give you access to information not only through my family's past experiences but also through a lifelong online resource, now and in the future. Visit vaulttoinvestmentrealestatesuccess.com for inspiring blogs, podcasts, resources, and products.

Life is ever-changing. Making investment real estate part of your philosophy can shape your financial foundation, unlock sustainable wealth, and create a living legacy. Now is the time to develop the right combination of investment strategies using your own personal real estate.

Let's start laying down the cornerstones to your vault, building a strong financial foundation, unlocking sustainable wealth, and creating a living legacy. Are you ready?

Thank you for giving up the most valuable resource you have in life, time, to read and execute the principles in this book.

Thank you for staking out thirty-one days to make this difference in your life.

If *31 Days to Purchasing and Renting Your First Investment Real Estate Property* has delivered value to your financial and personal life, please recommend this book to others whom you feel can benefit from it.

APPENDIX

- 202 Income Statement
- Application for Personal Credit
- Application Form
- Business Plan
- Vault to Investment Real Estate Success Net Worth Calculator
- Vault to Investment Personal Income and Expense Worksheet (Sample)
- Vault to Investment Real Estate Personal Income and Expense Worksheet
- Vault to Investment Real Estate Success Net Worth Statement Net Worth Calculator (Sample)
- The Investment Real Estate Way Starter Kit Checklist
- The Move-In Checklist
- The Move-Out Checklist

REFERENCES

Quick-Start Guide

- The Everyday Millionaire Podcast. Patrick Francey.
- 31 Days to Purchasing and Renting Your First Investment Real Estate Property Workbook and Planning Guide.

Preface

- The Richest Man in Babylon. George Samuel Clason.
- "Whether you think you can, or think you can't—you're right." Henry Ford.
- The Suitcase Entrepreneur. Natalie Sisson.
- "If you want to live a happy life, tie it to a goal, not people or things." Albert Einstein.

Acknowledgements

- "Spirit, Growth, Success." Sir George Simpson Junior High School motto.

Welcome

- My Ten-Thousand-Plus Hours. Malcolm Gladwell.
- Tri-Ya Racing. YouTube. New Orleans, Louisiana
- MelRadCoaching. Melanie McQuaid. Victoria, British Columbia

Value

- Vision Statement. Susan Ward.

Introduction

- Before Happiness. Shawn Achor.
- "Failure is success in progress." Albert Einstein.
- No Excuses!: The Power of Self-Discipline. Brian Tracy.
- Metro. Mike Goetz.
- Cheryl Connelly, Futurist. Ford Motor Company

- *Transcend: Nine Steps to Living Well Forever*. Ray Kurzweil and Terry Grossman, MD.
- "How to Make Money by Staring at the Ocean." Preston Ely. *Success Magazine*.
- "Evidence of positive impact on the customer when the salesperson leaves the sales call." Jim Mansell.
- "Richer generation Canadians 18 to 34." Dean Beeby. CBC News. February 24, 2016.

The Secret Sauce

- Toastmasters International.

Day 1

- *The Canadian Real Estate Action Plan*. **Peter Kinch**.
- *Retirement Groove: Finding Yours!* **Alexis Leclair**.
- *Alice's Adventures in Wonderland*. Lewis Carroll.

Day 2

- *Unretirement: How Baby Boomers Are Changing the Way We Think About Work, Community, and the Good Life*. **Chris Farrell**.

Stage 1: Ready

- Ray Dalio.
- *Outlier: The Story of Success*. **Malcolm Gladwell**.

Day 3

- *The Five Secrets You Must Discover Before You Die*. **Dr. John Izzo**.
- *COACH: Clarify, Outcome, Apply, Commit, Help*. **Hugh Phillips**.
- *Do the Work*. **Steven Pressfield**.

Day 5

- New York Stock Exchange.
- Toronto Stock Exchange.

Day 7

- The Real Estate Investment Network (REIN).

Day 8

- PadMapper.com.

Day 10

- "Timing Is Everything." **Natalie Nicole Hemby.**

Day 11

- Julian Hall.
- PadMapper.com.

Day 12

- The ONE Thing. **Gary Keller and Jay Papasan.**

Day 15

- Your FICO Score. MyFICO.
- Canadian Mortgage and Housing Corporation (CMHC).

Stage II: Set

Day 21

- *Money Honey: A Simple 7-Step Guide for Getting Your Financial Shit Together*, **Rachel Richards.**

Stage III: Goal

Day 25

- The Everyday Millionaire **Podcast. Patrick Francey.**
- PIVO.

Day 26

- American Automobile Association (AMA).
- Canadian Automobile Association (CAA).

Day 28

- *The Money Pit.*

Day 31

- Habitat for Humanity.

www.ingramcontent.com/pod-product-compliance
Lightning Source LLC
Chambersburg PA
CBHW071801080526
44589CB00012B/636